2018

Writing from Inlandia

An Inlandia Institute Publication

INLANDIA
INSTITUTE

Editorial Board

ISBN: 978-1-7324032-3-9

2018 WRITING FROM INLANDIA

Work of the Inlandia Creative Writing Workshops

This publication is the end result of a three-season run of Inlandia Creative Writing Workshops held in a variety of locations throughout the Inland Southern California.

The Creative Writing Workshops are part of the Inlandia Institute's Literary Professional Development Program, which also includes seminars and boot camp workshops on writing, publishing, and an annual Indie Authors Fair. The purpose of this core program is to foster creative writing and support the emerging writers of Inland Southern California.

These workshop participants are diverse in age, gender, culture, and writing experience. Their writing, compiled here, is just a taste of the multitude and range of voices and stories this region has to offer.

CONTENTS

Redlands Joslyn Senior Center Contributors

Janet Goeske Senior Center Contributors

Riverside Public Library Contributors

Colton Public Library/Colton Area Museum Contributors

Tesoros de Cuentos at Casa Blanca Public Library Contributors

Rowe Branch of the San Bernardino Public Library Contributors

Ovitt Family Community Library in Ontario Contributors

Corona Public Library Contributors

* Poems denoted by an asterisk were originally generated in Stephanie Barbé Hammer's Poet-TRY online workshop. Thanks, Stephanie!

INTRODUCTION

Happy ten year anniversary to Inlandia's Creative Writing Workshops program!

Welcome to the long-awaited 2018 anthology, compiling work from writers in Inlandia's ongoing creative writing workshops produced during the workshop year. In recognition of ten years of excellence, here is a brief timeline breaking down how the program has changed over the years, and what we have to look forward to.

2008 Ruth Nolan leads the first creative writing workshop for Inlandia Institute; a chapbook bringing together the work of participants, *Slouching Toward Mt. Rubidoux Manor*, is published.

2010 Jean Waggoner leads an Inlandia writing workshop in Idyllwild. Immediately thereafter, Maureen Alsop begins leading a Palm Springs workshops, thereby tripling the size of the workshops program overnight.

2011 The first combined Writing from Inlandia anthology is published; Cati Porter leads a workshop series at the Ovitt Library in Ontario. And then there were four.

2012 Myra Dutton joins Jean in co-leading Idyllwild; Charlotte Davidson takes over for Cati at Ontario.

2013 Alaina Bixon takes over for Maureen in Palm Springs; Mike Cluff takes over for Ruth in Riverside; Matt Nadelson leads a workshop at the Corona Public Library.

2014 Mike Cluff dies unexpectedly; Jo Scott-Coe takes over the Riverside workshop.

2015 Andrea Fingerson leads a workshop at the San Bernardino Public Library, bringing the total number of workshop locations up to six; Maureen moves to Australia and Jean and Myra begin a hybrid mountain-desert workshop.

2016 A big year for turnover: Jean and Myra retire, Nikia Chaney takes over for Andrea in San Bernardino while Andrea moves to Corona to take over for Matt who's moved to San Pedro (not quite as far as Maureen, but certainly not commuting distance!) Charlotte retires and Ontario is handed off to Tim Hatch; Mae Wagner's Joslyn Joy Writing Workshops are welcomed to the fold; and we begin a new series of "boot camp" workshops led by Stephanie Barbé Hammer, among others.

2017 Frances J. Vasquez and Rose Y. Monge join the family with Tesoros de Cuentos at the Casa Blanca Library, Marj Charlier with memoir and fiction workshops in Palm Springs and Rancho Mirage, and Jessica Carrillo with a new bilingual workshop in Colton.

2018 James Ducat pilots a second section of the Riverside workshop; CelenaDiana Bumpus' long-running Poets in Motion workshop at the Janet Goeske Senior Center is brought into the fold; Allsyon Jeffredo takes over for Nikia in San Bernardino.

To summarize, in ten years we've grown from 1 to 12 workshops, plus a host of other online bootcamp workshops. Writers in the program have had the opportunity to work with 22 different workshop leaders, from the mountains to the deserts and all parts in between. I'm sure I may be forgetting something, but with so much, how could I possibly remember it all?

So, what's next?

We're continuing to grow the program with a new workshop next fall led by James, tentatively proposed for the A.K. Smiley Library, and a new partnership with the Palm Springs Art Museum led by Marj.

Inlandia is, above all else, about people and the stories we all have. Helping you tell your story is what we're about. Thank you for being a part of Inlandia's story.

As I am every year, I am grateful to all of the people who make up Inlandia. We are all Inlandia.

Every year, as we pull together to publish this anthology, I am reminded of how special this book is, and how reliant it is on the talented and dedicated writers and workshop leaders who participate in Inlandia's Creative Writing Workshops Program, a sampling of whom appear here. Thank you.

Inlandia's workshops program, including the annual publication of the *Writing from Inlandia* anthology, are made possible by grants from the E. Rhodes and Leona B. Carpenter Foundation, the City of Riverside, and Poets & Writers Readings/Workshops Program, with particular thanks to the director of their west coast office, Jamie FitzGerald Lahey. We also wish to thank Inlandia's members for their generous donations of time, talent, and treasure. Special thanks to our readers for appreciating the good work found here.

This issue also marks the return of Jean and Myra—as editors! For those wondering why the long wait for this anthology, we discovered too late that we were experiencing growing pains. The anthology as it originally stood was as big as a New York phone book. Jean and Myra had the task of whittling it down to a mere 321 8.5x11 pages, set in 12 pt. Times New Roman. Phew! That's a lot of WORK! Literally and figuratively speaking.

Additional thanks goes to the newest Publications Committee Chair, Mark Givens, who took on the task of copyediting and laying out this beast for publication. It was truly a team effort this year.

Of course and as always, we wish to thank our host venues for allowing us to use their space free of charge to hold our workshops: Riverside Public Library, Corona Public Library, San Bernardino Public Library, Palm Springs Public Library, Rancho Mirage Public Library, the Ovitt Family Community Library in Ontario, Joslyn Senior Center in Redlands, Janet Goeske Senior Center in Riverside, and the Colton Area Museum. Special thanks to Mike Murphy, CAM board member, for showing up for us.

We are grateful for all of your support.

—Cati Porter, Executive Director

REDLANDS JOSLYN SENIOR CENTER

Led by Mae Wagner

Memorable Moments of the 1960s

When I think of the 1960s, the personal and what happened around me in the larger society get tangled up and I can't think of one without thinking of the other. The 1960s was when everything happened.

I got married because that was what you did then and moved to California from New York. I started working as a secretary to the dean of a law school in downtown Los Angeles. I took three buses to get to the office because I did not yet have a car.

Robert F. Kennedy was shot not too far away, at the Ambassador Hotel. There had been so much hope attached to his candidacy and he may have won the presidency, had he lived. A few days after the shooting, I stood and watched as a caravan of limousines coming from St. Vincent Hospital passed by, the black silhouettes of Jackie Kennedy and Ted Kennedy visible through the car windows, a personal tragedy for them and a tragedy for the country as a whole.

Martin Luther King had been killed earlier in the year which was also a great calamity although I did not relate to that situation particularly well. Part of it was that I was a fairly recent immigrant and did not yet know or understand all the social problems and undercurrents that existed in the United States at that time. But I remember very clearly tall, slightly rumpled Professor Ogden standing in my office, declaring that attending the funeral in Atlanta was the most moving experience of his life.

The students at that time were up in arms about the Vietnam war. They also protested against unfair treatment of farm workers and led a boycott of grapes and lettuce grown in California. A leader among those students was Miguel Garcia and he used to tell me not to buy lettuce or grapes. I didn't quite understand what it was all about and kept buying grapes. I liked Miguel Garcia;

there was something very earnest about him. He protested against the Catholic Church as well, demanding that it should share its wealth with the parishioners who lived in poverty. Miguel Garcia became a lawyer, fighting for those same causes he so ardently believed in. Unfortunately, he died young.

The protests against the Vietnam war were violent at times. I remember Professor Rank coming back from a visit to UCLA, all shook up. He had been in the path of several cars the students there had set on fire and rolled down his way. He was shaking, saying he had almost been killed.

I did have an understanding of the Vietnam War. I never liked the vilification of the United States' motives and the simplifications used by those opposed to it. Like most people, I dreaded communism, not so much because of its pretense to social and economic equality as because, in order to maintain that fiction, it required the enslavement of men's souls. It required that you accept that truth was what the regime told you it was, not what your own "lying eyes" told you it was.

Then, at the end of the '60s, Richard Nixon was elected president, promising law and order. I could understand that people were fed up with the riots and the disorder. At the law school, it didn't go over too well. The students' new rallying cry was "Take to the streets!" But, it seemed as if the age of protest had played itself out; high emotions can't last forever. Also, Nixon had promised to end the Vietnam war, a promise he kept.

Another memory from that time is of a neatly dressed, middle-aged woman on the bus, looking extremely self-satisfied at the news. Clearly, her candidate had won.

The Girl in the White Dress

I was driving home in the rain one night after an evening over indulging in alcoholic beverages when the high beams lit up a girl standing in the middle of the road like the proverbial deer in the headlights. As I slammed on the brakes and spun the wheel madly the truck skewed wildly out of control, off the road, through the ditch, and finally by itself, shot backwards up onto the roadway covered from front to back with mud. I jumped out of the truck certain that I had run over the girl but she was still standing there. After that scare I was out of control and screamed some things in her face that I regretted five minutes later, but eventually I calmed down enough to talk to her in a civil manner and invited her to ride to her destination. Now, I've lived in these parts all my life and thought I knew everything about it but I couldn't visualize where she was talking about. She said "no problem, I'll direct you."

The truck was so covered with mud that I couldn't even see the front of the hood through the windshield and ended up carrying several buckets of water out of the ditch to wash the thing off enough to drive. With that done, we climbed in and took off. As we drove, she asked me what I was doing out in such miserable weather and before I could think I blurted out something that I thought I could not have told anyone. My wife, light of my life died in childbirth four months earlier. Our daughter had only lived an hour due to an unsuspected congenital abnormality. I exploded into pieces and cried. You know, more than cried; I howled until finally I was empty. I had not wept at all since Karen and Allie died and it was all bottled up inside me like arsenic in a rusty hypodermic syringe.

I looked at her and she seemed familiar, I mean not like someone that you think you should know but someone that you know damn well that you've never met but even so there's still something familiar enough to cause a little gut sliding unease. It would be almost like running into an old girlfriend's sister that you've never know about, you know what I mean. There's some kind of weird connection that you shouldn't recognize but you do anyway.

We talked more, or to be truthful, I talked, she listened; threw in a few things here and there that really struck a chord with me and made me talk even more. I couldn't shut the hell up. I told her about Karen, how she saved me from myself, how she completed me, how I didn't think I could live without her, how I didn't even want to. I told her that I could die tonight and be glad to see it coming. You know what I mean? To hell with living like this. It ain't life, it's just, well, plain old hell, you know.

We went on for a long time. I don't know how long, just a long time and all at once I realized that I didn't have the faintest idea where I was. Like I said, I was born here and never left. Getting lost here is like getting lost going from the kitchen to the bathroom down the hall, but there I was, just the same, lost. She was giving me directions and I kept on driving, but I was beginning to get scared because nothing looked familiar. I didn't know what was going on there but I know that we'd been on the go for what seemed like several hours and the gas gauge had not moved and my watch had quit. Finally, she said, "ok, this is my stop." I looked around and didn't see anything but black woods. I was about to open my mouth to say something when she reached out her hand and just said "don't." When she opened the door and the dome light came on, I got a full look at her. She was like Sunday morning choir, clean as a new penny. Bone dry. not a hair out of place. She was wearing a long, white dress that didn't have a spot of mud on it nowhere, not even on the hem. She had some shoes on that were made out of some kind of fabric. Snow white. Clean, you know. On the ring finger of her left hand was a ring. Now, I ain't usually much aware of ladies' ornamentation, but I sure know that ring. I had put it on Karen's hand when we said our I do's and it was still on there when I saw her go into the ground. She got out, then turned back inside and whispered, "We're fine, John. Don't wonder, don't worry. We're just fine. Love life, love everyone in it.

Look for and find truth. Believe."

With that she closed the door without slamming it, turned and walked toward that stand of dogwood trees that grow over where the tracks cross the creek.

I felt myself slide down into the seat and sleep covered me. When I woke up, the sun was just starting to crack the ridge. The truck had run out of gas during the night and the lights had drained the battery. Oh well, no matter; I had a jerry can of gas and a tractor battery in the truck bed. When I got to out to get the truck going, I looked at the ground. No tracks. I knew exactly where I was, you know, down by Daltons crossing, about five miles from home. As I drove, I yawned and said out loud, "damn, what a fine morning!"

I stuck a Johnny Cash tape in the slot and sang along. Johnny's better than me. I felt good.

Love Like This

Connor Anderson was deep in the bowels of an ancient steamer, mid Atlantic, wishing he had thought of something else—anything rather than working his passage from Scotland by feeding coal into that leaky boiler's fiery maw. Ten hours on shift, eight hours off. Every shift brought him closer to New York harbor though, and the certain knowledge that nothing, not even misery lasts forever.

One of the fire room rules was that while working in that inferno, you were supposed to wear a long sleeve shirt, buttoned at the wrists and neck so that in the event of a burst pipe or a broken fitting, even that much protection might keep a worker from lethal scalding. Of course, nobody really cared about the boiler rats and in a place where the temperature could easily reach 120 degrees, the men usually worked in their pants only, sweat running down their bodies in sheets.

The owners provided washed clothes every shift plus hot water and raw soap to try to scrub the black mess off of their skin. After a few weeks, however, it became obvious that it wasn't going to come off, and most of the men just gave up and lived with it.

Connor's shift partner was a wiry little fellow with so much body hair that Connor later said that it was like working with a monkey. The man jabbered constantly in some language of which Connor never understood a single word. No one even knew where he came from, but it was commonly thought that he was hiding out from the law in connection with a bar fight in Wales. One of the other firemen, talking to Connor said "For crying out loud, kid, if you just got to kill someone, do it in some grungy little shit hole of a port where don't nobody could car less." That sounded like good advice Connor and he kept to himself as much as he could.

During his off-shift hours, his mind took him away from that pounding, wallowing, flat bottomed wreck back from the arms of sweet Nancy Gregor. She had wanted to marry him right away, but Connor had said no, that he would marry her as soon as he could take care of her in a fashion that he could be proud of. Try as mightily as he could, Scotland just didn't have the resources to produce that and so Connor proclaimed that he would immigrate to America, where a man could pick up a fortune while only half trying.

After becoming rich in a couple of years, he would send for his love they would spend the rest of their lives trying to spend all the money he was certain to make. After a few more weeks the ship finally reached New York harbor. He didn't even get to see Lady Liberty on his way in; he was down in the fire room shoveling coal when they passed her.

His first actual look at America was the boiling, brawling pier at Red Hook, across the East River from Staten Island. He was supposed to stay on board to load coal for the return trip, but he cashed out and left the ship. Appalled at the city, with its crowding and squalor, he cried out to God that the place looked like the underside of hell. What had he gotten himself into? After sleeping two nights in an alley, he found a room to share with four other men in the same predicament. He saw an advertisement for men to work on a railroad line heading west, and he figuring that nothing could be worse than where he was, he went to sign up. The busier took one look atheism and said, "Chappie, you may not know what you're in for here. Truth be told, we don't recommend that white men try this."

"Why?," responded Connor.

"Well, white men just die out there; work's too dam hard; it's best for Chinamen, Mexicans and niggers." Ignoring the warning, the next day he found himself on a train headed west to lay track and true to the employment office man's word, and when he got where the crews were working, he found the work to be brutal, back breaking hard labor. The only rest that came along was when the machinery broke down, which happened with amazing regularity. The crews were paid by how much truck went down, not by the hours they worked, so, no trackie, no money.

Connor soon saw the most of the breakdowns were caused by lack of maintenance and didn't seem to be all the difficult to fix if a man only had the appropriate tools and spare parts on hand. He noticed that most of the things that broke on the track gear were due to the failure of the same six parts and if he had replacement parts and tools, he could cut the down time significantly. Better than that, if he had a few barrels of grease and a few cans of oil, he could keep a lot of that gear from breaking at all. He designed and sent back drawings and diagrams to improve rolling stock and the company was ecstatic with his performance. Connor Andrews was a first class design engineer when nothing like that even existed. He loved the work and many of the things that he designed and built were to be used in the next century. He was particularly keen on locomotives, and he just couldn't walk by one without stopping to simply admire the iron beast. All this was not, however getting him any closer to bringing his love from Scotland.

One fine day Connor found himself in a dirty little frontier town call San Bernardino, as lonely for Nancy Gregor as he thought he ever could be. He had written her letter and letter, running over with anguish and love. It could sometimes take a couple of months for a letter on the way, month in and month out. He had heard nothing from her because in a year and a half, he did not have an address. Connor was now at the end of his rope and he wondered what there might possibly be in San Bernardino that he could possibly use to make enough money to bring his Nancy Gregor from that far away country into his arms. He was absolutely adamant that she would cover that six thousand miles in ease, comfort and safety. No grubby tramp steamer for her, grinding through that danger fraught north Atlantic. Every year several ships were lost to those rough, cold unforgiving seas, and he was going to make sure that her passage would be safe and comfortable.

By that time, rail lines were in place across the continent and a person with sufficient means could ride a train from New York to San Bernardino. Actually, it was a little more complicated than that, but it could be done and Connor fantasized about the day when he would meet a train in San Bernardino and there sweep his Nancy Gregor into his empty arms, never to let her go again.

One day Connor wandered down to the rail yards where he was now working as a locomotive and rolling stock mechanic, and came upon a small, filthy shop with only one set of tracks in and out and nothing being worked on. He walked in, narrowly avoided being bitten by a mangy dog and found the owner, passed out in a drunken stupor lying in a puddle of urine. He went back the next day with a couple of pounds of bad smelling meat that he found behind his boarding house, made friends with the dog, and make the drunk an offer to buy the place. Cleaned up and painted, the shop attracted attention and getting a few small jobs, Connor started to make a name for himself. Small jobs turned into major overhauls and before long, Connor had move from the small shop into a much larger facility with six lines of track. He had twenty employees and as much business as he could handle. His heart turned to Scotland. Only one thing remained to be done. He drew up plans for a house and hired a builder to do the work. He bought several acres of land with a small stream on it and watched the progress on Nancy Gregor's house with a leaping, glad heart. He was still sending letter after letter to her and since he now had a place to receive mail, he received a letter from her. The day it arrived, he picked it up at the post office and was so overcome that he stood in the middle of the room and wailed like an idiot, tears pouring down his face, kissing the letter over and over before he got up the nerve to open it. People thought that he had lost his mind. In the next month he sent her an avalanche of letters and in one proposed marriage.

When he had gotten his post office box, she had started writing him as furiously as he wrote her. He had all of her letters in a trunk, where he went every day to read those lines of love and passion, but one day they stopped without one word of explanation. He was devastated to think that she might have changed her mind. If that be the case, he had to hear it from her and he almost doubled his output of mail to her.

Finally, a letter appeared from Scotland. It was from a local parish Priest. Connor carried it home to the house that he had built for Nancy Gregor and there read the words that ripped the heart out of his chest. "———regret to inform you that Miss Nancy Gregor died this January first, 1901, from pneumonia. Birth records indicate that she was twenty years old. Since she had no blood relative and no money, she has been buried with Christian rites in the Kirk yard as an indigent. Sir, I am in receipt of an astounding amount of mail from you. I have found these letters to be intensely personal and I ask you for any advice you may be able to provide me concerning the disposition of them———"

Connor wrote the kind man of the cloth, requesting that he box up the letters and place them in permanent storage. He provided a check large enough to store them into the next century and provided under separate cover a sizable donation to the church.

Connor finished the house but never invited anyone in for a social visit. He became a virtual Hermit, going to work every morning and going home every evening. Often, he could be seen sitting on his porch, reading though a hug stack of letters. Someone had given him a Labrador puppy that was his constant and sole companion. The dog went where Connor went and if the dog wasn't welcome, then neither was a Connor. Not many people turned down Connor Andrews' attention because through good business practice, he had accumulated a fortune of several million dollars of which he was inclined to give generously when he found reason to do so. Connor had no social life and he was so withdrawn that he made people uneasy and invitations stopped coming in. He was relieved.

In late 1946 he began having low back pain. He figured that it was just the old rheumatiz and didn't pay much attention to it. The mild ache became real pain and he saw his doctor about it; the result was a diagnosis of metastasized prostate cancer. Six months to a year left to live. He went home, sat down in his rocker on the porch, petted his old dog and thought, "Well, that's time enough."

He had a shop foreman who caught Connor's attention every time he came around. Abel Martinez seemed to know exactly what would need to be done and exactly how to do it. Connor shook his head at the level of confidence and competency he regularly saw in his foreman. Abel was married to a Mexican woman who exemplified the Mexican idea of a Mexican wife. Maybe a little loud, and brash, quick to laugh, and quick to love. Connor was withdrawn, but he was not unobservant. He watched these two citizens of the new world as they showed a love that equaled that which he still had for Nancy Gregor.

Flor Martinez was a school teacher. Not as in the usual gringo system because in those days, Mexicans were seen as second class and so she, as her personality led her, opened her home to all the little kids around the shops. She taught English, she taught arithmetic, she taught Spanish, she taught cooking for both boys and girls. The children around her noisy house learned social graces and how to navigate polite society. For the girls, there were many girl things to master because each of them would grow into Mexican women who would need to know such things. One day Connor came to Abel's house on business and watched Flor. Teaching a squad of little girls learning needlepoint. Something clicked in Connor's mind and he asked her to do a needle point work for him. She said, "Sure, Señor, what do you want?" He told her he would let her know in a couple of days, and sure enough, in a few days he showed up with a drawing of what he wanted. She took one look at it and said, "Señor, what the hell is this? It doesn't make sense. Looks like writing but what language is it?" Connor look at her, looked at the drawing and said, "Someday you will understand. Until then, you don't need to. Just do the picture and stretch and frame it. I want to hang it in my house." Connor spent time with his bankers and lawyers, and finally sold the business to Abel Martinez for pennies one the dollar. The house he transferred to Flor Martinez for good will.

Connor didn't even bother to clear his belongings out. He said that everything there went with the house. He checked to make sure that the flower he had planted on Black Dog's grave was thriving and then walked down to the train station where he caught a train for New York.

Flor had never seen the inside of her house when she and Abel walked into if for the first time. She was so flabbergasted that she had to force herself to keep walking. They expected the place to be a filthy old bachelor's den and they couldn't believe what they were seeing. Light, airy, and very feminine. Crochet doilies, pastel colors, a bait displaying porcelain dolls, several cabinets full of beautiful china, trivia, paintings, pictures, and in a prominent place, that needle point that he had commissioned Flor to make. She still hadn't a clue as to what it was, but Señor had said that someday she would understand, and that was good enough for her.

Abel casually opened a closet and gasped. Flor came to see and was amazed at the sight of a full closet of beautiful women's clothes, gowns, dresses, and with the tags still on. None ever worn. A truck full of undergarments, a rack of shoes, some leather, some silk, and all beautiful. Almost everything so out of date that at her age she would never be able to wear more than a few of them. They were speechless.

Another closet contained a riot of blouses, scarves, belts, ties, and in the back a cardboard box. Abel pulled it out and with some trepidation opened it. Letter, hundreds of them all from Nancy Gregor.

Connor enjoyed the train ride and the ocean voyage much more this time. He even made sure that he saw Lady Liberty as he passed her. When he again set foot on Scottish soil, he was a tired, dying old man. He had longed every day for Nancy Gregor and now he was so close. He finally found the old man who was the caretaker of the little church that he remembered as a young man. As he strolled among the headstones in that rattly little Kirk yard he asked the old man if he knew the grave of Nancy Gregor. The old man said, "Oh yes, she's right over here," and slowly led Connor to a place that he would have missed had he been alone. Over grown with rank weeds and fallen leaves, was a small vertical rock without a trace of inscription. Connor asked the old man how he knew exactly where she was. The old caretaker replied, "Ah, but I loved her. She didn't care a whit for me, though; she was going to go to America. Never made it, more's the shame. She died back in '01. Her beau would have made a lucky man."

Connor came up with an exorbitant amount of money to establish in perpetuity a fund to rebuild the chapel and clean up the Kirk yard. It is now a pleasant place to meditate. Smooth, close grass, trimmed trees, People come by the chapel for a few minutes of prayer. Some bring a sandwich and have lunch there. There are comfortable benches all around. All the old stones are still there and if they are so old that the inscription is unreadable, well, that's alright, known only to God, their bones resting in this beautiful place, their souls resting with Jesus. Actually, one stone was changed. Connor commissioned a dual headstone. Connor wanted to marry Nancy at the time but the priest, a youngster said, "What? You can't marry a dead person! Are you daft?" Connor argued long and hard, saying that yes, he realized that you can't marry a dead person, but had she been alive, he surely would have! At last an old retired priest was brought in, Connor greased the wheels with money and the old cleric performed not a full ceremony of marriage, but what he called, "A full intent to marry." On the new stone, on the right side the inscription read, Nancy Andrews, faithful wife to Connor Andrews. Born 1880, died 1901. On the left side, the inscription read, Connor Andrews, faithful husband to Nancy Andrews. Born 1880, died 1948. The stone carried another inscription. Deeply carved into that heavy, polished marker were words in Gaelic, that ancient language of the Scots: "with a love like that, nothing more is needed".

Connor wrangled a few more promised from the local authorities. He would be buried the day he died. He would not be embalmed. He would not be buried in a casket. He would be wrapped in a soft blanket and laid directly into God's sweet earth, as close to Nancy Andrews as the workers were comfortable with digging. He would be buried with a bouquet of roses in his arms. The old caretaker, who was in charge of the proceedings, said "What, roses in your arms?" Connor said "Yes, they will be for somebody I'll meet. The caretaker, understanding everything, fulfilled Connor's wishes to the letter and he was laid to rest in accordance with his desires.

Legend has it that on cold, clear moonlit nights, their ghosts can occasionally be seen strolling hand in hand across the verdant fields, and some have sworn to feel the breath of roses on their skin even when no roses are abloom.

After much debate it was finally decided that it was alright to bring dogs to play in the Kirk yard. They play joyously, and then tired and clam, many go to the graves of Connor and Nancy to sleep. Some folks grumble that it seems a sacrilege to allow dogs to sleep on graves, while others say "No, it's right and proper. Look how peaceful they are. It's the love of those tow that brings them."

Abel and Flor Martinez were sitting in their house, still not sure what they were going to do with it. Flor was studying the needle point that Connor had commissioned her to make. She was sure that the words held a deep, rich meaning and she longed to understand. Suddenly, she jumped up, ran across the room, jabbed her finger at the art work and cried out, "By God, Abel, I know what language that is! It's Gaelic and there's an old woman down at the library who's from Scotland. I'll bet anything she can translate it."

Flor didn't want to take the needle point off the wall for a couple of reasons: first it was very large. Almost four feet long and only a little less than a foot tall. The second reason was that Connor had fixed the artwork so firmly to the wall that it was plain to see that he wanted it to never be moved. Flor, however, still had the full-scale template that Connor had made for her to create the needle point from and a few days later, they took the scroll to the library, met the ancient Scottish lady and asked her if she knew what in the world it said. She glanced at it and cried out "Oh! Where in the world did you get this? It's beautiful! I haven't seen Gaelic calligraphy like this since I was a girl in Scotland. Can I buy this? I want to frame it and hang it in the library!"

Flor said no, she would never part with it because a treasured friend had made it by hand. The old dear was disappointed but understood. Flor finally took a deep breath and asked if she could translate it. "Oh but of course," she replied. It's so touching. "It says, with a love like this, nothing more is needed."

I Remember

I remember a couple of years ago when we had three humming-bird feeders going at the same time. We were filling them every 2-3 days in order to keep up with the demand. We would stand at the window and try our best to count the birds that buzzed around the feeders and at best, we were able to count approximately 25 or so. Each feeder had 4 flowers/feeding holes and the birds didn't seem to fight too much for a chance to eat like they did when the population was smaller. Sometimes the feeders would be a total blur with birds zooming back and forth from the feeders and a place to just sit and rest. I really don't know how they kept from having a mid-air collision but they seemed to have it handled. Some of the birds were very nice to one another and would even share the same flower with a buddy, where one would take a drink and they sit back and allow the other to drink or even drink at the same time. Others seemed to have a "me only" or "me first" attitude and were unwilling to share, sometimes even would chase off anybody that was in their way. At this same time, we had some friends that said they had five feeders and approximately 40 or so birds.

Fish

When my sister and brother-in-law celebrated their 50th anniversary the table decorations included a bowl with shiny flat blue marbles with a bright yellow ribbon tied around the neck and had a beautiful male beta fish swimming around. There were twelve tables for all the guests with all these lovely bowls of fish and my great niece had stated that all the fish bowls needed loving homes and she was not interested in taking them all home with her. So I proudly took my bowl with fish home. The problem was that I didn't have a safe place to keep it at home as I had a cat that definitely would not leave it alone. So I took the beta to work and placed it on my desk. It made a nice addition and I really enjoyed glancing at it from time to time. My co-workers also enjoyed looking at the fish as well and if I was out of the office for my flex day one of the co-workers would feed it for me. Also, before the weekend she would add the small piece of vacation block so he would have food while we were closed if I was off that Friday. When I changed offices then I had new people to admire the fish and carry on the tradition of "fish sitting." One of the co-workers was sad that my beta didn't have a name and decided that his name should be Hairy (where that name came from, I'll never know) and even made a label for the bowl with his name on it. As the years have passed on there have been 10-15 or so beta fish and I have named them all Fishy 1, Fishy 2, etc. Now over the years there is still a beta and I have lost track as to how many fishes there have been. I now have the beta at home in a different fish bowl and the cats have been no problem.

Serendipity

The reason that I started flying was because Steve (husband) had taken flying lessons and after he got his license, I went flying with him. I had never considered that I would ever learn to fly, but decided that maybe I should learn to find an airport and land in the event of an emergency. I set up to take a few lessons as a passenger pilot in the right seat with an instructor. Lina was here from Sweden with her boyfriend and both were teaching flying. After four or five lessons they had to return to Sweden and I got placed with another instructor. After a lesson or two Sean said to forget this passenger pilot stuff and he moved me to the left seat and saying "you are going to get a license for yourself."

I continued my lessons and started moving through the training process that proved to be much more intense than the program that Steve had gone through. It was called a 941 Program that required me to do three flights with the Chief Instructor and be signed off before I could advance to the next training module. I also had to do another check flight and be signed off before I could go for the check ride with the FAA Examiner for my actual license.

In my 4th month of training I took a training session with yet another instructor and Mark told me that he was going to steal me to be his student. Within a few weeks there was a student swap and I now had my third instructor who turned out to be much harder than the other two had been. He was really picky and more demanding but I feel he made me a much better pilot because I had to work harder.

During this time, I was also working full time and was a full-time student in the School of Business at University of Redlands for my bachelor's degree and had to spend a lot of time studying for school. I was also studying for the ground school portion of the pilot's license and taking flight lessons. When I finally had to take the written portion, I was really stressed out as I didn't think I was ready. Mark made me take it then anyway and I did pass and was glad that portion of the process was past me.

After all my training was over, I sailed through the last flight with the Chief Instructor and all that was left was to finish the last preparation to go for my license. Thanks to my instructor, I was so prepared that I sailed through the process with the FAA Examiner and became a pilot in my own right.

This was so funny because I didn't even think that I would want to fly myself or be licensed, but found out that I really enjoyed flying and being able to control something that is so unique to most people. It was truly and unexcited outcome.

Unexpected Happening

I had been gone a couple of hours on a shopping trip and when I came home the screen door was standing wide open. The door opens on the back of the house and my husband is really inclined to leave everything open so the cats and dog can come and go at will. I went in and put my purse on the bed and was on the way out to get the bags from the car when I heard a strange sound coming from the bedroom. I found a hummingbird flying around and around the room. Steve was taking a nap. I woke him up and we went back to watch the bird fly around the room. The poor bird was getting really confused with the entire wall of mirror doors on the closet and the large mirror on the dresser. He would fly and fly and finally land on the blades of the ceiling fan and then fly some more and land on the top of the doors that run along the top of the mirror closet. I tried to get him to land on a dowel or on my finger so I could take him outside, but that was not going to happen.

Steve pulled the blinds up, opened the window and removed the screen in the hopes that he would just fly out the open window. The first thing that happened was Muffin, our cat, jumped up on the window sill and was very interested in what was going on. So I grabbed her and put in out in the hall and closed the bedroom door. Hummingbirds need a lot of energy so I decided to get a feeder in the hopes that he would land on it and eat, and then I could put him out the window. When I came back into the room, he had finally found the open window and was gone. A few months after this we had one flying around the living room and with much work, we finally got him out of the house too.

It was really a treat to watch them fly in a confined area while it lasted. I just hope that there were not any bad affects from the amount of flying that they were doing as I don't even know how long each of them had been in the house. Hopefully they went on to have a long hummingbird life.

Early Experiences with Musical Training

It was important to my mother to do "what was considered to be the right thing" in raising a child. During the time I was growing up, music lessons for all children was one of the expectations of properly raising a well-rounded child.

When I was in grade school, my mother and father bought a brand new piano. I don't think the money for it came easily. I loved it. It was the most beautiful piano I had ever seen. It was mahogany. I loved learning to play on it. I loved practicing. I even loved polishing it on weekends.

My mother hired a man from our church to give me piano lessons. I only knew his name was Brother Dewey. He was an old man. And I don't mean old, like a child thinks everyone over 20 is old. He was probably the oldest man in our church. Part of the respect paid to him was because of his age, but mostly it was because of his zeal in bearing his testimony.

On the first Sunday of each month, Brother Dewey would be one of the first to stand up and declare his love of God and his assurance of his belief in the church in a loud and passionate voice. He would form his right hand into a fist and pound it into the palm of his left hand to emphasize his points. After the service was over, a crowd of people always gathered around him to praise him and thank him for his wonderful and inspiring words. Sometimes, I was brave enough to stand up and bear my testimony. It was intimidating as a small child, but we children were all encouraged to participate. Once in a while, someone would come to me after the service to praise me for my efforts.

My mother started working-probably to pay for the piano–and because Brother Dewey couldn't come in the evenings, he came after I got out of school and before my mother got home from work. The weeks passed and I learned to play little songs that could be performed for company. I knew it made my mother happy. Although she never said anything, I could tell from her face after I finished playing for friends and family that she was proud of me.

One afternoon, when I finished playing, Brother Dewey told me what a wonderful job I had done. He was more enthusiastic in his praise than he had ever been. I was happy and eagerly accepted his praise because it came from this person who was not only well respected, but revered.

Then he turned towards me on the piano bench and hugged me so hard and so tight that I felt uncomfortable and trapped. I waited for him to let go of me, but instead, he kissed me on the lips. His lips were pressed so hard on mine that my gums were smashed onto my teeth. His eyes were closed and he had the same look on his face that he had when he bore his testimony. No one in my large family or our many friends had ever kissed me like that.

I don't remember the rest of the lesson, but when I walked him to the door when it was over, I waited impatiently by the closed door until I was sure he had gone. Then I ran out of the house to my neighbor's house to tell my friend, Darleen, what had happened. In her bedroom, I made her promise she would never tell anyone, especially my mother. When I was finished, Darleen didn't say anything at first. Finally, she said, "We need to tell my mom." I reminded her that she had promised not to tell anyone. She said that she would keep her promise, but I needed to tell her mom, Ella.

We all called her "Old Ella," even though she was younger than the other women on the block. She was divorced with four children and didn't do anything all day but drink coffee, smoke cigarettes and rock back and forth in her rocking chair. She looked and seemed older because she appeared shapeless, covering her body in a shapeless dress, and her hair was greasy and unkempt. Really? What could it matter if I told Ella what had happened? She probably wouldn't get out of her rocking chair anyway. After I told her, I made her promise not to tell anybody—and she promised.

The next day after dinner, my mother and father were talking in that quiet, secretive way moms and dads sometimes talk. As my mother walked towards me with an extremely serious face and my father was looking at me with an expression on his face that mirrored hers, I knew that somehow, Old Ella had managed to get out of her rocking chair long enough to tell my mom what happened. And, I must admit, I was relieved because I didn't want to keep anything from my mom, but I was afraid to tell her.

We went to my bedroom and sitting on my bed, I repeated everything to her. She didn't say much. I couldn't really tell how she felt, except that she was very serious and tight lipped. I knew she believed me and I felt a great weight had been lifted from me. I slept better that night than I had the night before.

Brother Dewey never came back to give me a piano lesson. Eventually I had another teacher who came in the evening after dinner. I still saw Brother Dewey in church. We never spoke again. He got up on the first Sunday of the month and bore his testimony with ardent passion, forming his right hand into a fist and pounding it into the palm of his left hand for emphasis. Afterwards a group of people would gather around to praise him and thank him for his inspiring testimony as he stood with his arms folded piously across his chest accepting their words with a look of modesty.

Later, when I was brave enough to stand up and bear my testimony, others would praise me for my effort. If Brother Dewey ever happened to look my way, it was remote, detached, as if I did not exist.

Moving On

My daughter, Andrea, and I were at dinner. Over chips, salsa and a Margarita, I told her about a woman I had met that morning with lung cancer. While she was in treatment, a nurse she grew to know over time, asked her why she fought so hard to stay alive. The woman answered her, thinking the nurse must have admired her bravery through this ordeal. She was surprised when the nurse said that the reason she was asking was because she had told her family that if she had cancer, she didn't want any treatment; she would just die.

I was very upset that someone had said something so awful to this woman. I was outraged and indignant. I expected Andrea's response to mirror mine. Instead, she said, "Do you mean like when you told your oncologist you weren't sure you wanted to accept treatment?"

"I said that? I don't remember saying that."

"Yes, you said that. When the doctor told you that you had cancer and would be having surgery and then radiation treatment, you asked him what would happen if you chose not to have treatment."

"Really," I asked. "What did he say?"

He said, "Then you'll die."

She looked at her plate a few minutes as I sat trying to remember back to that conversation. Then she continued, "That's when I found out I was pregnant with Colin and you said it was a gift, a sign of life to come and you started treatment.

I smiled, "Yes, yes. That part I do remember."

The Year 1955

Charles Dickens wrote "It was the best of times, it was the worst of times." 1955 was the best of times because I got married and the worst of times because I got married. Did he propose? Did I? We had known each other since second grade and dated since high school. We mailed wedding invitations, found an apartment near the San Bernardino County Library where I worked, and after we said "I do" went on a one-week honeymoon.

It was the worst of times because he left a week later. The U.S. Navy requested his presence in the Philippines for six months. When he returned, he was stationed at Port Huenume, ten miles south of Ventura. Sailors stationed at Port Huenume are Seabees, short for Construction Battalion. Seabees construct bridges, run ways, roads, any construction requiring heavy equipment, any place the Navy needs something built, the Seabees are sent to build it.

While he was in the Philippines, I bought my brother's old 26 foot house trailer. It was parked at the trailer park my parents owned and since rent was only $25 a month I moved out of the apartment and into the trailer. So smart of me I thought, saving $20 a month on rent—$120 in the six months he would be gone. I moved my treadle sewing machine and chair into the trailer and made curtains for the windows, pillows for the couch, put dishes in the cupboard, went to work and waited for his return.

He came home the first of November. Although he was impressed with the trailer, he informed me our car didn't have enough power to pull the trailer. Any excuse, I thought, for him to buy a car. He bought a 1951 Pontiac hard top convertible, green on the bottom, white on the top, white wall tires, and white leather interior. Plenty of power he said.

Had he ever pulled a trailer? No. He bought a trailer hitch, hooked the trailer to the car and white knuckled it one hundred and fifty miles west to the navy base. When he told me he would park it in a trailer park at the beach, I imagined Balboa, Newport, Laguna, beaches I was familiar with, white sand, blue water, blue sky, white clouds. Boy was I in for a big surprise. There was no beach, no white sand—just dirty gray ocean.

Three things I learned very quickly—two cannot live as cheaply as one, a sailor's pay is not enough for two people, and the mournful, beeohhh, beeohhh, beeohhh, sound of the fog horn bellowing across the bay, day and night when the fog rolls in can drive a person crazy. After he went to work, I sat inside the little trailer which seemed to get smaller every day, hearing the annoying fog horn and counted pennies trying to figure out how to pay rent, car payment, car insurance, gas for the car, and groceries for two on less than $100 a month. Not much money, Oh, but honey, Ain't we got fun. No, we ain't!

November—everything shrouded in gray, gray sky, gray ocean, gray sand, gray seagulls, gray vegetation rotting in nasty smelling marshes. Across the road on the gray sand was an abandoned fish processing plant, its weathered wood bleached gray, its tin roof gray, loose and banging in the wind. Gray house trailer. Gray yard. Navy equipment painted gray. Gray depressed me. The green car provided the only spot of color. Gray skies are gonna clear up, put on a happy face, brush off the clouds and cheer up, put on a happy face. You bet I will.

Monday, five days after arriving, I drove north ten miles, walked into the Ventura County Library and asked for a job application. The lady at the desk asked my name, told me to wait a minute and disappeared. In a few minutes she was back with an application, and a woman who asked me where I had been, they had been expecting me! I was confused. She explained that California county libraries publish a monthly newsletter reporting news from county libraries in California. In October's newsletter was an article about me stating I was moving from San Bernardino to Ventura. They thought I might come in looking for a job. They were happy to see me. She asked me to take the application home fill it out, bring it back the next day and they would process paper work. She asked, "When can you start?" I could not believe it. I was ready to start that minute. I completed the application that night, returned it on Tuesday and started working on Wednesday.

That weekend we moved the trailer to a park close to town. Beautiful bright colors everywhere, green grass and trees, flowers, neon lights and blue sky. Gray skies cleared up and I put on a happy, happy face.

Moving On

My dear L.C.

I am writing to express my thoughts about our relationship. What a great trip these past ten years have been, but maybe ten years is enough time together. Maybe time to spice up our lives, time to move on.

I will always remember the good times we've had, the trips we've taken together, the Route 66 trip, National Park trips, visits to friends and family. We traveled many roads together and we hit some rough spots now and then, but we stuck together. You were willing to go along with the plan, go that extra mile. You were dependable except for the time you got all steamed up, almost blew your top. I left you alone for a while and let you cool down, give you something to drink and you were okay. And one time you refused to move. Remember that? Nothing I said or did to encourage you helped. You just sat there, not making a sound, like part of you had died. I had to ask for help and we got passed that problem.

The first time I saw you I was shocked. I had not heard a word about you. I had been released from the hospital after surgery and a fours day recovery period. He dropped me off at the hospital Monday morning, checked me in, stayed until I was wheeled into surgery, then he left returning in the evening. He never discussed what he did during the week I was in the hospital. Now I know he was with you. He wanted you, but let me tell you, you were not the first. Oh, no! Before you, there was another, younger, and more beautiful.

You are still young with many good years ahead. I see you getting the once-over, from top to bottom. People looking for a new, exciting and long lasting relationship ask about you all the time and leave their names and phone numbers.* They would love you and take good care of you, give you a complete make over. I plan to start looking around and see what's available for me.

Wishing you the best and thanks for your dependability and the wonderful experiences we shared—great memories. I will miss you, L.C. He wanted you—but I want a car and so I'm moving on.

Author's note: *L.C. Stands for El Camino, a 1985 Chevy, white exterior, blue interior, white wall tires. Names and phone numbers, business cards left under L.C.'s windshield wiper when parked or handed to me while talking about the El Camino.*

Reuniting with Linda the Dish

She was downright cute, brown hair and eyes, a few freckles sparkling across her nose and checks, a Mona Lisa smile, like she was enjoying a story she was telling herself, embellishing, exaggerating, dramatizing, even fabricating to make the story hilarious. She was nineteen years old, tall, slim, smart, funny and single. And like I said, cute. Her name was Linda.

We met in 1959 at the Point Mugu Naval Missile Test Center located on the California Coast midway between San Diego and Santa Barbara. We worked at the front desk in the technical library where classified documents received from aerospace companies were cataloged and stored. Our job was to shelve reports in the vault and check them out when requested by both civilian and military personnel.

Navy officers in their magnificent uniforms, winter blues and summer whites, as well as civilians came into the library to check out reports, or hmmm, I wonder, did they come to check out Linda? She had her pick of all those good looking, brilliant hunks. And who did she pick? Cal, an enlisted sailor who worked in the photo lab down the hall. He was of average height, but shorter than Linda, earned less money than officers and civilian personnel, and personally we, the married women of the tech library, thought Captain Tucker was perfect for her. Oh, well, love beats all.

One Monday morning Linda waltzed into the library smiling from ear to ear, her left arm extended, her hand waving, her ring finger sporting a dazzling diamond engagement ring. Several months later she married Cal. Her name changed from Kaiser to Dishman. She became known as "Linda the Dish."

In late 1959 and early 1960 there was a pregnancy epidemic in the tech library. First Phyllis announced she was pregnant, then Rosie, then Jeannie, then Linda. As for me, I had been married five years and had no intention of having kids, ever. I was the seventh of nine children. At age five I had two younger sisters, at age seven,

WWII began, there was a housing shortage, my oldest sister and her two little girls moved home. I was the designated baby sitter. No kids for me I decided at age seven!

My husband was in the Navy and I enjoyed my job and friends in the library. We bought a house, I signed up for UCLA extension classes on base and he bought an Austin Healey Roadster. We were having fun, road rally's, week-end drives up and down the coast on Highway 101, in the roadster. Life was good until I got sick. One morning at work I felt queasy and rushed to the restroom. Linda followed, took one look at me and said, "You are pregnant." "I am not," I snapped, "I have the flu." "No," she insisted, titling her head slightly, grinning in that superior way, "you are pregnant, definitely pregnant." She was right. Within three months Sue announced she was pregnant. Wow! Six pregnancies in the tech library!

Linda made a little book for me. On the front cover she wrote "The Bump" by Linda Dishman, November 22, 1959. It began— once upon a time there was a lady with a bump—namely me. Phyllis, Rosie, and Linda had boys, and Jeannie had a girl. They all became stay at home moms. On July 23, 1960 "the Bump" became Sandra Elizabeth. Six weeks later I returned to work. In October, Sue gave birth to a girl. She also returned to work, but seven months later was pregnant again. She had a son and became a stay at home mom. I transferred out of the library, away from the chairs that, according to our supervisor, were the cause of all the pregnancies.

When my husband was discharged from the Navy we moved back to Redlands where we grew up and where our families lived. Life went merrily along and on December 26, 1968 we had a son. Years flew by and for my birthday in 1986 Sandra gave me two tickets to see Phantom of the Opera at the Dorothy Chandler Theater in Los Angeles. I thought she was going with me. No, she said, the tickets were for me and a friend. After asking seven friends if they would like to see the show and getting seven no thank yous, I called Linda. "Oh, yes," she said, "I would love to go." "When?" she asked. "Next Wednesday," I replied. "Oh, perfect, I think I am going to be sick that day and I'll have to ask my boss if I can borrow his car."

She drove to LA from Oxnard, in her boss' pickup truck. I drove from Redlands and we met in the underground parking garage at the theater, ate lunch at the theater while she told me about the divorce. Her best friend, Kim, and Cal were having an affair. He asked for a divorce. She agreed on four conditions: first, she wanted a percentage of the profit from their business, second, she wanted Cal to refinance their house, she would get half of the equity, third, she wanted Cal to stay in the house with the boys so they would attend the same school, keep the same friends, and fourth, she wanted unlimited visitations. Cal agreed. "Let Kim and Cal deal with four adolescent boys" she said—she would be the fun Mom. We saw the show, parted company in the parking garage, promised to stay in touch, but didn't.

Cal died in October 2013. Jeannie emailed me his obituary. It stated Cal was "survived by his loving wife of 25 years, Kim, and four sons." I met Jeanie and Sue for lunch recently. We reminisced about our days at Point Mugu and wondered what became of Linda. After agreeing to locate her we didn't even try.

Last Friday, as a result of a writing assignment titled "Someone I would Like to Reunite with and Why," I googled the white pages and searched for the names of Linda's sons. I found one who now owns the family business and found a web page with his phone number. I called. His voice mail answered. I left a message, my name and phone number. He hasn't called. I will try again.

Why would I like to reunite with Linda? Curiosity. I wonder what happened after the divorce? I wonder what stories she would write today. I would like to tell her what happened to the Bump, tell her I still have the "Once Upon a Time" story she wrote so long ago. Most of all I would like to talk and laugh with Linda like we did—Once Upon a Time.

I did locate Linda and we talked briefly on the phone. She was recovering from recent brain surgery, her second. We agreed to stay in touch. We haven't. I have her address and phone number. She has mine. Maybe I will send her a card. Or maybe I won't. Maybe I'm afraid to find out what has happened to my cute and funny friend—Linda the Dish.

Popsicles

In 1905 an eleven-year old boy living in the San Francisco Bay Area named Frank Epperson accidentally invented a summertime treat. He mixed some sugary soda powder with water and left it out overnight. It was a very cold night and the mixture froze. In the morning he ate the icy concoction, licking it off the wooden stick. He said it was an Epsicle, combining part of his name with icicle. For many years Frank sold the treat around his neighborhood. The years passed, Frank married and had children. His children referred to the Epsicle as "Pop's sicle," and that is why we now have this great summer treat—the Popsicle.

The original six flavors and colors are: lemon lime (green), grape (purple), tropical punch (pink), orange (orange), berry punch (blue), punch (red). New flavors have been added: banana, strawberry, root beer . . . What? What did you say? You mean . . . ? I wrote the wrong . . . ? I should have written what? The assignment was obstacles? Are you sure? Obstacles? I thought she said Popsicles! Well, okay then. Let me tell you the obstacles Frank encountered trying to get a patent on his little concoction.

No?

Okay, seriously, she wants to know the most difficult obstacle in my life? That would be me.

Then she asks how does it (me) affect my life? I cannot stay focused. I have too many irons in the fire or in my case, too many UFOs in my life—UFOs are unfinished obstacles.

Can it (me) be fixed? Can I be fixed? I am trying. I made signs saying—STAY FOCUSED.

Put one by the computer, one on the fridge, one over the kitchen sink, and one in the window over my sewing machine. So far, those darn signs have not done one darn thing to keep me focused.

Next she asks—or do you just accommodate it (me)? I am very

accommodating. It's so much easier to go with the flow or maintain the status quo.

People who have goals have obstacles. I say get rid of the goals and you get rid of the obstacles.

And eat more Popsicles.

The Bus Boycott

Mr. Rios was a regular customer at our grocery store on south Waterman Avenue in San Bernardino during the late 1940s. He liked to converse with my mother about happenings in our neighborhood. He fished in Baja and would often peddle some of his catch in our neighborhood. His fish were the freshest and tastiest no matter the variety.

Mr. Rios was the foster father of two girls named Verna and Etiwanda Feltz. Both girls were very polite and very well groomed despite their modest income. My mother would chastise my sisters often and exclaim, "Why can't you be as neat and presentable as the Feltz girls?"

One afternoon Mr. Rios asked mom about our use of the school bus.

"Mrs. Gonzalez, I notice your children ride the bus to school."

"Yes, Mr. Rios. We live exactly one and a half mile from school. So, they can ride the bus."

"Well Mrs. Gonzalez my children have to walk to school."

The Feltz's lived approximately one block closer to the school so they were technically no eligible to use the bus.

"Mr. Rios, have your girls walk south and stand across the street from the store in front of the Morse's barn and the bus will give them a ride to school."

"Yea Mrs. Gonzalez, but will the bus stop for my children?"

"Yes Mr. Rios, if they stand across the street, they'll be exactly one and one-half mile from the school. The bus will pick them up."

Mr. Rios started to leave but he stopped and asked again several times, "Yea Mrs. Gonzalez, but are you sure the bus will stop for MY children?"

Mr. Rios left but was clearly agitated and concerned about whether the bus would stop for his children.

I remember thinking Mr. Rios is not very bright. He was almost in tears. Isn't mom telling him the bus will stop because the girls will be at exactly one and one-half mile from the school?

I thought this even as I wondered if the bus would in fact stop as the bus driver would know the girls didn't live at the designated spot as it was in front of a horse barn. It is a sign of the times and an example of my ignorance as to why Mr. Rios kept asking, "Will the bus stop for my children?"

I was very worried about the situation the next morning as I boarded the bus because I didn't want mom to be wrong.

My sister and I were the first on the bus route. I was the person in charge of operating the manual directional signal flag. It allowed me to crouch next to the driver and achieve a level of protection against the few thugs that were always creating a great commotion on the bus. It was a very responsible job. But my experience as an altar boy came in handy, and I was privileged to have that responsibility.

The bus driver was a gentle and quiet old man whom we all called "pops." He managed to control the situation as there was always a lot of chatter and pushing and shoving.

The bus route traveled south beyond Mill Street to pick up Paul Brown. Paul was the designated door opener and closer.

The bus would then return North and turn right at Mill Street and head East toward "Okiville." This was an enclave half way between Waterman and Tippecanoe Avenues. The folks who lived there were mostly low-income Whites and Mexicans. The bulk of the passengers on this route were from there.

The bus continued its route and as it headed North on Waterman Avenue, I could see the Feltz girls standing across the street from our store in front of the old barn. I was very nervous as I didn't want Mr. Rios to be disappointed at my mother's assurances that the bus would stop.

I was ready to signal stop when Bobby Irwin, a certified bully, jumped up and started screaming, "Pops, you're not going to stop for this nigra, are you?"

The bus started to slow and I was quick to signal a stop.

"Pops there's going to be problems if you stop. Pops are you crazy, you old man?"

Pops responded as he stopped, "They have a right to ride this bus."

Bobby went berserk. "Pops, you crazy fool. I ain't gonna ride no bus with no nigra."

With that Bobby jumped out of the bus and he was quickly followed by two other cohorts.

The Feltz girls quietly got in and sat by the empty front seats by the door.

Bobby and his cohorts were yelling and screaming at pops.

"Ain't gonna ride no bus with no nigra."

Pops asked one more time, "Are you going to get in?"

"Ain't gonna ride no bus with no nigra."

Pops ordered Paul, "Close the door." And with that we were on our way. I was pleased that mom's advice had prevailed as I signaled our departure.

During the commotion the bus was quiet. As the bus picked up speed, suddenly as if by some pre-planned synchronization, the kids pulled down the windows and started a mocking chant, "Bobby Irwin you're a fool, now you'll have to walk to school."

"Bobby Irwin you're a fool, now you'll have to walk to school."

An ugly situation was suddenly very festive and filled with laughter. Bobby became the butt of many jokes as he maintained his school bus boycott that lasted four days.

On the fifth day Bobby and his buddies showed up at the pick-up spot in Okiville. Bobby hadn't recruited any additional boycotters. Why walk three miles to school if a free bus is available?

Bobby marched to the back of the bus and with a prominent swagger commandeered the back bench with his two sidekicks.

He declared loudly, "Ain't gonna ride no front of the bus with no nigra."

And, so it went. The rest of the semester with two colored girls in the front of the bus and three rednecks at the back of the bus. That's the way things were in San Bernardino in the year 1949. We may have been ahead of our time, as this happened six years before the Rosa Parks encounter in the South.

Verna Feltz went on to a very promising academic career. She made history in San Bernardino when she won a National Thespian Society Award. She broke the color barrier when she was featured in the *Sun* newspaper as she posed with her teacher mentor. That photo was one of the few instances that the *Sun* printed a photo of a colored person with a white.

Etiwanda followed in Verna's footsteps and also achieved promised success. She later married a very popular student, Clarence Goodwin, who later became an Assistant Superintendent of Schools in San Bernardino.

Whatever happened to Bobby?

Don't know. Perhaps went into hiding when his pals needled him that he rode the back of the bus in order to protest a racially integrated bus?

As I age and recall this incident, I can only surmise the anguish in the Feltz family the night before when Mr. Rios instructed the girls that Mrs. Gonzalez assured him that the bus would stop for them if they followed her suggestion. What if the bus didn't stop?

Oh, the humiliation. Better to walk than to be left standing on the highway. Isn't being colored in the USA punishment enough?

As for me, I am forever grateful that pops had the decency to stop that ol' bus.

Thank you ol' man! RIP

LBJ Visit

I was a volunteer at the Democratic headquarters in early October of 1964 when we learned that President Lyndon Johnson would visit San Bernardino for a rally in his campaign for his first elected term.

President Johnson had worked as an elevator operator at the Platt building at the southeast corner of Fifth and E Streets in downtown San Bernardino in the summer after he graduated from high school. He wanted to have a rally there in order to operate the same elevator for a bit of nostalgia.

The news was enthusiastically welcomed. The headquarters became a very busy place in helping to coordinate a successful visit.

I was informed that I would be a part of the cadre of supporters who would stand in a cordoned-off area in front of the speaker's podium. We had to be cleared by the FBI. We thought we were especially selected VIPs, but, we learned later that we would constitute a barrier against any plot to approach and harm the President.

Two weeks later the preparations were complete and the big day for San Bernardino arrived.

Security was very tight. The intersection of Fifth and E Streets in downtown San Bernardino sported multi-storied buildings at each corner that enabled the Secret Service to station snipers at each roof top.

Today, only the J C Penny building remains as the other three have been razed. The Platt building was at the southeast corner and that landscaped parcel is now part of the Rosa Parks State Building complex.

The city crews erected a raised deck in front of the J C Penny building to house several dozen policemen who were eyeballing the crowd for any problems. It seems the Secret Service wanted them out of the way.

Finally, the hour had arrived. A throng of some 20,000 supporters went wild as whirlybirds hovered overhead and the San Bernardino High School band struck up a version of the President's campaign song "Hello Dolly." The band played on as the President ducked inside the Platt building to check out the elevator to ensure it complied with the American with Disabilities Act (ADA)—no wait, that law was enacted years later in the first Bush Administration.

President Johnson started his speech and opened with the expected compliments to local dignitaries when I was startled by the emergence of an imposing tall well-dressed gentleman. My god! It's Lyndon Johnson himself. That person giving the speech is a double. It makes sense. After what happened in Dallas in 1963. But before I could rationalize that nonsense, the man introduced himself.

"Hello sir, my name is Sam Houston Johnson, and what is your name sir."

I had a quiet chuckle as I thought who but a Texan would name a child Sam Houston? But I maintained my composure as I gave him mine.

"I'm Richard Gonzalez."

He was very polite.

"Mr. Gonzalez I am so pleased to meet you, sir."

Sam Houston Johnson was sharply dressed in western attire with a swanky suit, kerchief, boots and an elaborate Stetson.

John Kennedy had changed our culture about hats, but it seemed the Johnson were bringing them back.

Sam Houston Johnson carried non-stop as he had a gift of gab. I soon felt like we were long lost friends.

"I am so proud of my brother; 'They' let me go on the campaign trail wherever he goes provided I stay out of the way. You see Mr. Gonzalez, I am an alcoholic."

I needed to know that?

He invited me to celebrate his brothers' accomplishments with a drink. With that, he whisked out a pint of Old Forester from his jacket and popped it open. I was startled. Me? Drinking at a political rally in a hot October afternoon in the middle of Fifth Street?

I then noticed there were Secret Service Agents beside him calmly taking care of the situation.

To drink or not. Gee, if it's okay with the President of the United States and The Secret Service, why not!

So, I took a swig. He then chugged without doing the expected wiping of the lip of the bottle and handed it back to me.

And, so it went, back and forth until the bottle was emptied. I caught only some the President's comments including one where he urged the crowd to support. A newcomer Ken Dyal for Congress.

I remembered there was a rumor that a Republican, Jerry Pettis, might crash the event by getting a photo of himself with the President to use in his own Congressional campaign. Pettis was vying for the same seat in order to replace retiring Congressman Harry Sheppard who had severed for 35 years, mostly as chair of the House Defense Appropriations Committee.

Harry Sheppard wielded a lot of power and was responsible for acquiring appropriations for Norton Air Force Base in San Bernardino, George Air Force Base in Victorville, and it was rumored he set up the Twenty-Nine Palms Marine Base in the desert on a bet with a drunken sailor that he, Harry, could put a base "anywhere he damned well pleased." It turns out that Harry was ahead of his time. Marines were traditionally amphibious warriors. Who could have known that one day Marines might be deployed in the Iraqi desert landscape?

On Election Day we learned that the Pettis plot was quite simple. He used an old photo of himself with Vice President Johnson when they met years before at a meeting at Loma Linda University where Jerry was an administrator.

Then, I noticed that one of the cops on the deck was looking intently at our drinking caper. Manuel (Manny) Quevedo was a detective with the force. I thought I was okay as I was in good company.

But it was clear Manny was disgusted at witnessing two Democrats drinking in public at a Presidential rally that I am convinced he decided to become a Republican at the precise moment.

In any case he organized a group of Hispanic Republicans and supported Jerry Pettis to replace Ken Dyal after only one term. He also helped Richard Nixon and Ronald Reagan with the White House.

The speech was over and Sam Houston Johnson was whisked away as the President had a rally planned in Riverside. I've read he quit drinking in 1972 and died in 1978 of lung cancer complication.

I was elated by my unusual experience and I wanted to tell my father about it. My dad always felt I was wasting too much time in political activities.

When I arrived at our home in Rialto my father was beside himself.

Giddy! Prancing and holding out his arm, "Mijo, you won't believe what happened to me."

"What, what?"

"I shook the President's hand."

"Whaaaat! Where?"

"Well I was coming home from work up E Street and Second Street was blocked off. 'What's happening?' I asked.

'The President is coming.'

Oh, yea, I reminded myself. So, I scooted in between some people to get a better view. [Dad was a little over five feet tall] I saw this long caravan of black limousines on Second Street and it stopped at the intersection of E Street where the President stepped out of the car. Mijo, I got so excited I ran to him and told him how happy I was to see him and I shook his hand. It was so emotional. Then the crowd rushed in and I was crammed up against the car and couldn't get out. I felt I as asphyxiating.

I yelled, 'Hey let me out.' A man in a suit was holding me tight against the car. I couldn't move. He was shouting, 'Why did you run?'

I told him I just wanted to shake the President's hand. 'Well. Okay but don't run.' Then he let me go.

How about you mijo, did you shake the President's hand?"

No dad. "I didn't."

"No? Why not?"

I had to do some fast thinking.

"Well dad it's this way, ugh well, you see it's this way…"

I smiled as I told him.

"You see dad, I had the special assignment to entertain the President's brother."

My dad frowned. His face showed his disappointment as he contorted his face.

"Humph! I thought you were an important person in the Democratic Party that you would have shaken the President's hand."

With that my dad turned away in utter disgust all the while he held his right hand away from his body.

What a letdown. Upstaged by my own pop. ON MY TURF!

Oh well. It turns out that my father, Angel Gonzalez, an immigrant from Mexico, a naturalized citizen, and a lumber clerk at the W M Day Lumber Company in San Bernardino, on his way home from work, and without any preparation became the unofficial Greeter to President Lyndon Baines Johnson on his triumphant return to the city of San Bernardino.

Sigh!

60

A Young Man on an Oklahoma Farm in the 1940s

As a young boy on our Oklahoma farm in the 1940s, I was with my dad every hour of every day until my mom said "that is enough!" I rode on the tractor with him, walked repairing fences with him, accompanied him as he laid brick or any of the many other skills he had.

Mending fences was a job he did in the cold of winter as spring, summer and fall were much too busy. When we mended fences, we did not need to carry the fence posts or digger. Instead, we had a nanny goat that voluntarily followed dad wherever he went. Before we would leave to mend fences, dad would tie one end of a posthole digger and a few posts to her. As we walked and repaired problems on our fence, the digger and posts were always as near as this devoted nanny goat. She was very happy to be with us and never seemed to mind dragging the digger and posts.

This goat was also my lifeline as I could not tolerate cow or even horse milk during my early years. Her milk turned me from sickly to thriving.

I dreamed of being a farmer just like my dad and saved all of the seeds that I found. One day I was sorting them on the concrete walk, between our house and the cistern, when my mom called me for lunch—which always took priority over any other activity! However, while I was eating, our chickens were having lunch too—on my seeds!

Those chickens were not very popular with me for a while but this experience probably was a lesson for my later life. Bringing one's work to a good and secure point takes precedence over food.

Later, during my high school years, I rented plots of land and farmed cotton. After that, my farming career ended as I earned a living in many other ways over the next 60 years. Even though I no longer farm, it still gives me a sense of security in owning the family farm in Oklahoma that was my childhood home.

Nowadays, a man who grew up a mile from our land now farms it on a share basis. This is a very common arrangement where the land owner typically receives one-third of the crop and the renter "share cropper" receives two-thirds of the crop. This is how my parents started out. They were renters until they bought our farm. This is a totally voluntary arrangement and farmers compete to rent land from owners who no longer wish to farm it.

My First Love

My first love was a beautiful little girl named Willola Jane Hardin. She had long black hair, a very friendly outgoing personality and was part of my youth group in our church in Clinton, Oklahoma. I fell head over heels in love with her but she never developed the same feeling. She and most of the other members of our group could often be found riding around in my other love, my 1952 red Ford convertible.

Sometimes we traveled to church youth groups in other towns. On one of these trips we were traveling on a dirt road when I saw a flooded section ahead. I made a split-second decision to by-pass it by veering left through a farmer's field. That was a bad decision for two reasons, first the field was very soft and I just barely made it through. Second the farmer saw me and his hand signal let me know his lack of approval. This was a very stupid thing to do and I felt bad about messing up the field, especially since my dad and I were farmers, too.

Normally, I drove very safely when I had people, especially her, with me. But when I was alone, I often put the car into a slide in order to practice taking it back out, I guess I was practicing safety.

As for my other love, Willola, I made up new words to a song that our group often sang. "I have decided to follow Jesus, I won't turn back, I won't turn back." My new verse was "I have decided I love Willola, I won't give up, I won't give up." I am sure that no one ever heard me sing it. Although she never accepted a date with me, she was always very nice to me—even when I visited her in the hospital after her appendectomy. In the end, contrary to my song, I guess I did give up because she may have been part of the reason I bailed Clinton for California.

As a side note, Willola had one brother and a single mom. After Dad was widowed, he believed that Willabel Harden, Willola's mom, was after him but he was not interested. If he had married Willabel, Willola would have become my stepsister!

I Am From

I am from Otto and Lena Meyer, Fred and Katy Meyer, Jake & Agnes Sawatzky.

I am from Jacob Hoeppner, my mother's great-great-great-grandfather, who traveled to Russia, negotiated with Katherine the Great and moved his people to the Ukraine for over 100 years.

I am from a mother who very nearly died bringing me into this world.

I am from a mother who protected her two children from the dust bowl by placing us in an inner closet, with wet towels covering the door cracks, to trap the dust and give us breathable air.

I am from a mother who would not allow us to go to town with dirty clothes, except during harvest time.

I am from a mother who prepared five meals per day for harvest crews and delivered two of them to the crews in the field. To get to the crews she drove our 1936 Chevrolet across the roadside ditch across the field and to the combine location.

I am from a mother who shuttled plow shears from the field to the blacksmith & returned with a sharpened set. This allowed her husband to continue plowing without interruption as that was very time consuming.

I am from a mother who hated credit and a father who loved it.

I am from a mother who fought cancer for four years and then lost the battle at the young age of 42!

I am from a father who worked, for a trailer park owner, to provide a safe space for our car. We three lived in it while mom was in a Missouri Hospital.

I am from a father that had complete faith that he could learn to do anything he wished—and he did as he learned to design and build custom homes in their entirety.

I am from the hot-dry or cold-wet western Oklahoma plains, California's beautiful San Diego area, the west San Joaquin Valley, and the crowded Inland Empire, CA.

I am from Redlands, CA, a very lovely university city with many cultural activities and events to enjoy.

I am from a farm family that learned to work together and to love the good earth.

I am from early to bed and early to rise.

I was a "burn the candle from both ends" person. I worked full time, flew half time and got some college education half time during many years.

I am for reality: not the make-believe fiction stuff.

I am the owner of my family farm: I consider it a bit of ultimate security and never intend to sell it.

I am a Christian, a husband, a father, a grandfather, a friend, a gleaner and a neighbor.

I am a Child of God who has worshiped with the German Mennonites, Church of God, Methodists, Swedish Covenant and Calvary Chapel people.

I am one who believes in charity, provides for it and strongly believes all recipients must do what work they can for it.

I am a military man who believes in "Peace Through Strength" and we need much more strength than we have now.

I am getting old, slowing down and naps are not so guilt ridden any more.

And I am a Conservative Republican that loves this nation and its Constitution.

History of Grain Harvesting

As children on our Oklahoma farm, we wanted gum to chew. So, we'd grab a ripe head of wheat and rub it between two hands to break the chaff from the grain. We'd blow away the chaff and chew the grain into a gum. Throughout history, this was likely a simple way of processing a very small quantity of grain.

In biblical times, long before the days of power machinery, heads of grain were placed on a hard, flat, smooth surface at the top of a hill, the "threshing floor." People would tread on the heads of grain or use animals to drag a heavy object over the grain, breaking the chaff from the grain. The Bible says, "do not muzzle the mouth of the animal when he is treading out the grain." So, farmers would allow their animals to eat grain as they were "treading out the grain." Later, on a windy day, the farmer would go to the "threshing floor" and toss the material into the air. The wind would blow the light chaff and stalks away as the heavier grain fell to the floor and was collected.

Much later, the invention of steam engines and threshing machines made this work both easier and faster. These machines used the same method as the farmer on the hilltop. A cylinder rotated above spaced bars breaking the heads apart. As the heavy grain fell and was collected, a fan blew out the chaff. Devices called "straw walkers" were used to move the stems out. These machines were moved into location with a steam powered tractor and set up in a fixed location in the field. The steam tractor powered the thresher through a flat belt. The alignment had to be precise or the belt would not stay on the pulleys. Harvesting started when the crop was mature but not yet dry ripe. A horse pushed machine called a "binder" was used to cut the crop off at the ground and bind it into bundles with twine. Workers walked the field, picking up these bundles and placing them in a tepee shaped "shock." Shocks allowed the grain to cure and dry out. With the grain dried and the thresher ready, young men with teams of horses and wagons picked up the bundles from the shocks and delivered them to the thresher. The twine was cut from each bundle as the bundles were fed into the thresher. The straw and chaff blew out, forming a large pile. When the straw was removed, the base was used to grow strawberries or watermelon. As a young man, my dad used a team of horses and a wagon to gather the bundles and deliver them to the thresher. He also positioned and operated steam tractors when he worked in the plains of the Texas Panhandle.

Much later, a machine was invented that combined many of these processes. It was called a "combine." Combines relied on gasoline engines, but they were pulled by tractors. As a result, part of each crop was mashed into the ground and lost as the combine made its first trip around the field. Combines had a header with a sickle that cut off the crop below the heads and moved them into a machine that functioned much like previous threshers. The first combines had headers about 6 feet wide. Later combines had headers 12 feet and larger. Initially, tractors and combines were mounted on steel wheels. These tractors required a lot of power to move. My dad had a 12' Minneapolis Moline combine on steel wheels. When Clinton Sherman AFB closed, they scrapped some of their airplanes. My dad bought some of their wheels and rubber tires. We mounted those wheels and rubber tires on our combine. It was a great improvement.

Much, much later, self-propelled combines were developed. These combines didn't require a tractor and didn't damage crops as earlier combines did. These combines were designed with large drive wheels mounted at the front just behind the header. The rear wheels steered the unit. I was working as a farm hand and had the chance to operate one of these machines before my dad did. What a thrill! My dad's three brothers were very poorly educated and considered backward, but they pieced together their own self-propelled combine!

In recent years, "rotary machines" use a completely different method of threshing grain.

Waiting

Knowing to wait is a virtue, that like other virtues, is a challenge. Worried you wait with patient for someone to arrive or for something you are expecting to happen.

International travel involves a lot of waiting. Waiting for pick-ups, waiting in the check-in line, waiting for boarding-time, waiting for take-off, waiting for a connecting flight, waiting for your turn in the immigration line, waiting for a taxi, waiting to check-in at the hotel, waiting for your room to be ready.

Waiting involves patience, waiting involves expectation, waiting involves change of some sort, such that when whatever you are waiting for arrives, you are either happy or unhappy, you are either satisfied or unsatisfied, you are either pleased or unpleased.

Like during one of my frequent trips to South America. At the hotel in Sao Paulo, I turned off the alarm clock and slowly crept into the bathroom, struggling to keep my eyelids opened, I turned on the shower.

The chilly water did help to further awake me. I assumed so early in the morning, the water heater was still off-duty. After a few moments I heard the bubbling of the coffee maker I had prepared the night before. I was hoping the coffee aroma would finish waking me up. I stood for a moment waiting for the aroma. I then realized that the cheap Nestle coffee, was, after all, complimentary in each room, and I could not expect anything better.

Ten minutes later I was checking out of the hotel and getting into a taxi that took me to the Guarulhos Airport. My flight to Bogota was leaving at 7 AM and I had to be there two hours earlier, at a time when all coffee shops in the airport were nicely closed.

Checking in at the airline's counter I received the news that my flight had a delay, because of the heavy fog at the originating airport in Porto Alegre. "Stay put, we will announce when we are ready to board," said a ground crew member with one of those charming smiles that give you the confidence that you are in capable hands.

I took a seat in a comfortable sofa in the roaring waiting hall, too tired to focus on my Kindle. And I waited, and waited, and waited.

At 1 o'clock in the afternoon I stood up and approached the counter again.

I barely heard a voice saying,

"Yes, the flight just took off from Porto Alegre and will be landing in Guarulhos in about 80 minutes."

Finally, around midnight we arrived in Bogota. The same procedure to get out, when you are sitting in the rear part of the airplane. Of course, no more connecting flights to my next destination, Cartagena, until early next day. Again, I waited, and waited, and waited in a comfortable sofa.

Traveling is moving in space and time, but for me traveling is a succession of waiting periods in unusual places.

GARY NEUHARTH

Anger

Dark horses running with the wind
    you should be careful—anger's not a toy
    fast gallop across a sea of coals
    feet dancing—fire racing as the road rumbles
Who wants to be humble
    flared nostrils sucking in cool wind
    and breathing out a scouring fire
    you hould be more careful

Their voices sound like leaves
    they make no noise when they touch the ground
    just ahead there's a threshold yawning in the dawn of the
    profound
    you'd like to say "do you hear me now"
    but the growing fire is instinct and it festers deep within
There's no longer need for questionings
    the elixir of rage has become of age
    and hot anger incinerates reason
    the pleading voices sound like cowardly choirboys
    dressed in powerful black robes but unable to sing

You better be careful
    they caged men in Brooklyn for doing what you feel
    but you'd rather be dying with a spirited wind
    than bowing at their heels
You're been storing this for a long time inside
    Someday you're going to explode
    Their words feel like spit on your face

As you feel your temperature rise
    as your temples throb and your forehead tightens
    and your knuckles whiten
    no time for reflection now—you're moving swift and strong

A preacher waddles
 his head and hips wagging in a stupid false waltz
 saying "stay out of trouble"

Time is slowing down and the walls buckle as your knees slam
 into them
 like a battering ram
 it's pain—it's power—it's pleasure
 as you rain down resentment like the hail in hell
 their voices fade away in the wind
In a glimpse you rode the fire
 and flew on a dark horse
 and felt no remorse

You didn't like it when the winds died down
 or when you felt the ground beneath your feet once more
 you had been full and now
 you were empty again.

GARY NEUHARTH

The Dawning

When he ran for deep green grass it was morning
    stark, cold, and dark
    you could hide in the dark
        in the morning light
            and feel safe

Then the light would roll over the hilltops and flood the valleys
    and the world would wake up
    flinging reason to the cold chaos of morality
    and the children of the night would shudder and sigh
    for the night had passed them by
    and left them stripped and naked
        to the searing gaze
                of the moral majority

A cardboard box or thick hedge or an empty field
    was the sanctuary of oblivion to them
    some stood in solitary places in the early hours
    watching the rays gleaming from the newborn sun
        as it cut a swath
            through the morning mists

They looked like eagles
    noble and lofty
        as they watched the vision for the day unfold

Some stretched and went about stalking the courteous man
    after all, they were easy prey for lions in winter
    and the streets were full of them today
        they wouldn't even be missed

For some the inevitable man appeared
    he was always in the right place at the right time
        just when you needed him most
    some called this a miracle and others called him a nuisance
        I called it the harmony of chaos.

The Perfect Kiss

As a boy of sixteen I suddenly became aware of the mysteriously overpowering presence of girls. They had been around me all the time and I had never noticed them until now. I fully intended, therefore, to seek out the most attractive, foxy beauty I could find. After much searching, I found a willowy brunette with a Rod Stewart haircut and a body like an Israeli machine gun. Her name was Starla and her eyes were like two glittering emerald pools of light. Her hair was sandalwood blonde and her lips were pomegranate red. Her nose curved up into the most spectacular full-blown ski jump. To top it all, she was strangely attracted to my intense admiration of her. My heart beat noisily in my throat like a diesel engine. I wanted to kiss her pomegranate lips, to sweep her into my arms and smother with kisses. Regaining my fractured senses to some degree, I told her I would like to kiss her but not in the ordinary dull way. I wanted it to be very special, spectacular and timelessly unforgettable.

It sounded good to her and to my amazement she agreed. We laid out our strategic plans of action. I had seen a commercial of two lovers running with arms out-stretched through a field of grain to meet together in a beautiful embrace. So we got into my Dodge Dart and drove about looking for the perfect field. Finding no grain field, we had to settle for alfalfa. It was twelve noon and the sun was just at the right angle to light up our features and make us look more attractive. We stood back to back in the lush alfalfa and began to walk away from each other in brisk paces. At my command to stop we stood about twenty paces apart. Like two daring duelers we turned and began to run to each other. We collided unexpectedly and she sprained her nose and I had a large mouse swelling up over my right eyebrow where her forehead had banged into it. We were both dazed and it took us a few painfully long seconds to realize we had forgotten to stop just before meeting in our dashing embrace. I apologized for my oversight and we decided to try again.

This time we waited until it was very romantic and the sun was setting, throwing beautiful hues of color across the sky. We would hold each other with our eyes closed and slowly draw our faces together and kiss. We embraced slowly, lips parted and full of anticipation. My teeth caught her squarely in the cheek and her mouth wide open landed on my cheek smearing saliva extensively. I remember her muttering, "This is so gross I could gag." We were both quite unnerved by this encounter.

After some quick talking I managed to get her to agree to one more try at the perfect kiss. This time we drove to the Greyhound bus station. We would try a new approach. We would pretend to look for an empty seat and both walk slowly to the same seat. As we both met, we would say, "I believe you have my seat." As we had seen on TV. We picked out a seat in the center of the bus station waiting area and each of us took up a position on the opposite end of the bench. We approached each other casually and I said, "I believe you are about to have my seat." She answered, "I will have more than that if you don't come through this time." Quite gracefully I swept her into my trembling arms and miraculously we had the most perfect kiss with no further injury or interruption. We both let out a sigh of glorious relief. We had done it right! We could scarcely believe the satisfaction of our achievement, the perfect kiss.

The Piano

It was just a piano—an old piano with black and white keys in the middle places half way down the front side of the dark maple.

The front cover was off and you could see all those heavy piano wires.

You could look right at them, stripped down and laid out in the open.

Pretty wires with that cast-iron earthly frame holding the whole pretty heaviness in place—just waiting for some fingers with no destination in mind to set themselves down with soul driving in mind and a spare pick up laid down just in case soul came to lightly.

So I put my fingers down and stepped right into the bass section.

You know, the deep and low down side, where the keys rumble and the thunder kind of slams into you with just a little effort in a bass finger dance.

Out there with the thunder pulsing erratically from those velvet hammers, pounding and slamming into the coiled taut and twisted cables, over and over again, caught up in the rhythm of the dance, bouncing in a bawdy pulse that leaves the bass player breathless with anticipation.

Each wire going into a thunderous bolt of tingling reverberations as those hard, straight velvet hammers strike it again and again so that a chaotic frenzy rolls from the keys long after they are played.

Oh, the ecstasy of this mindless rhythm dances through my every nerve and fiber!

My head arches back, and my eyelids flutter as the sensuous pounding goes into my temples.

My mind, and body, and fingers connecting.

Write with Mae

Prologue: *It may surprise people to know that Black culture carries with it a tremendous amount of guilt stigma. Part of a legacy, it still accentuates nearly everything we do. In order to keep us under plantation laws, we were given gospels that taught us to be ashamed because everything we did was sinful. About 150 years later rampant drug use and varieties of exploitations caused many Black People to lower their guard or be less inhibited. Stronger ones adapted and appear to have overcome, or at least be comfortable with the situation. However, such progress carries a risk of becoming complacent. Other casualties are those with an exceptionally milder, even docile temperament. In today's environment many such ones feel prevented from pursuing passions.*

SHADOWS IN DREAMS: What Keeps Me from Pursuing My Passions?

I used to, and still suffer from bad dreams where I'm being at first being sought after or pursued as a person of value. The pattern is usually the same. Second, things start to get ugly when I realize that I've been duped and trapped into some dangerous situation. I try to escape by staying in well lit, populated places. Then all of the people fade and disappear until I find myself alone again. Shadowy figures follow me, getting larger and longer with every step. Clearly, there is no escape. The next option is to look for somewhere that the shadows won't chase me, somewhere high enough to just jump from. As I start to pray, I become confident that God will save me and if He doesn't that would be okay well. I spot a ledge and quickly jump, weightlessly gliding among the lights as the nightmare fades into the past. Finally, I awake wrapped in empty darkness gasping for air and thanking God for having saved me yet again.

So in daily events, when opportunities to engage in pursuits of passion come up, I need to take the initial step of clearing my mind of certain omnipresent stigmatisms from the legacy of negative baggage. It's a time-consuming consideration that people unmarked by skin color do not have to process. By the time I get through this step, often the spontaneity of the moment has passed. Counselors advise me to just shrug it off and let it go; but be prepared and wait for the next opportunity. Nonetheless, thoughts of failure to bridge connections become even more engrained when links continue to be missed. Such occasions, brief and fleeting, slipped away winking. The shadows in my mind keep tally is what I'm left thinking.

Socio-political mechanisms also come into play, as they have seeped in through a series of historical developments, creating a kind of pressure cooker effect. That for me constricts ventilation leading to impaired growth. Once manifested, this condition is displayed as a form of arrested social development. Some might still label it in the no longer acceptable expression "retarded" in growth. In any case the outcome is the same. For me even miniscule amounts of success sometimes translate into yet another disappointing setup, which I will wish to escape from. After so many close calls in life, I spend lots of valuable time sort of looking over my shoulder for those shadows, and praying in an undertone.

Older now, it seems that oppression has won. The political elite (AKA The pointy hat crowd) are completing their goals, their jobs well done. They have prevented those like me from pursuing our passions. They use quazi-Peace Officers (formerly Pinkertons) smartly uniformed; carrying badges and guns to keep a lid on things. They've applied a tried and true societal formula that at first goes: Create a cauldron with walls that restrict the target's mobility. [This may be accomplished by financial means, imprisonment, or death] Second, to this add the essential ingredients of helplessness and despair. Shake well, or agitate vigorously over time in order to destabilize. Then crime will certainly begin foaming towards the edges; and "presto-change-o." Emerging will be a fully developed, living, breathing case of stay in your place (in the shadows), and be reconciled to failure. More recently expressed as "Just shut and dribble!" [To use a sports-related term]. This has been a story about things that have prevented me from pursuing my passions.

The end

Maverick

As a fellow veteran I was familiar with his legendary story of courage. However, the state that he represented (Arizona) has a persistent history of being anti-Black. In my opinion, policies of his political party have come to represent symbols of oppression towards "Poor People" [An analogy, another way of wrongfully implying Blackness]. For example, Arizona alone opposed recognizing M. L. King's day as an official holiday. Therefore, I wanted to dislike him. But I couldn't. I fell in love with him when he took the microphone from one of his supporters and corrected her attempt to slander Barrack Obama, and again when he famously gave the thumbs down in defense of Universal Healthcare for all Americans. I left my green patio light on all night in memory of John 'The Maverick' McCain.

KARL PETTWAY

What Makes a Hero?

To me the word "hero" signifies actions more than a designation. However, for this delightful assignment I will continue. Heroes can have a tremendous affect in a person's life. They give a valuable gift. A precious gift in return would be to make them aware of their heroic deeds. Heroes can be just for entertainment or they can be a real key source of motivation. As it is said about beauty, that is in the eyes of the beholder. If we haven't done so already, it is not a bad idea to try to create one. If you have an open mind they can be found almost everywhere. For others to understand our choices we may need to narrow them into categories such as: everyday or famous; powerful or intrepid; even historic or potential. The fun ones for me are in my cinema fantasy world and sometimes in sports. They are the ones who usually perform for large audiences and deliver under incredible pressure or against great odds. For example: Gordon Liu, Jet Li, Wesley Snipes, Denzel Washington, Scarlett Johansson, Milla Jovovich, Tom Cruise, Bruce Willis, Arnold Schwarzenegger, Jonny Lee Miller, Robert Downey Jr., Angelina Jolie, Joy Reid (a news show host), Johnny Depp, Antonio Banderas, Morgan Freeman, Gene Hackman, etc... However, in the real world they range from ones who exemplify courage and strength as they continue to fight just to live. Of course, doctors, scientists, engineers, and inventors work to keep the world livable and functioning. Educators, coaches, mentors, writers, and artists bring color and meaning that add depth to our quality of life. Among those are obviously places where many heroes can be found. But then, there are the unsung ones. They are the great heroes such as moms, dads, as well as others who have stepped up to fill the void or take the lead. These ones are too numerous to count as most of them have passed on in death. They often never even thought it was possible for them to have the honor. Therefore, this would be the time to them let them know that someone considers them a hero.

Music: Then and Now

Home shoppers almost always have one request in common. They want their prospective dwelling to be quiet. My earliest memories of life in NYC include a kind of background music. The whole neighborhood breathes to a musical rhythm that starts midweek with the faint but distinctive baseline. It's almost mouthwatering because it is accompanied by smells of varieties of evening meals being prepared. By late Thursday many types of cultural melodies announce their presence. However, that Latin Cuban baseline is relentless. It does not compete, nor does it try to overtake other noises that provide bouquets of sounds auditioning to be heard. It is more of a feeling than a sound at this point, seeming to communicate patience as the much-anticipated weekend approaches. Other musical stylings, of which there are many, may take front stage while nightclub restaurants and bars are open. But whether you are asleep, awake or somewhere in between all will be nodding their heads or tapping their fingers and toes to the persistent, combined rhythm of Cuban bass and drums. They will fade sometime Sunday morning but their richness will by then have penetrated and fully saturated you by then, and never ever really leave you completely.

These are musings from the viewpoint a young boy who lived it in that place and time. Now, as an older man, my musical tastes have run the gambit. Growing up in Polish Hamtramck, MI. I have touched by Hungarian style, Eastern European folk melodies that seem vaguely familiar to me. Then the music of Motown exploded onto the scene as a birth child of Doo-Wop era music. It was in my face and everywhere. When it sparked the British invasion of music, it transformed American Rock and Roll which had been widely used partially to suppress profits and progress of Black music artists. As a young teen I embraced it all. Then cultural awareness and social issues made me retreat from mainstream music. I hung out with older guys returning from the Vietnam battle front. Together, we withdrew from an unwelcoming society into a world of hard drugs and very hard jazz, almost exclusively. My musical descent was so deep that it took an overused and still misunderstood genre of music referred to as P-Funk, Uncut Funk, AKA the Bomb. After the military I returned to Detroit to connect with my "American roots." That journey took me through the urban jungles of Cleveland, Baltimore, and then to the musical motherland—"Chocolate City" (D.C.).

I am currently in a state of perpetual growth, musically speaking. P-Funk strangely provides a home where the aforementioned, Latin Cuban baseline lives on with persistence. I'm guessing it is a part of who I am. And now, with the aid of modernizing technology, don't be surprised to notice parts of your body moving with a life of its own when listening to this intoxicating rhythmic brew. After all it was created by and is still piloted by funkateers (Funkadelic, aka Parliament) and funkmasters (George Clinton and Bootsy Collins et al.).

Graduation

My high school graduation story starts with society's changing attitudes towards educational accomplishments. Like many New Yorkers, the early 1950s found me modeling myself after characters like James Dean, Paul Newman, or Marlon Brando. The thing that was "cool" back then was similar to the depiction of life from the *Happy Days* TV show. So, having the "Fonzerelli" mystique was admirable. In those days there wasn't much emphasis being placed on education. For me all of that somehow translated into wanting to be a rebel. As much as I tried to slouch around my parents kept beating some sense into me until I realized that I was really no tough guy.

Still, when the sixties came along with popular slogans like, "turn on and drop out," I managed to screw things up by not respecting what an education could offer. During the Civil Rights Movement people all around me were fighting and dying for the opportunity to have diplomas, certificates, and degrees. But silly me; I could hardly wait to drop out of school as soon as I turned 16 years old. It was an important missed opportunity because when I moved back and forth from Michigan to California, I would skip up a grade. Had I been on my toes I could have completed highs school well before turning 17.

My dad viewed my quitting school as an opportunity for me to work and to begin paying rent to help out. After a year of being a full pledged working adult, I was clambering to return to our old agreement. Which was: I stay in school, rent free, meals included. But there was no going back for me. From that point on I had to support myself. I still had to maintain an air of jazzy coolness in the community where I lived. But social awareness's of that time period had adjusted my attitude. Becoming educated shot right to the top of my list of priorities. I worked, gambled, and hustled while attending Metropolitan Continuation School on skid row, in downtown Los Angeles. My older brother returned to adult school after being out for more than 10 years. My father returned to attend the same adult school after a lifetime of no formal education. And very, very amazingly the three of us graduated from George Washington Adult High School in the summer of 1968. It is 2018 and I have been in college ever since. That is nearly 50 years of college; and I still plan to return... There is just so very much to learn and I'm still playing catch up.

Not the End

Aging in America

Steering a course through your senior years is like driving an old car on a two-lane mountain pass. Will the car hold together until you reach your destination? Will a sudden, blinding storm make driving impossible? And, what about the next curve, the one you can't see around? What waits just beyond your sight? If you worry about these things long enough, you'll find yourself applying the brakes, slowing down, pulling over to the side of the road, and just plain giving up.

But my car isn't that old, I tell myself. Okay it's old, and it's not as fast as it used to be. But it still runs. My mind circles the what-ifs and the what-nows, even as I ask myself what happened to the stronger, braver, more courageous me? The me who was willing to venture beyond her comfort zone?

Truth is, the world is a dangerous place for the living, old and young. While the young worry about their jobs, their families, their futures, the old worry about Medicare, heart disease, and memory loss. And those of us who aren't willing to take some risks, to move outside the safety of our own comfort zones, are likely to retreat to the safety of our beds, pull the covers over our heads, and call it "Game Over."

If we do that, though, the Dark Side wins. We miss the very things that bring light to our lives. Our sense of purpose, our families and friends, the faith, hope, and love that remind us life can be so much more, so much better if we are willing to put ourselves out there.

So, if you are sitting on the side of the road, it's time to put your key in the ignition, turn on your headlights, and get back on the road. Take the next curve, the one you can't see around, meet the challenges that give life joy.

JANET GOESKE SENIOR CENTER

Led by CelenaDiana Bumpus

CRAIG STONE

Beyond the Door

How seldom I see a dog
in the clouds, an elephant or tree.
Not often much, if at all anymore.

How seldom I laze
in the cool grass,
on a warm day,
staring blankly skyward.
Not often much, if at all, anymore.

How seldom I see a child
eager to bring home a tadpole.
Not often much, if at all, anymore.

How I enjoyed seeing chalk marks
in the street keeping score.
But alas, not often much, if at all, anymore.

I no longer see children in line
for a turn at bat.
See hide and seek, football or catch.
Not often much, if at all, anymore.

How seldom I see a child at play
unless it is head down,
unable to look away.
Often much it's a device
that keeps you
from your adventures,
beyond the door.

Forbidden Love

I just want to love you in my own language
I'm sorry if it turns you blue..
I can't change how society views our relationship
And I'm sorry if you feel my love is the end for you.

I just want to love in my own language.
I chose not to live my life a lie.
As for someone who sees their sweets as I do.
The rest of your still, warm brownie friends can only watch us
and cry.

The Kids Learned to Say

The kids learned to say:
>"We'll help you with that"
>"We'll carry that for you"
>"Allow me to get your hat"

The kids learned to say:
>"You can have my seat now"
>"We can hold that door for you"
>"We'll explain that somehow"

The kids learned to say:
>"You have no right to be here"
>"Go back to where you came from"
>"We don't care if you disappear"

The kids learned to say:
>"You're a lesser person than us"
>"Spray paint swastikas and see no wrong
>with the back of the bus"

The kids learned to say pretty much what parents dole out
They remember what they see and soak up what it's about

The kids learned to say "We love" or "We hate"
So put it on adults, the future of the state.

What Did It Just Do?

New phones can be daunting
as some already know.
Swipe left. Swipe right.
When it's on mute, it'll glow.
Got to be on WiFi
to get information through.
If you grab your phone wrong
you'll cry, "What did it just do?"

The buttons I now push
are flush like the glass.
Sometime I wonder if
it's worth the pain in my ass.
Then pictures come in
from far off places:
grandchildren, nieces
all with smiles on faces.
I'm now rethinking my problem
I'll revisit this in June.
But, I'm sure when
I get the next bill,
I'll sing a different tune.

Thomas Vaden and Duncan Webb

Truckstalgia

White with surface rust
lost from the '60s.
Never restored
from my memory, sometime—
I had to let it all go.

My Ford pickup protected
from the sun for years.
Not like me now.
I had to let it all go.

Like parts of me disappearing
the truck bed boards
wasted away, remind me
that if not replaced
I had to let it all go.

Now I have to decide
if my love for that truck
carries me like it would
have if I had been more
careful not to let it all go.

CRAIG STONE AND PHYLLIS MAYNARD

Ode to An Elf

I wish I was someplace else;
perhaps on a beach, with a reef type shelf.
But here I am, with snow all around.
Pining for that warm island ground.

I wish I was someplace else,
instead of making toys for someone's shelf.
I'd lie on the beach, relax and I'd tan.
"More drinks with rum." Would be my command.

I wish I was someplace else,
instead of working for the guy with the thick black belt.
But all it takes is to see one kid smile
and I forget all of that, at lease for a while.

MARY RODRIGUEZ BRIGGS

When It Rains It Pours

My hairbrush ran away
I heard its moans and whimpers
as it tucked into its bristles
handfuls of my silver hair.
I swallowed a sob
as I saw it 'round the corner
training like stardust in the night sky,
strands of my silver platinum hair.

My underwear moved to a new home.
It refused to tell me where.
It left a farewell note, simply stating,
    'You call this a home?
    Spare me!
    Good luck!'

My boots stomped a dance in dirt and mud
and refused to take a bath

My hair threw a fit!
Screamed and stood on end—
where it had a heart attack
and is now lying dead flat.

My jeans insist on. Having an outing—
just one more time.
Tears and smudges add to glamour
they insist.
My blouses and shirts fought it out.
I'm too confused and tired to determine
if the best one won.

My socks say they like the new aroma.
'Sweet as a daisy is out of style,' they say.

My toothbrush cries,
    'It's too early.
    I'm too sleepy.
    Let me rest until tomorrow morn.'
My face insists that grime and grease
add to its beauty.
Perhaps, it's right.
I'll check tomorrow, when I'm awake.

And off I go!
Stumbling out the door—
intact as much as I can be.
Hoping my beautiful facade
holds up far beyond the front door

Pettie's Complaint

Arf! At last. Cool and comfy.
No more roasting in this coat of fur.
No more panting 'til my tongue
sweeps the floor.

Finally, winter's here. What a treat!
Mommy, open the door and let me free.
Don't want to be in this stuffy house.
Want to smell the pines and feel the breeze.
Want to romp and feel the grass beneath my feet.
Want to run wild and chase the squirrels.

Yak! What the heck?
What furnace blaze is this?
Indian Summer, did I hear someone say?
More like Indian Hell.
Let me back inside!

No, don't make me lie on that flea-infested rug.
Let me sit beside you on that cushy chair—
or better yet, on your fat, cool lap.

I am panting. I cannot breathe.
I'm having a heart attack!
My tongue is dry and hot.
Give me a drink of your icy lemonade.

Grr! Arf! Arf!
Why did you kick me?
I didn't do anything.
I was only trying to clean your dirty feet.

The sun's at high noon.
Where did my breakfast go?
You haven't fed me since yesterday's dinner time.
I'm hungry! That ham and eggs you're eating
smells good and yummy.
Don't eat it all!
Leave some for me!

The fleas are biting. I'm hot and hungry.
I'll die of thirst!
Can't you see the tears well in my eyes?
Why do you tease me so?
Mommy, don't you love me anymore?
I'm needed here on earth.

Dance Of The Stars

When the stars come out to play
in the beauty of the moonlit sky,
I will tiptoe out my door
in my gown of golden silk
wearing shoes spun of golden webs.

I will dance to the music of the stars
on my dew et grassy lawn. Swaying,
whirling, trilling, pirouetting to the moon.
I will waltz the night away
until the sun comes out to claim the day.

On A Dark Night

In the last days of autumn, on a gloomy foggy late night, as I laid a slumber bone tired and weary a she-wolf came pounding on my door. Startled by the vicious pounding, I stumbled to the door. Cautiously I opened just a crack through which it growled from froth-spitting lips, "Where is he? Where is he?"

Its hair was henna red, frizzled and stood straight up. Its red eyes blazed forth tongues of fire and it had a foul evil smell. Dumbfounded and confused, I stood there in my stocking feet. Disgusted, I brushed its spit from my frightened face. It growled again, "I know he's here!"

Now startled and wide eyed, I swallowed hard and whimpered, "Who ever do you mean?"

Hearing this is snarled again, foul breath and frothy spit issued from its mouth and nose. I held close the door with all my might, until it went away.

With the first rays of dawn came bitter cold and misty gray. I heard a soft tapping at my front door. Opening the door, there he stood, "the wayward one," bleary eyed and shyly grinning. Angry and accusing, I said, "Your rabid dog was here last night. Where were you?"

With downcast eyes he muttered incoherently. As I slammed shut the door, I angrily cried out, "And don't come back no more!"

The Plum Adventure

Today is like any other Sunday, Shaya, age twelve, a middle child, was sandwiched between her brothers: Bradley, age fourteen, and Clem, age ten. Shaya and her brothers had gotten up early, dressed themselves in their Sunday best, then sat at the kitchen table waiting for Grandma to make breakfast. Sunday breakfasts were the best as there was a little more time to sit and eat than on the school days.

Vegetables, poultry (Leghorns, Rhode Island Reds, turkeys, ducks, pigeons, guinea hens raised from eggs), bread baked from scratch, goats, sheep, and milk were farmed and made at home. Breakfast—as most meals—was made with fresh vegetables and meat. This morning's breakfast consisted of scrambled eggs laid by Leghorn hens, which are prolific layers. Also, bread, butter, hot chocolate made from beans grown in one of the outer garden plots, and fresh guava jam. Artificial additives are an alien concept to Shaya.

After breakfast the trio left to go to church—an Episcopal (Anglican) church, most parishioners were of this faith. On the way to the church other children joined in the trek. The walk took about thirty minutes to get to the main road. Shaya wondered why the adults did not have to attend church as often as the children in her community. Most times, the adults not seen in church except for Easter and Christmas. Shaya often heard phrases like, "do as I say, not as I do,"or "adults are examples for the young." She concluded that adults get to make all the decisions, for now. At least, she mused, we get away from home for a little while and get to spend time with our school friends.

The siblings arrived before church started. Father M, also known as "beet face," was not around and neither were the sextons. Hmmn, we know where they are, back in the vestry having pre-communion wine, thought Shaya. It was the rumor.

Most of the parishioners who had been mulling about in front of the church headed into the church, found their pews, genuflected, and sat down with reverence. After all, this was the service. Shaya was sure most of the parishioners were thinking "one hour to go." Father M was not in the habit of letting the mass go beyond the requisite time limit. One could count on his punctuality after the mass. Once the mass started with the procession of altar boys, priest, choir in place, organist playing, the parishioners knew everything was on track. They knew they were getting out on time.

The trio had a mission planned after church and each child thought, May the best kid win. Usually Shaya's older brother won because he was at least a foot taller that she was, and maybe half a foot taller than her younger brother, so she was "out heighted" and sure to get mowed down in her brother's quest to get this once in a season "first fruit." But this season, she was faster and stronger, in her mind.

Father M's voice faded as Shaya was consumed in her thoughts of success and lauding it over her brothers as she ate this illustrious fruit. The fruit was small enough to evade the grasps of her brothers if she got it first. Father M's voice came droned closer. It was time to receive communion.

Shaya looked around to see who was leaving their pews to take communion. She spied Martin and Umzie, the class bullies on their way to the altar. I can't believe those two had the nerve to go to the altar, Shaya thought. By then, the two were kneeling at the altar. Well, Shaya thought, if those two bastards are going to receive communion, then I'm going to receive communion. As Shaya searched her memory, she thought, I haven't done anything really, really wrong this week. She remembered she hadn't gone to confession in the past two weeks either, but decided to risk taking communion anyway.

Shaya got out of her pew, genuflected, and walked to the altar. At the altar, she knelt and cupped her hands in anticipation of receiving first the wafer, then moved on the next go round for a sip of wine from the chalice. She had noticed that Father M, after blessing the wine, would take more than a sip then rinse the chalice with more wine and a drop of water. Hmmn.

Observation seemed be Shaya's strong trait. She dismissed this as an adult act, maybe something that most priests do. She'd question it later.

With communion over and the parishioners reseated in their pews Father M finished the mass by saying, "Go with God."

First in church, last out of church and vice versa. Shaya and her brothers sat in the last pews to be the first to the door. And they were. The stampede to the doors began—down the steps and through the graveyard to the main street. The siblings would be in a race for home and the plum tree.

Shaya looked around. Checking for her brothers. They were a few paces up the street. She took off after them knowing that if she could catch them at the street gate, she had a chance to beat them.

Bradley and Clem were holding onto the street gate panting and trying to catch their breath. Earlier when Grandpa left, he linked a rope through the fencing and the gate. Thanks Grandpa, thought Shaya. It slowed Bradley and Clem down.

Clem unlatched the gate, swung it open and ran up the steps to the next gate, taking two steps at a time. Bradley was on his heels. At the second gate, a much larger iron gate, Bradley got in first and tried to slam the gate to leave Shaya and Clem on the outside. Shaya and Clem both pushed the gate inwards together to keep it open. Bradley turned and ran towards the plum tree trunk, but Clem caught up to him. Both boys struggled a little. Shaya thought they would be duking it out for awhile, and saw the opportunity to climb the tree. But as she got to the trunk, Clem grabbed her arm and pulled her back towards the house. Bradley climbed up the tree while Clem and Shaya watched from behind a pillar under the house, just in case Grandma poked her head out the window.

Bradley climbed onto a branch he thought could support his weight. He stood on the branch and held onto another branch overhead. He reached out to pull the branch with the ripened plum towards him. It was wedged between two partially ripe plums. Here it was: the first and only ripe plum, the sweetest.

Bradley told us after the incident that he got excited, let go of the overhead branch to pull the branch with the 'plum' towards him. The branch snapped and he slid off the bottom branch and was left holding onto the branch with the plum. Fortunately, the branch twisted making it a little stronger, but not for long. The branch began to peel towards the tree trunk, then stopped. Bradley was forced to decide to jump. But where?

Bradley was dangling over a cliff; a good 20-foot drop. At the bottom of the cliff, there were trees. Bradley just let go of the branch and fell into a banana tree, then slid into a guava tree. He didn't suffer any broken bones. But, best of all, in Shaya's mind, Bradley didn't get the plum either.

Bradley pulled himself over the fence onto their yard just as Grandpa was walking up the steps. Bradley's church clothes shredded when he fell. There was no way the boy could explain what happened without confessing his sin. As Grandpa scolded Bradley, Clem and Shaya crept up the back stairs to avoid being seen. They knew if Grandpa saw them, they would get a spanking for being a part of the plum adventure. Bradley got a slap for reckless behavior. Then the family ate lunch.

Leaf Art

Squash, cucumber, grapes, bean leaves
no matter, the artist, at full steam.
Get that pesticide.
Halt! See the beauty, not human design
the artist hide, works displayed.
Not angry anymore, just transfixed.
Appreciate the beauty, enjoy the design.

Inland Empire

It's just a wrinkle, not the end. It's all hope.
Not every good heart is attached to a beautiful face.
    Good things are always beautiful.
Life is creating the right relationship.
    Finding the right person is not life.
Architect, builders of bridges created
    for two-way crossings, or walls as barriers
No alarm clock wakes up the dead, just the living.
Day of rejoicing. So dance like King David,
    rejoice with promises of hope

Energy gives and forgives, not a human characteristic.
Manna is still the culture, undeserved but expected.
People throw words like stones or daggers
    again and again. Who benefits?
It's honorable to play your cards well.
    It's not important to hold the high and low jokers.
Readily you build the blocks of life,
    barrier or bridge. Your choice
End life caring as much as you cared in the beginning.

One is...

One
    is

       respectful of self and others
           speculates about one's future usefulness
       thoughtful, well versed and present
       funny, colorful with flavored language
       outgoing, knowledgeable, fast,
           perceptive and expressive
       quiet, reserved, and at ease with self
       a lover of dance
       like a robin, colorful and beautiful

       One is hawkish and designing

With This...

Two rings of gold—their story told
    is mine, and oh so sad!
They symbolize the sweetest love
    a person ever had.
One ring is mine—the other his
    (he's gone from me, you know).
His death had left an emptiness
    that doesn't cease to grow.
I never thought we'd be apart—
    in life we both were one.
But now he's gone and I'm alone
    (my life is all but done).
I have his ring. That's all I have
    (it's nestled next to mine).
It's part of him to stay with me
    for my remaining time.
He had a message etched within
    (I did this, too).
We swore our love forever—
to each other we'd be true.
I loved him so
    (I love him so).
I did and always shall.
He's still so much a part of me,
    I need him with me now.
But that can't be (can't possibly)
bring back the times we shared.
Sweet secrets...talks...(and most of all)
adventures that we'd dared.

Echo

There's an echo in my room
    a deep and hollow din.
I feel the room's not filled
    with warmth or love...or him.

I've got my bed and things
    all nestled close around.
But nothing seems to take away
    that empty, silent sound.

The unfilled space expresses
    the sound that's never been.
My hollow room's not filled
    with warmth or love or him.

Ode to A Safety Pin

Oh, little twisted wire
—important as the atom—
you've held my hem,
you've sutured my seam,
you'd close my cleavage
(if I had 'em).
But, as time wears on
(and on, it must)
your brilliant brass
has turned to rust.
You've been exiled to some old purse.
Until some day when something "pops,"
you'll take your place
as "my wire nurse."

PHYLLIS MAYNARD

My Boomerang Never Came Back

My dad's name was Chapman ("Chappy"). He was my role model for many years—many years ago he seemed to possess boundless energy. He was always working on a project, whether it was music—his first love—or something the family needed or wanted. He always seemed to be moving. I think there was a tempo in his head they kept him moving to its rhythm. Unhappily, his final ten years were spent in nursing a stroke—when his only activity was from a wheelchair. During these sad times, he would lament how sorry he was that he was not able to complete the many plans that he'd made prior to surrendering to the stroke. He felt that life is full of rewards to be enjoyed by the hard work put into it, but thought that the "enjoyable" part of his hard life had somehow evaded him. He asked me to make up a poem for him with this with his title, "My Boomerang Never Came Back".

Your rewards are great
(they say) if you're kind,
and do well in all of your deeds.
I've been moral and straight
and stayed on the track
—but my boomerang never came back!

Education (they say)
is almost Divine
and God will smile if you're smart.
I've learned to read
and I'm smart as a tack
—but my boomerang never came back!

Do good in life.
Help those whom you can.
It's done. You can be on that!
I'm gently defensive and never attack
—but my boomerang never came back!

I've been good.
I've been strong.
    Kind thoughts all day long.
    Compassionate to a fault.
I wouldn't hurt critters.
Never swat a gnat
—but my boomerang never came back!

Now, God knows I'm good
    and kindly and smart.
He knows all my virtues an sins.
He tells me, "Be patient.
    Be cool and kick back!"
Your boomerang, Chap, will come back!

A Mouse in The House

A little after 7:30 in the evening shadows were just beginning to creep through the house when the perpetrator suddenly dashed from under the furnace room door. Icy fingers of fear clutched my throat as droplets of anxiety begin to gather at my hairline.

The enemy!

This threatening foe was right there in my home. Scurrying across the living room carpet, he was taunting me with invitations to war—his actions silently shouting at me, "I'm here and I'm near and I'm going to stay! So whadda ya say?"

After some shrieking and tap dancing around this unconscientious invader, I decided I'd have to develop a superior maneuver to block his direct route, which was back under my bedroom door. I immediately jammed a bath towel at the bottom of the door to prevent any exit he might consider.

Why do I worry? Why do I fear this tiny rodent so? And why is he in my house? He is tiny, ugly, black and brown, and—eech—no larger than a hummingbird. But this is war and one of us must go.

Allies are an important part of war strategies so I called my son (an ally) shouting on into the phone, "Bring mouse traps! I have cheese!"

Day one passed quietly with no snap of the mouse trap. We were approaching day two and still no response from the enemy.

In the meantime, I'm sleeping on the couch. Enter the bedroom? No, sir.

I'm trying to mentally plan my life without my bedroom. I'm glad he isn't barricaded in my bathroom. Meanwhile, life must go on. I have things to do. Errands to run. I'll begin today without dwelling on this conflict that has been thrust upon me. I'll begin by having a cup of tea and reading a newspap...SNAP!

That was the fictional finish to my "mouse story." The actual conclusion to my tale is stranger than fiction:

On day two I gathered enough nerve to peek into the bedroom—all quiet—and I could see the mouse trap was still set with the enticing chunk of cheese. I crept further into the bedroom with the door closed door behind me. What a chance I was taking!

What was that? I thought I saw a long burly tail under my desk. I looked further and at the end of that tail was a tiny, ugly, black and brown (eech) mouse appearing to take a snooze. He was lying on his side not at all disturbed—probably wanting a short nap before taking on the cheese.

My back-up ally at that moment was my daughter, who I talked into investigating further the sleeping vermin. She was totally composed—unlike her mother—and picked up the little thing by its tail and informed me the little critter had taken the "long nap." My daughter tried to convince me I had scared the little nasty thing into a heart attack. But I preferred to think it was just very (very!) old and was trying to find a suitable place to bite the dust.

The Rose and the Thorn

The rose and the thorn, the rose and the thorn, one so young and beautiful—the other: old and worn.

Someone said "How can they stay together, they cannot last." But with God, the present and the future is the same as the past.

The rose and the thorn, the rose and the thorn, the rose looks so beautiful, the thorn looks so forlorn.

I will tell you a secret, which no one else knows. God created the unsightly thorn to protect the beautiful rose.

So if tomorrow by chance a rose you should see, look upon the face of the thorn, for the smile there, that will surely be.

If the thorn could speak, his last prayer would be—to kiss the lips of his fair rose then happy, he would be.

The rose and the thorn, the rose and the thorn, each have their purpose in life, and for each other, we were born.

Dancing and Running

My parents put me in ballet and tap when I was eight years old because they caught me dancing and jumping on our furniture like Fred Astaire did in his movies. My dance instructor's name was Charles Lockmiller. At this time my family lived in Galveston, Alabama. Mr. Lockmiller was the best instructor in all of Alabama.

My first year, I danced in two different classes: one of ballet and the second in tap. I was in the class with five other young girls. Mr. Lockmiller told us we had to keep a notebook with the name of our dance steps written inside the notebook—the steps, ballet and tap, had French names. I have no recollection of whatever happened to my notebook later on in my life.

At eight years old, I caught the bus on Pioneer and East Broad Street. The bus took me over the bridge to downtown Gadsden. The Coosa River separates East Gadsden and downtown Gadsden. The bus would let me out in the front of the post office. The dance studio was one street behind the post office. My lessons were an hour twice a week.

After my lesson, I would walk back to the post office and wait for the bus back over the Coosa River. Mr. Brannon drove the bus I took going home. He was the father of my best friend Mary Frances Brannon, "Pug," for short. Pug and I were the same age. When I boarded the bus, Mr. Brannon would ask me to show him my new steps: Tuesday was ballet steps, Thursday was tap dance steps.

When my father came home from work, he wanted me to show him my new steps. Dad loved tap dancing. Dad was as good as I was after awhile.

I danced all the time. I practiced all the time. The lesson sparked a light and a love of the movement my body did.

The second year of dancing, there were two of us girls. We started with our ballet recital first, then after the other dancing (other students), my partner and I did our tap routine.

My third year, I danced by myself. I was happy because I felt like I was getting personal attention and learning new routines.

It should be noted that right before my recital, I usually fell on both knees and wore bandages on both my knees. My mom would try her level best to keep my knees Band-Aid free but to no avail. I wore these beautiful costumes and my knees were hurt.

My parents were at all my recitals. My dad would praise me for the big smile I had on my face when the music started. My teacher, Charles, gave me my cue to go on stage.

Sometimes, I would get scared right before my dance came up. I just knew I would not remember the dance routine. But as soon as the music started and I danced on the stage, somehow my feet took over and I danced like Fred Astaire. I would look out at the audience and find my parents smiling at me. I could tell I made them proud, skinned knees and all.

We moved to Riverside, California, in 1957. Two years later, my parents enrolled me into dance classes with Freddie Finn. He was one of the best of all-around dancers in Southern California.

Freddie Finn did not have the fancy costumes and recitals that we had in Alabama. Freddie taught me modern jazz dancing. He taught me more up-to-date tap dancing. I did not sign up for ballet this time.

In 1960, I decided to try my hand at square dancing. I did some square dancing in the sixth grade and liked it. I joined the Teen Twirlers of Riverside. We danced at White Park and at Cow Town on Van Buren, Riverside, in Woodcrest. I enjoyed country music and the steps we did as the caller called out the routines we did. My brothers, Ed and Doug, square danced, too.

Dancing helped me in my track and field training. I beat all the boys in sixth grade in the 50-yard dash. I had to run against the boys again because I was a girl and girls can't run faster than guys. It was fun. I beat them again and again.

I always enjoyed the Standing Broad Jump. I'd pick a spot in front of me and that is where I landed. We didn't have these kinds of sports in Alabama elementary school. It was a new experience for me. I stayed in Track and Field up to high school.

I joined the Riverside Sheriff's Department in March of 1975. I didn't get back into running until February of 1979. I went through the Riverside Academy in Box Springs, Riverside. It is no longer there. We ran every day. We called it "PT," physical training: sit ups, pull-ups push-ups, climb the rope, run Mount Rubidoux, run around Wheelock Field, track, etc... Our class had to run the stairs up and down in the gym. We had to jump rope.

After the Academy, I kept up with my running. I ran Mount Rubidoux once a week. I ran all over Riverside. In 1985, June, I competed in the Police Olympics, in Ventura, California, in Track and Field. I walked away with two silvers and two bronze medals.

In June of 1986, I walked away from the Police Olympics in Orange County with a gold medal. The name of the Police Olympics was changed to the Police Summer Games. I have competed in sixteen games in Track and Field: the 100- and 200-meter races, throwing the javelin, throwing the shotput, and bench-press.

When I became a Deputy Sheriff, I had to keep up my cardio conditioning. Lifting weights helped with my upper body strength. Being a female in law-enforcement did not make me or any of the other female Deputies popular. The female Deputies and myself had to earn the male Deputies' respect.

I could've sat in the front of the television with the remote in my hand, on the couch. There were days when I would get home after work and change into my running clothes. You have to push yourself constantly and have self-discipline. My body tells me when I overdo any workouts.

I can see and hear my dad telling me, "Your body will tell you your limits." Dad was a butcher but he was a weightlifter. My brothers and I have followed in Dad's footsteps.

In all the years I've participated in the in the (now) Police and Fire Games I have won over forty metals. In the hallway of my home, I have a shadow-box of gold, silver, and bronze medals. One of the backs of the medals says, "To Promote Physical Fitness Among the Law-enforcement and Firefighting Community. We Are the World's Primary Defenders of Life and Property. We Are the Peace Officers and Firefighters."

There's another story that law-enforcement officers carry, "Every time we leave home to go to work, we try to come home at the end of our shift, alive."

I find humor in fitness—if I get shot, I'll bleed slower. Starting out as a dancer brought me to my career in law-enforcement.

Phyllis' Story

Phyllis Leslie Perry was born on June 9, 1946, at 10:00 a.m. to Barbara and Jessie Perry in Gadsden, Alabama. Two of her brothers, Edwin and Douglas, were born in Birmingham, Alabama.

Ed had asthma and he was sick all the time. Mrs. Perry had family in Riverside, California. In 1956, Phyllis, his mother, took Ed with her when Mrs. Perry went to visit her family in Riverside. Ed did not have another asthma attack during their visit in California.

In the summer of 1957, the Perry family moved to Riverside, California. The climate in the west improved their son, Ed's health one hundred percent. Phyllis had one more brother born in 1959.

Phyllis graduated from Riverside Poly High School, in June of 1964. She married her childhood sweetheart and worked as a waitress for about four and a half years. Phyllis and her first husband divorced in April of 1967.

Phyllis' first son, James, was born May 23, 1967. Jessie was born August 27, 1969. Phyllis became a stay-at-home mother and wife.

Phyllis' second husband, Ron, was born in the big Island of Hawaii. He adopted James so all of the family carried the last name of "Ah Puck."

In order for the Ah Puck's to buy a home, Phyllis had to go back to work. She was hired as a Sheriff's Aide in the Riverside County Jail in March of 1975. Within four years, Phyllis had been promoted twice. She became a Deputy Sheriff for Riverside County, California.

In February of 1979, at the age of 32 years old, Phyllis began training at the Sheriff's Academy in Box Springs, Riverside, California.

After Phyllis completed the Sheriff's Academy, she was reassigned back to the old Riverside Jail.

In 1981, Phyllis was assigned to Riverside Patrol and Investigations.

In 1987, Phyllis left employment with the Sheriff's Department and was hired as a Riverside Marshall. She was assigned to Hemet Court. Phyllis also assisted in Banning, Lake Elsinore, and him and Temecula Courts.

In 1991, the Riverside Sheriff's Department took over the Marshall's Office. Most of the Marshalls became Deputy Sheriffs. Phyllis was back in Riverside as a Deputy working the Riverside Superior Court.

Before Phyllis retired, she married John, her third husband. Ron and Phyllis were still closed because of their sons, grandchildren and great grandchildren. Phyllis retired in 2005. She was asked to return to work part time as a Bailiff in the Courtrooms in Riverside, Corona, and Moreno Valley, California. Phyllis work another eleven years; bringing her a total of forty years working in law-enforcement. In 2016, when Phyllis was seventy years old, the Riverside Sheriff's Department thanked her for her service and let her go.

Arrangements

and so, this is how it goes
she thought
as she bent
to collect the pieces
of herself
and
arranged them into a bouquet
    to share them
        with another.

Bioluminescence

The swaying creaky mast
from where I see it, far below,
looks as if it sweeps across the sky,
windshield-wiping stars from my eyes.

Our hull bounces across the salty waters,
jolting us from one side to another.

The darkness is heavy here
and we grab onto the railings,
                onto the lifelines,
                      onto each other

The stars never budge, though,
except the ones we find in the ocean:
some lighted little creatures
that awaken in our wake—
the fireflies of the sea
slipping past us
as we trudge forth
in our ocean passage.

I feel lucky as I begin to realize
that everything is illuminated
and has been all along.

Cleave

A pebble fell
at the center of my forehead
then my body,
fragile
split down the middle.

Each of my organs chose a side to belong to.
    My right half dropped to the sidewalk
    and it spilled and it spilled and I gasped
    with half a mouth.
    I spilled muscle, I spilled blood while
my left side wobbled but stood upright.
I thought, how odd to be still living with intestine
exposed and only one leg to walk on.

The left of me left—
went for a hop through the park
and I wondered if my horizontal side
was my weaker side as a bird stopped to sing
awhile and perch on the shoulder I still had.

I thought of abandonment, of and by my selves
while a tree above me shed a tiny spring blossom
which glued itself onto my liver,
still moist from the split.
The sun warmed me, burnt me,
caused a sweet stench to rise.

Which half of me would they write about in the books,
which half of me still had a heart?

Conscious

I ran, feverishly
to all parts of everything
to taste it
to drink it in.

I reached for fistfuls of wind
and ether and light
of earth and dust and words—

More, and faster
I drank, I saw, and I felt it all.

And why,
        why,
                why
they asked,
did she make it about everything
when she went to look for herself?

Oh, but— they did not know
they did not know
that everything is me
and I

I am everything.

Elixir of Life

We frame things
We want to remember:

Certificates
People's faces
Specific places

If we could frame feelings
we would
    the sunny ones—
the ones that smell of love.

We would
hang them on a wall
near where we wander often
or better yet
reduce them to a liquid
and sip from them daily.

Home

Water on lips,
Hands on hips,

I welcome you.

You, the human
You,   the bringer of light
You,   both healer and hurter

because you are me
and you are he
and you are she
walking in sand
while waves come to erase
mistakes.

Space

The inexplicable
Void
Starry skies,
What lies between thighs
A pause...after uttered words
The air between us—
    tense or sweet
    sweet space
    within us
What we take up
and what we leave
when we go.

Summer Storms

I'd be the rain, the warm summer rain
dropping in on you
in the middle of a pleasant lunch, or
perhaps a brunch

I drip
    drip
        drip
                into your drink
inviting you to look up at me, with difficulty.

I baptize you with warm water
    one in your eye, you blink
        the hell is this? you think

Some dance in me, bare skinned
    as I quench desert lands,
        pooling in their sands
Sawing palms with my breeze
whipping up Caribbean seas
rocking boats, flooding moats

I thunder—

    while you all run under roofs
    awnings, trees
disappearing fast, drying quickly

leaving some feeling free

leaving only a memory.

The Human

I touch

       I tangle

I toss around
the parts of me
the darkest shades of black
the flowers that bloom from pain
A—a—a puzzle of hues
A hot-blooded fuse

I am
I am
The survivor of me
The one who hurts and heals,
The human.

ROWENA SILVER

Tempest Fugue

Soon, I will tell you sea tales
tantalize you with sagas of typhoons
and cyclones—yarns so vertiginous
you will fall overboard,
then, I will carry you ashore,
resuscitate you until you undulate
in sea rhythms and become salted
to my taste
Afterward, I will marry you
to adventure—as you lie
so deliciously
on the blue couch
hypnotizing my cat
with twisted yarn

Swim for It

The silver goldfish
I bought at Petco
went belly-up last night
Even more translucent
It's caught under the bougainvillea
swaddled in gluttonous swarms
of teeming angels
who furiously reshape
fins and gills
into a primordial mulch
of glorious resurrection

The Parting

I'm afraid of water
so the sight of you diving naked
into the gleaming millpond
engenders dread and longing

Ah, the slope of your calves
the sweet curve of your back
the prayer of your hands
parting the water in one delicate thrust

The pond sequesters you
surrounds you in shadows
leaves me outside the miracle
drowning

The Familiarity of Assumption

Beautiful things can turn on you in a second
like that Picasso etching you loved your whole life
only to have an expert tell you it is a fake
and not even a good one
Yet you continue to love it,
but in secret, more like a mistress than a wife

Then there was that week-end at the beach
when you complained
about dogs that barked all night
and you turned to me and said
"But, my dear, those were seals"
and suddenly the din is protected
and it would be useless to
report the noise to anyone

except perhaps a lifeguard
but he or she would laugh and point out tiny
croaking frogs and the pounding surf
which will not be hushed by
any will or mandate but the moon's

it is useless to love seals and Picassos in the abstract
and now I am wondering if I actually did try to talk to dolphins
would they would have anything interesting to say

or would they simply complain about the lack of
kelp and someone's cousin who ate all the anchovies
in the last buffet before sunset?

Pleasure Cruise

A person will have to give account for those permitted
things that his eye saw, but of which he did not partake.

Jerusalem Talmud: Kiddushin, Chapter 14 66b

Much as he once refused his mother's breast
he will not take the wheel or drink the wine

is so determined to detest the feast
he snacks on rice cakes, unadorned and dry

an unsubstantial mix of salt and grain
evocative of wandering and want
evocative of deep and ancient pain

He grasps at railings, shivering and gaunt
afraid the breaching whale will wet his shirt
lurks deep within the cabin's lower tier
Still clinging to the comfort of his berth

and yearning for the boat to come to pier
he glances out a porthole at the sky
and sees a comet flash—
and pass him by.

At the South Kensington Station

How could I recognize you in the haze?
remembrance has withered you away
into sweat-beaded face and measured grace
You're particled into my memory
as soft, synaptic murmurings of light
I keep you safe and warm inside façade
a caricature, hovering, unarmed

and lightly dusted with a decade's salve
a masking balm, more real than artifact
that somehow strengthens nose
and straightens spine

I did not know you, as I did not know
a mongrel when she came to lick my hand
when I returned, from two years travel
dog-less, in Bhutan

But, in that instant she transformed herself
from limping, scruffy cur
with cataracts, to my beloved
most amazing, Kate

Since you remain immutable and cold
yet huge, like Mayakovski's "cloud in pants,"
I'll file away this moment in the fog
and dash to Heathrow on the morning train

Waiting by the Curb

This is the click of new shoes in an empty hallway
hologram hope battered by time and the acrid fumes
of burnt memory. This is a remnant of gardens
built in separate deserts. We have sought out
and destroyed each other's secret places.

After long journeys we have returned to the same season
of banter and ruse
I planted yellow roses
in the full knowledge that things fade
desire seemed promise enough

But this is not what could be, or even enough of what was
This is something painted on the side of an ice cream truck
A dreamsicle—luscious looking—but never in stock

Rushing Headlong West

the locomotive sways
travelers awake
to faded cushions
haggard velvet
memories of red

Once, a czarina rode
in such a sleeper car
now Pepsi bottles mirror birch
trees through lace curtains
yellow with cigar

this train no longer
takes them to specific
rendezvous—they wipe
the frosted window
but the fog obscures the view

Donna Slezak

It Was A Dark and Stormy Night

It was a dark and stormy night. That's the way the old timers told it, and told it and told it. They said the sky was so black it looked like God had left heaven and turned off all the lights in the universe. The wind howled so loud it sounded like a pack of wolves inviting all the neighboring packs to a party. Yep, they did talk about that night.

It also was Christmas Eve. The night I chose to make my debut into the world. I was the first child, the only one for that matter, born to Joseph and Mary Gardner of Gardnerville, Indiana. My father, Joseph, was the son of Martin Gardner, owner of the largest and the first farm in the area. As it happened, my father was badly injured by a tractor accident when he was a boy. His left leg was badly damaged and he could no longer work on the farm. When he and my mother were married, my grandfather bought them the general store in town as a wedding present. They lived above the store and became strong, supportive neighbors to the little village that grew-up as a supply center for the farmers in the area.

Now on that particular dark and stormy Christmas Eve, Mom was just a few weeks away from my birth. She was having a difficult time, and the Doctor was concerned about my delivery. The day started with dire-weather radio reports. Stuttering through static, the announcer warned that a blizzard of biblical proportions was gathering on the horizon, and the storm was headed straight for our little village and all parts beyond. Travelers all along Indiana's roads were advised to find shelter and dig in. Everyone was told to stay indoors. Not exactly good news for Christmas Eve. Since there were few radios and fewer telephones in our area, spreading the bad news befell on those of us who did possess such devices. Disappointment and concern brought neighbors scurrying into the store to use our phone to get in touch with their relatives to cancel visits. While there, they purchased last minute supplies for Christmas at home. Mom was up and about helping Dad with the surge of business. As they worked, the menacing clouds hovering on the horizon began to move in. The sky grew gray, and by noon there was no doubt that something mean was happening in the atmosphere. The store had quickly sold out of most everything "holiday" and town had become very quiet. Folks were hunkered down in their homes as they had been instructed to do. Dad didn't like the way mom looked; pale and hollow-eyed. "Honey, you look really tired. I want you to go upstairs and lie down right now. I'll close up. No use to stay open any longer."

She wanted to argue but was too tired. She did as he told her.

It was four o'clock in the afternoon. The temperature was hovering near the thirty-three-degree mark and dropping. He closed up and hurried upstairs to find Mom lying down. "How you doing?"

"Okay. All done?"

"Yeah. It's so dark already. The wind is something fierce. It almost blew ol' Hal over. All 200 pounds of him."

"My goodness. I hope everyone got home alright."

"I'm sure they did. You lay still for a while." he said, as he lit the little kerosene heater. It was getting chilly in the room. "I'm just going down to call Doc. Just to make sure he's going to be around."

"Oh, don't bother him, dear. I'm alright. Just on my feet to much today. He said just yesterday that it would be at least another week. And he doesn't really have any place else to go does he?"

"I know all that. But I'm going to give him a call, anyway."

The Weaver's farm was ten miles out of town. Doc had a new Model-T Ford and it could take the rutted dirt-roads pretty good. But that was in good weather. This storm was a horse of another color. The wind was already slamming the first snowflakes against the windows. He left a message for the Doctor and hung up. He turned on the radio only to be met with static. The lights flickered as the electric lines were buffeted by the wind. To keep busy and his mind off of the doctor's tenuous journey, he filled some oil lamps for when the lights went out. Electricity was a recent luxury and not always a reliable one. The poles were hard pressed to withstand Indiana's normal storms, let alone a blockbuster; they came down on a regular basis. He carried the lamps upstairs and checked on his wife. Something was smelling awfully good. Mary was in their cozy kitchen peeling potatoes. The meat was already browning in the stew pot.

"I thought I'd do something simple tonight. Maybe turn in early."

He went over to her and gave her a kiss on the cheek. "Sounds good to me. You okay?"

"Sure. I'm just tense with the storm and all. It sounds just wicked. Did you get a hold of the Doctor?"

"It seems little Billy Weaver got the measles for Christmas."

"Oh, poor baby."

"I just hope the Doc gets back before the worst of the storm hits. We are already without the radio. I brought lamps up. The electricity is sure to go, too. It's already snowing. It's going to be a dozy."

As fate would have it. Record setting blizzard or not, I chose this night to come into the world.

As the story goes, Mom and Dad had dinner and turned in about seven o'clock. Even before the storm, they had planned on a quiet Christmas. The Doc didn't want her to travel, even the twenty miles out to the big farm; didn't even want her on her feet helping to cook for the whole clan. So, the two of them were planning to have Christmas for just the two of them. But quiet, it wouldn't be. It was about nine-thirty that night when Mom woke up in horrible pain. Dad raced down stairs to call the doctor. He tried to turn on the light but was met with just a click. Yeah, the lines were down already. He could hear the wind hurling itself in relentless fury against the front of the store. Snow was smashing into the window piling itself beneath it in wet piles. He fumbled around under the counter of the store in search of a candle, wondering why he had taken all of the lamps upstairs, finally he found a candle and a match. He picked up the phone and in the dim light he picked up the dead receiver. "No," he screamed softly. "I should've known. These things are no good for nothing! God! Now what do I do?" He didn't wait for the Almighty's answer. He raced back upstairs to see about Mom.

She was in agony. Bleeding and crying. He lit a lamp and put another cover over her to keep her warm from the creeping bitter cold that had taken over the house. "Darling I have to go out to get Doc. The lights are out and the phone is dead. I don't know what else to do."

"No—don't leave me—" she bent over with another contraction.

He bent down to hold her. When it was over. She told him. "Okay, Go, Hurry. Please, I'll be alright until you get back. Be careful."

He relit the little heater then grabbed his jacket and scarf.

Bundling up as he descended the stairs, he ran out into the dark, stormy night. The snow hit him in the face, and he couldn't see where he was going. But he knew the street. He could walk it blind folded. Even so it was slow. For every step forward the wind blew him back two. The five-minute walk to the end of the street and two houses around the corner took him almost fifteen minutes.

Meanwhile, Mom was trying to stay calm. She wasn't so much frightened for herself as she was for me. The pains were coming closer together and they were harder. Dad had been gone for what seemed hours. It shouldn't be taking so long. Then she heard something. She wasn't sure at first, but she thought she heard a knock at the door. But who; on a night like this? It was almost 10 P.M. She was sure it was her imagination. It's the storm, she thought. The doctor maybe? He could have missed Joe in the storm. She listened closely. There it was again. It was someone knocking—or was it just the wind? She slipped into her slippers, wrapped a blanket around herself, grabbed the lamp and hobbled down the stairs, she had to be careful not fall or drop the lamp.

She made her way across the shadowy store and stood by the door.

Sure enough, someone was there. She could see a dark blob pressed against the glass that looked like a man. She set the lamp on the wood stove by where the old timers sat and timidly opened it a few inches only to be met by the wind's fury. She was nearly knocked down. But the man caught her before she fell. "I'm so sorry to bother you like this," he told her, yelling to be heard above the wind. "My car ran out of gas on the highway. The sign said there was a town—I hoped it had a gas station. This storm has the highway in a mess. My headlights didn't do a thing. Would you have a telephone. My wife is expecting me tonight. She'll worry."

"Come in," she yelled, "shut the door."

He came in, dropped a bag on the floor and with both hands pushed the door closed. The wind was quieter.

"I'm afraid the lines are all down. No lights. No phone," she told him."

"Oh goodness. Now what?"

"Well, you can't go back out—the highway will be impossible tonight…" she bent over in great pain.

"Oh—what—are you in labor," he asked, as he saw her in the dim light.

She cried out as a contraction hit her.

"Are you alone?"

"My husband went for the doctor. He's been gone a long time. I'm worried…"

"Okay. Here sit down for a minute." He ushered her to a chair. Then rushed back to the door to retrieve the bag he had dropped.

Mom looked at him in disbelief. "Are you a doc…?"

"Yes, I certainly am and a good thing from the looks of it. You need to get back to bed. Where….?"

"Upstairs."

"Oh it would be. Can you make it?"

"I think…"

"Lean on me. We'll do it together."

Upstairs he tucked mom into bed and did the cliché thing—boiled some water. Scrubbed his hands good—this I know from the many times I heard the story—dumped his instruments into the boiling water and set to work. "This would be easier with two—"

It was then that Dad returned without Doc. He was half frozen. Worried beyond reason and scared to death. Of course, he was surprised to find a perfect stranger in his house, but before he could ask too many questions, he was quickly put to work. After properly scrubbing up and for the next few hours he was too busy and too scared to question the presence of this gift of a doctor.

With my first cries and with Mom finally out of danger, all dad could do was thank God and the good doctor, who happened by at the right moment. Dad said God must have taken him off the highway to help Mom through my birth. Doctor Watson never did call, that night.

They put the doctor up for the night and awoke to a dazzling Christmas day. The sun made the deep snow-covered ground glisten like diamonds, and there was peace on earth—at least in Gardnerville. The Doctor wouldn't stay for breakfast. He checked Mom and me again, and urged dad to get the doctor over to check on us as soon as possible.

Then he went downstairs, out the door and down the road. Dad watched as the tall lanky doctor walked with long strides down the snow-covered street toward the highway. Dad scratched his head as he turned to go back to go inside—something bothered him but he couldn't put his finger on it.

Then Doc Watson's loud, "Joseph" took his attention away from the disappearing figure.

The doctor was trudging slowly through the deep wet snow up to his knees, down the middle of the street. Quickly, Dad's attention was drawn back to the departing, "Doctor Michaels………" he called down the street. But there was no one there. The doctor had completely disappeared. He'd wanted to introduce him to Dr.

Watson. Dr. Watson slogged up to the store's porch beside Dad. "Who were you calling to, Joseph?"

"The doctor. The doctor who saved Mary and the Baby. I wanted you to meet him. He was great, but I don't get it. He couldn't have disappeared that fast. Hey, that's it. He had to get gas—He didn't get gas! And he was walking on the..................."

"What do you mean saved Mary and the baby—did the she have the baby?"

"Yeah, last night. During the storm. Don't know what we would have done without him."

The doctor just tore open the door and ran upstairs, not knowing what to expect. Mom's delivery could have been very bad. He didn't know another doctor within fifty miles of Gardnerville. Joseph was acting very strangely. He took two stairs at a time which wasn't easy for a man of his years. When he got to the bed room he found mother and child cuddled together sleeping soundly. He fell thankfully into the big chair beside the bed. They both looked quite well. He was relieved, and astounded.

Joseph was right behind him. "Last night. When I couldn't get you. I was terrified. She was in such pain. When I got back from your place. I found her with this doctor. He had everything under control. We—he and I worked together—little Gabriel Michael was born about 3 am. Everything was fine—tired, yes, but okay. He said his car ran out of gas on the highway. He walked into town to get some. How did he do that? I could hardly make it to your place—the storm was so bad—-then he had to stay the night."

"I know. I got hung up in a drift just outside the Weaver's gate. Couldn't get out until this morning. When I got home and found you had been there and Mary was having pains, I was frantic— was expecting the worst. I don't know who this doctor was, but thank goodness he came along." He checked mother and me over and proclaimed us both perfect. "A Christmas miracle," he proclaimed and went home to thaw out and have some turkey and dressing.

Mom's recovery took a little longer than a usual delivery. But she did fine, and so did I. It got really spooky though, when the electricity got restored. It was taking the road crews some time to dig through the all the drifts. It was a sunny day in the area. A chilly Thursday, and a slow day at the store. Since my birth, Mom hadn't worked in the store too much. Dad wasn't too busy, so he was having a coffee break with the old timers who liked to sit around the warm stove, drink the free coffee and listen to radio since it was also free. They were listening to the local news. Today, the reporter was telling about the mess the crews were encountering on the highway near the Gardnerville turn off. "The crew uncovered a sedan that had become completely covered by snow. It had evidently hit the transformer. There was a single occupant; the driver, was identified as Dr. Gabriel Michaels from Indianapolis. It looked like he died instantly, sometime Christmas Eve night. An autopsy would give the exact time of death. His family was being notified. They said Dad turned forty shades of white. "No way!" he said. "It's just not possible. No way!"

Mom was just as incredulous. They could never explain it. Of course. It falls under the title of Unexplainable.

Me, the recipient of said miracle found it a bit of a strain growing up. It just really puts a lot of stress on a kid. You know, being a miracle baby. But then, I stepped up to the plate. I grew up reliving the story every Christmas Eve, and I still have to tell it to the grandkids, great grandkid and great, great grandkids every year. Gardnerville never did have another dark and stormy night like that one; it grew up to be a small town, the general store became a small supermarket and Dr. Watson's practice grew to include a young ob-gyn Doctor by the name of Gabriel Michael Gardner. Yep, that's me; now retired, of course. But there's still a Dr. Gabriel Michael Gardner in residence in town, though he's a GP; my son. But he'll be around for a while to the carry on the tale of that very dark and stormy night a long time ago. Who knows, after that. He has a son who finds the tale of a ghost doctor very intriguing.

Donna Slezak

Ancient American Warrior in The Sky

It was going to rain. You could smell it in the air. See the distant line of black clouds. Hear the low drums of thunder warning of the coming storm, but where I sat on my friend's stoop it was still a beautiful afternoon. The sky was a soul-redeeming blue with whip-cream clouds. Lighthearted breezes played with the trees. I had nothing to do but wait for her. So I scanned the picturesque sky looking for fun objects amongst the clouds. There, I found an arrow. Not a skinny arrow; but big blocky arrow. It said, "Follow Me." So I did. I was not disappointed. It ushered me straight to Him. He was trekking an invisible path across his azure world. An ancient Native American Warrior, he wore a head band that held his long straight white hair back from his face. It was an old face. Weary. His eyes were set deep under his wide, steep forehead. Sharp, high cheek bones pulled leathery skin taut across his weary features. A large nose dominated his face, eclipsing the slit of his mouth. His jutting chin suggested a stubborn adversarial persona. He wore leggings and a tunic with a long cord wrapped around his waist. A bulky blanket engulfed him, protecting him from the chills that plague the aged. His left hand hung straight by his side. In his right hand, he carried a lance. Not a Native American lance. The spear-head suggested a Roman or Spanish weapon. I didn't know what brought this warrior on this walk-about. Perhaps he had heard the thunder and mistook it for drums, drums that had once called warriors to council meetings. And so, he had come to do his duty to his people; as he had always done. He looked down at me for a long time, but we could not communicate. I could only gaze at him in awe. It was getting later. The storm was moving closer. The wind becoming stronger. I feared for my heavenly Brave. He needed to find another plane for existence. Only Demons would dance around the council fires tonight. I wished him the Great Spirit's protection and most reluctantly went inside. The sky grew black and the thunder splintered the silence. The rain came. I worried about my warrior. I hoped he had made it to other sunny-skies before the storm set in. Now every day when the sky is that heart-wrenching blue and the clouds are snow white and so fluffy that you want to reach up and take a handful, I scour the heavens for my friend, the Native American Warrior in The Sky. I am grateful for his awesome visit that day, but....I'm still hopeful that someday he will come to visit again.

Pondering

He asked me,
>   'If you knew for sure that you only had X number of years
>   left,
>   then what would you do with the time?'
Boring question. Tedious even.
Why ask about what would I do with time left
instead of what I would do with the words I have left?
I propose that starting at the age of 20
everyone gets 25 million words to throughout their lifetime.
That's it. When all those words are used up
the voice box shut down.

You must weigh each word the tongue forms
>   for heaviness or levity,
>   For value, clarity, and utility.
>   Tenderness, love.
The use of the word "like" counts for two words. Vulgarity, too,
>   will add on.
Speak silence, only.

Promise Yourself

"Did you get them?" a voice called from upstairs.

Mrs. Loper closed the front door. She sighed deeply as she put her packages on a chair. "Oh, no, dear, I forgot."

Karen scrambled down the stairs, her long black hair flying behind her and her face reddening. Flashing her dark eyes, she blurted, "Oh, Mom! How could you forget?"

"Karen, I had a lot of items to buy. It just slipped my mind. Besides you know you shouldn't be smoking anyway."

"Oh, no," Karen moaned, pacing around the room. "I just finished my last pack, too." She paused and looked up at her mother. Half-smiling, she said, "Well, maybe this would be a good time to quit for me to quit, huh?"

Mrs. Loper's eyes widened and brightened. She reached over, gave her daughter a hug and whispered, "It sure would be, honey."

Karen shifted her weight from one foot to another mulling over the idea. Her hands dug deep into her blue jeans' pockets.

The front door opened and a dark-haired boy, about eleven years old, darted in.

"Wow! It sure is getting cold out there. I bet it's gonna snow tonight. Hi, Karen. Hey, Mom, when's supper?"

Mrs. Lopez smiled at her son. "In about an hour, Roy," she announced, hurrying toward the kitchen.

Roy studied his sister, "Why so glum, chum?"

"Huh, what?" Karen turned quickly. "Oh, nothing, Roy. I've got a lot of homework to catch up on. See you later."

Karen bolted up the stairs two at a time leaving Roy shaking his head when he heard the door slam.

Strolling into the kitchen, Roy asked, "What's wrong with Sis?"

Mrs. Loper looked up from her potato peeling. "She's trying to stop smoking. She ran out of cigarettes today and I forgot to get her some. So she is withdrawing. Let's try to be very patient with her, OK?"

"Yeah, sure," Roy replied. "She's tried that before, remember?"

"Yes, I do," His mother murmured, as the potato peelings curled around her fingers. "Maybe Dad would be here now if he had quit sooner."

Roy glanced at her, then lowered his eyes to the potato peelings falling silently to the floor.

The bedroom door slammed again. Karen's voice trailed down the stairs ahead of her flying feet.

"Roy! Hey Roy! Do you want to take a ride with me?"

"What for?"

"I want to go downtown for some cigarettes." Karen's eyes met her mother's, the jingle of her car keys filling the silence between their gaze. "Come on, Roy. We'll be back in half an hour."

The frigid night air hit their faces as Karen opened the door, shaking Mrs. Loper from her memories of her children's father. She called out, "Karen, it may start snowing soon, maybe you'd better..."

"It's alright, Mom. I have brand new snow tires, remember?" Karen replied. "We will be back before dinner!"

The Loper children both jumped into the family Volkswagen. The engine sputtered and died. Karen pumped the gas and the car started up. She drove without speaking. The slapping of the wind-shield wipers soon interrupted the children's quiet mood. It had begun to snow and large, heavy flakes covered the car.

"I know what you're thinking," Karen said to Roy in the silence. "My sister is hooked on cigarettes and can't stop!" Her outburst bringing her foot down hard on the gas pedal. "Look, now this will be my last pack—I promise you."

"Don't promise me. Promise yourself," Roy retorted.

"I have."

Roy took a deep breath and began again, "I guess it must be real hard to quit. Dad went through this too. I'm never gonna start smoking. It's a prison house! Hey, could you turn up the heat? It's getting mighty cold in here."

Karen adjusted the heater knobs and turned the windshield wipers to a higher speed. The wet, large snowflakes pelted the windshield, blowing a white sheet around the small car.

"Karen! This is turning into a blizzard. Let's turn back!"

"No, we're only a half mile from the store. I'm not turning back now," Karen snapped, as she flicked on the radio. A heavy rock tune blared out from the speakers, the drum beat matching The beat of the wipers as they slapped away the heavy layers of snow.

The tree appeared suddenly; the wide trunk loomed ahead as a dark black specter. Karen spun the wheel quickly and hit the brakes. The sound of scraping metal screeched into the children's ears before the car stopped.

"Roy! Roy! Are you ok?" Karen's voice sobbed and screamed, as she reached for her brother.

Roy picked his head up from between his knees, blood dripped into his eyes from a gash on his forehead.

"Oh, Roy! I am so sorry," Karen cried as she began wiping his face with her scarf.

"I-I-I'm alright. Really, Sis. Yeah. I am ok!" Roy stuttered, holding the scarf to his head as looked outside. "Yikes! We just sideswiped the tree. We are really lucky."

"I will never smoke again. I almost killed myself and you for a lousy cigarette," Karen cried loudly.

"Hooray!" Roy shouted into the air. "And look! We even have a ride home."

Red flashing lights blinked behind their car as another car pulled up behind them.

"We might even make it back home in time for supper." Roy said as he opened his door. "Mom's making my favorite potato soup."

SHIRLEY PETRO-TIMURA

Eulogy Poem for My Mother-In-Law

I called her "Grandma" right from the start

It would not be easy to win her heart

But there was soothing balm behind her tongue

And her contagious laughter made her fun

She always treasured her family

And her kindness meant the world to me

When my new baby, Talitha, was taken ill

She was there with a hug and concern that was real

Her hot chicken soup always made our mouth's water

No one could match it, so why did we bother?

The secret was the garlic salt I was told

But the ingredient that made it special was really her soul

Now she's up there serving Poppy and Uncle Dan something good

I'd ask for her secret if only I could

And if she was cooking her soup, I would surely partake

Instead of tasting these salty tears through farewells we do lovingly make

Goodbye dear Mom and Grandma, we will see you by and by

Where your laughter will abide forever and your love will not die.

Marshmallow Trees

Tangled in their sticky cocoon
    of ME
They watch marshmallows grow on the apple trees
    in their backyards
And say nothing
Sitting with chin cupped in hand
    they watch the mighty rains
Pelt, batter, and melt the marshmallows.
The ear-shattering silence
    as the white glue slides down the trunk
And turns black.

JOSE LUIS VIZCARRA

Letter to My Fourth Child

As a very proud father of my fourth child I am extremely proud to see my daughter grow in age: physically, academically and socially.

Every day since I saw you the first time I was overcome by fears of not being a father that you deserved. You are my fourth and last child. The first three made my life oh so happy and filled my heart with joy. You were the only one that was not born through a C-section. You gave me the fantastic experience of being there when you came out of your mother's womb and created the most beautiful sound that is the first cry of your life!

I am very proud of being a provider for my family. As a responsible man I worked in two jobs so that your mother could stay home for your older sister and you every day. Your mother did an incredible job raising both of you and gave you the best education to prepare you for life.

As you grew, I loved seeing you become a very good student and a fantastic friend and leader. Your creative mind and your caring ways left many wonderful memories everywhere you went. The minutes that I shared with you are great memories.

You put your heart on everything that you were involved in. Several times you experienced disappointment and you matured and overcame each obstacle. Swimming and tennis helped you develop team concept that will help you for the rest of your life.

Your great attitude left a great impact in the animal shelter. That led you to choose your career, which I think, will be a successful decision. Everyone is wishing you a very successful life.

Now you are half a world away in Australia. That is a great experience for you. The professional preparation will guide you to be a great doctor in veterinary medicine. All the people who know you are so happy for you.

One day you will find your mate to form your own family and you will add to the two grandchildren that I have.

Daddy's Fears

Even though you see me big and strong,
oh, my little girl, you really don't know.
Every real dad has a big fear.
What is happening to my little girl now?

When I met your mom so many years ago
there was real fear in my heart.
Will she stay with me for life
or will she soon from me depart?

A few wonderful months together
your mother and I gave life
to a beautiful little girl
and a bright new star!

When I saw you that very special night
for the very first time
I was so elated to hold you,
but afraid at the same time!

As time passed, oh, so fast
and on to school you departed.
I was so afraid you should know
of the bad education people talked about!

Some of my fears were erased,
as you developed in all areas of your life.
Even though you turned into my beautiful champion
there were fears that you wanted a special man in your life.

Then that frightening day you announced to me
"Daddy I want you to meet Ronnie, and please
be nice to him!" But my daddy thoughts were on violence
and to turn that Ronnie into macaroni!

But Ronnie committed his life to her.
Every day, he is there to help.
He pays the bills and improves the house.
He works hard and shares the chores.

But God is great to daddies who are fearful.
Today I have the honor of every father
of walking my daughter down the aisle
so that she can be the wife of a very good man!

Ronnie, now I pass to you as a father-in-law
all those fears that a loving father must have
when you and your wife will have
a beautiful little daughter that you love!

My Story: An Excerpt from The Two Golden Rules

I was born in 1948 in the beautiful city of Chihuahua Mexico to a very hard-working single mother, who was abandoned by my father, when she became pregnant. This is not an isolated event, but a very frequent social crime experienced in too many homes around the world.

Men who feel the machismo of conquest. Men who assume no responsibility for taking care of their children. Not only was I abandoned by my father but also by my mother who had to come to America to search for income to support her son. I do not hate either of my parents, but their abandonment left a big void in my emotions.

My mother worked in very menial jobs in order to make enough money to bring me to America to live with her. I was reunited with my mother at the young age of fourteen, when she was able to bring me to America on a student visa. Years later, she was able to arrange my legal permanent residence status.

I remember arriving to Los Angeles with my uncle. I started counting palm trees—which I had never seen. Coming from the border city of Juarez, located in the desert, California was culture shock. I did not speak English throughout my six years of middle school and high school. Though I attended school, I felt as though I did not learn anything from my teachers.

My experience in public school was the main reason I became a bilingual teacher. I wanted to teach children and adults the way I wished that a teacher had taught me. It was not that I was stupid; it was that all those teachers were not interested in teaching students to learn the language faster. I enrolled in seventh grade and graduated from high school in 1967. That was the era of the Vietnam conflict.

I volunteered to join the Navy.

157

So many American young men fled to Mexico and Canada to escape their responsibility to serve in the armed forces and pay their dues as American citizens. So many of us immigrants served in the armed forces with honor for our adopted country.

I was unable to join the Navy, but the United States Army drafted me the week they murdered Dr. Martin Luther King, Jr., in April 1968. I truly enjoyed my stay in the Army. I learned so much and grew as a human being.

After serving two years seven months and fourteen days, I completed my service in the Army. Most veterans are very proud of the service they rendered our country. The United States is a place of freedom that is worth dying for.

Soon after leaving the military, I enrolled in college using my GI Bill to pay for my college education. Like so many students, at first, I did not know what I wanted to study. Going to college can be a very wonderful and rewarding experience if you know exactly what you want.

I became a teacher and thirteen years later I received my master's degree. My 33 years of teaching on the elementary level and twenty years of teaching ESL to adults changed my life forever.

I became a millionaire in paper. My earnings went over the six-figure income. Most people would consider that a true financial achievement, but that is not the case. It is not what you make that matters, but what you keep at the end of the month. Like most people I was struggling because I did not have a solid financial education. That is why I have dedicated my life to educate as many people about financial education.

All of my education, formal and informal, did not happen overnight. I am very grateful for the authors of the great books that I have read: "The Holy Bible," "Mind Is The Master," "Think and Grow Rich," "Rich Dad Poor Dad," John Maxwell advice on leadership and so many books of wisdom, leadership, the spiritual life, good nutrition, exercise, finances, investments, business and other fantastic literature from which fortunate people can benefit.

All the conferences, audio, video and multimedia that I viewed also contributed to my education. Great minds helped me focus on higher education in college and business opened my vision to greater thoughts. All the hours I invested in my education placed me in a higher-level mindset. Learning how to set goals improved my time and life.

The birth of my four children helped me become a better person. My marriages created in me a sense of belonging and responsibility and true love for others. It taught me how to become a provider for a family.

The years that I attended public education helped me to be aware that I needed to learn and master the language of the country in which I lived.

The years I was in college sharpened my study skills, which helped me take tests for licenses in the financial world. Attending the business meetings gave me more leadership training to help people with their finances, business and investing. It taught me that nobody can succeed alone in this society.

We need great leaders to guide us away from mistakes and to perform like true professionals. The experience prospecting people and setting appointments is crucial to be able to close business. The training will help in solving problems in order to create income.

America is the greatest country in the world. There is an unlimited amount of money around the world and people do not know how to access it. The lessons learned have helped me eliminate most of the mistakes that I committed by borrowing too much money. Now I teach others with experience and confidence how to eliminate all debt in order to be truly free in life.

To be truly free in America you must acquire wisdom in how you invest and not waste your most valuable asset that all living human beings can possess: your time. All wise people have understood very well just how important their time was. All ignorant people waste their time away doing activities that destroy their future, present, past, health, finances, relationships, education, culture and every area of their lives. Animals have a much better sense of living with a purpose. We must find a purpose in life to drive us to a better existence.

Advice to A Teenager

Kiss the truth and
if it returns the kiss
you are ready for love
that knows no limits.

Embrace ecstasy and pleasure
will inhabit your body so that
a touch will kindle passion
that will smother apathy.

Know yourself to be the source of all good things
and your life will never
cease to produce wonder for others.

Then love will come to you
on dancing feet with new
music written just for you.

And there will never be
another sunrise for you
without joy.
I promise.

Tamale Day

The dozen tamales were just a gift I brought to make myself welcome. It was Sunday and I bought them after church from the women standing behind two large metal pots on a table outside of my church. They were still warm when I reached his house. I was anxious to see my friend again. The tamales were my excuse to visit, if only for a few minutes.

When I called his wife, Elisse, she told me he was awake and that Laura and her husband, Rod, were there, too. When the door opened, Laura stood in the opening flashing her spectacular smile with a greeting that spilled out like the notes from a sonata. His daughter had his eyes, exposing a soul so compassionate it made my concerns about him drift away, like the temporary retreating sea from a breaking wave on the endless beach of my angst. Somehow, the surprise of seeing her again—the daughter of my cherished friend who was wasting away from a terminal illness— to bring him the joy of her presence, caused me blurt out something which made her laugh and greet me with a hug. I knew I was welcome. I was his friend, but not his family. And my place among his many friends was only in that long line of memories we all carry.

Eliud grew up in a large family and they were all there placed together in a painting just inside the first room of his house. Almost as large as life, they looked out at you with sober faces binding them together but not without distinction. He had painted them long ago when his siblings were young adults. One sibling and his parents had died, but the rest were still alive. His two daughters, Laura and Tanya, were in separate paintings as was his wife, all women who reflected the beauty of his creative soul.

He was first an artist and that is what he brought to everything he did. As a teacher, he touched students with his insight into their better selves; that I learned from his students and felt it when he told me my writing should continue.

Teaching English literature made his artistic talents take a different turn. The mechanics of writing disappeared into that dimension where words evoke images without describing them as a sculpture makes you feel without touching it. This was his gift to his students. Beyond instilling self-confidence, his gift to them was an invitation to be aware of the power to hear their own voices in words that came out of the dark corners of the truth in their lives that was so hard to reveal to anyone. He was the first comfort to that pain and was there when the infant message lay at last in the open waiting to be read. And he held up their stories like a proud parent in publications that would have never been seen without his kindness.

So it was with me when I first wrote for him, or was it for me? I cannot tell the difference now. His impact on me was so subtle. I came to recognize good writing was never meant to be just a record of events past or imagined. It was an art, mastered by a few, that made stories about people's lives or their perceptions of life, thoughts and things, pierce the demanding reality of living. Reading good writing was a learning experience for many through a special sense of compassion and empathy awakening when we can see ourselves in words written by others.

What could I write about Eliud that had not already been written? We were only fifteen days apart in age, but now the gulf between us widened as he drifted away from his body that was helplessly in a sea of pain. Why was love so powerless not to possess the source of understanding of that pain we must all have at the end? I can only see I can do nothing to stop it. I can say nothing that is a comfort. I cannot even be a presence replacing the solitude of his suffering. I can only watch with everyone the inevitability of life. Tears come. I cannot stop them even to rejoice about the time we had together.

But I can start. I can remember his love for Mexican food—the food of his childhood—hot and spicy like his lust for life. He made his own hot sauce from peppers he got at specialty stores

162

that we all remember made us grab our glasses of water or beer. His eyes still light up, like his daughters do when good things happen or darken when things go wrong. There are no blank moments there. His intelligence could never be suppressed by things that would be boring to others. He still can find emotion in everything. And that is what worries me about the suffering of sensitive people. It must be as deep as they can feel about everything. But they will not tell you so.

As I tried to leave, he watched me from the comfortable seat on his couch, smiling and waving that hand I held earlier. Laura had held his other hand then as she knelt before him when he was seated at the table eating one of the tamales I brought, covered with hot sauce. She put her face next to his and told him she loved him. I looked at her face next to his and wondered how he would have painted her at that moment. Her eyes shone with such compassion and love for her father I could not ever forget that moment even if I tried. His grey hair next to her face made her dark eyes burn into my memory a reflection of that love he had given to us to share.

My dear friend, Eliud: He thanked me for the tamales and thanked me for coming to see him. I cannot remember what I said in return as I tried to say goodbye to everyone thanking me for bringing tamales. I felt I left with more than those tamales I brought that day but he always seemed to make that happen, somehow.

My Last Bicycle

It was September 30, 1990, and I had four days left to reach home on my new custom bicycle. I had peddled it 5,600 miles for three months across the country from Boston and now I crossed the Arizona border on my solo, "unsupported" cross-country trip. I spent that night in El Centro. The next day, I climbed up the steep curving road to Julian and camped again for the night. I could smell the sea when I got up and started down Highway 78 the next day. I first saw Oceanside stamped on a highway marker just before I had to swerve to avoid a car that moved next to me. I needed to adjust to the notorious California traffic quickly. The politeness of drivers in the twenty-one other states I traveled through was over. Enjoying the scenery now was risky.

Then I saw the Pacific Ocean as I came around a curve. It looked like a thin line on the horizon at first, but the landscape seemed to disappear as the ocean loomed into view. When I reached the beach, I leaned my bicycle up against a wall, took off my shoes and ran into the water. Soon the urgency of making my scheduled stop at my father's house in Laguna Hills made me dry off and pedal up Highway 1 to Newport Beach.

I got to their senior condominium in "Leisure World" as the sun was going down and was greeted by Dorothy, his third wife, when I rang the doorbell. Divorced, widowed, remarried and financially secure in a gated community, my father looked mildly content. He was still a consummate gentleman and host. He took me to his Kiwanis club lunch the next day mistakenly introducing me as Jim, who was my stepbrother I had met only once. My cross-country trip was not mentioned.

That afternoon I left for San Bernardino where I was expected at the weekly meeting of my Rotary Club. My friend, California District Court of Appeal Justice, F. Douglas McDaniel, was ecstatic when I told him by phone I would time my arrival for late morning, just before the lunch meeting. He and I had planned the entire trip to raise money for our Rotary Club's promotion (conceived by him) encouraging the teaching of basic moral values in public elementary schools.

I camped for the last time in Green River that last night—on the grass in the park. The next morning, wet from the automated nightly water sprinklers, I rode back roads to San Bernardino where I was met by a TV camera van and later by Dan Robins, our Police Chief, proudly driving his police car with its lights flashing.

When I got to the city limits, I followed Dan to the meeting place. As I rode around the last block, I saw dozens of people gathered on the street and our club President standing next to my smiling and waving wife, Gayle. Cheering and hugs for me by everyone were abundant, but I did not see Doug.

Then I saw him walking alone up the street from the opposite direction. He later said he had tried to be the first to greet me by walking a few blocks toward my expected route but did not anticipate I would be taking a route chosen by our Chief of Police. He looked very disappointed and I spent the much of following meeting trying to cheer him up.

Doug had mapped out the plan for the entire three-month bicycle trip across the country to make sure I was on a safe route and could visit Rotary clubs on their meeting days and times in 22 states and the District of Columbia. I had faithfully followed his plan and did not miss one meeting, often giving a speech he wrote for me about our program. It was a structured method designed to show teaching methods for making value judgments and we added a cash prize annually to teachers who are chosen, by a committee, as the most competent with their elementary school students in promoting what he called "character education."

I rode my bicycle each year for nine years afterwards, from Sacramento to the San Bernardino Rotary Club Awards lunch, an average of 538 miles in a week to keep the interest in our program alive. Now it hangs in the garage at our home in Riverside. But even after I moved away, Doug never stopped giving me credit for the program by promptly buying a large perpetual trophy with my name on it, that is awarded, engraved with the annual first place winner's name, at a gala luncheon each year thereafter.

Doug was a WWII marine pilot, decorated with the Distinguished Air Medal for his heroism in the battle at Iwo Jima. He was my hero, too. Many years later, Doug got hit by a car on his daily walk. When I visited him in the hospital, he introduced me to the hospital staff as his son. He never recovered fully and died at age 84 just before some new members of our Rotary Club changed the name of the "Duncan Webb Award" to the "Teacher's Award" but I heard they did not change the name on the trophy.

My First Car

The summer of 1949 in Livermore was still hot in September. But our big two-story Spanish-style house with its red tile roof kept us cool inside. It sat alone in the middle of two acres of rows of grapes and 57 English walnut trees, surrounded by miles of brown rolling hills of wheat fields. State highway 50 went by our driveway with traffic going 45 miles west to San Francisco and the ocean and 60 miles east to Sacramento through the fertile Central Valley that produced enormous amounts of fruits and vegetables. We saw much of that substantial harvest going by our house in hundreds of trucks that often stopped at a gas station at the intersection of highway 17 that went into our small town and then south to San Jose. The gas station was about a half mile west from our house towards town and I had made friends with all of the attendants. I rode my bicycle down there regularly and they let me wash windshields after school and throughout the summer.

That spring, my father had left for good to live near his office in San Francisco with his secretary and their new baby. Our wonderful summers in Oregon at my uncle and his sister's farm were no longer allowed. Luckily, I had gotten tall and strong from working on their farm with my cousins for many summers before. I was only fourteen years old, but was big enough to be able to reach the center of the windshields of cars and trucks that stopped for gas or food at the restaurant opposite the gas station. I got to earn tips that helped us buy food that we could not grow.

I saved some money too. And when not busy, I watched the men in the gas station do simple maintenance tasks or repairs by lifting cars up on a hydraulic hoist to change oil or fix them. They patiently taught me how to fix cars and when I saw a dismantled Model T Ford pickup truck in a junk yard behind our hardware store in town, I was confident I could fix it too—and make it run again. The hardware store owner sold it to me for $25. He also helped me bring some of it that I could not take on my bicycle or in a wheel barrow to our house, where I put it in one side of our garage in back that had been used for my father's car.

That side of the three-car garage was used by me now. It was where I hatched my chickens in nests I made under a light bulb from fertile eggs and kept the grain and straw for my growing flock. No one seemed to notice as I labored for the next month to put my pickup together with tools I had bought. Then early one afternoon after school, I finally got it started. It was wonderful and the engine ran smoothly.

The noise made my mother come to a window overlooking the driveway. She stood there looking out at me drive it around the front of the house, down the driveway and out onto the highway. I remember she had a cup in her hand and the usual cigarette in her mouth. She just looked at me as if she were in a trance. I drove my truck to the gas station where I was greeted with grins from the attendants. We used the car hoist to inspect my work and make adjustments for the rest of the day. Then I drove home before dark and put it inside the garage. No one said a word about it to me at dinner and I was not surprised. Our family had been in shock for a long time.

RIVERSIDE PUBLIC LIBRARY

Led by Jo Scott-Coe

Condensation

Dark heavy clouds remind me of my beloved Seattle—so far north, it may as well be Juneau. The weather here in this dry city teases. I know these clouds won't give me the rain I crave, I miss. These smatterings of meager droplets, like blowing wisps of sand, are no more nourishing than a zephyr. What I wouldn't give for a hard, steady downpour! Those thunder clouds seem like weak mewls compared to the roaring skies of Toledo, like lions fighting to mate. Riverside's storms are lonely cannon blasts of blanks, like a third-rate circus act: every sad rumble, I expect a clown to tumble from the clouds to my feet and bow for applause. I remember laughing a lot as a child in Seattle. Here in this desert, my humor is a sapling still struggling to break the hard surface of the dry ground.

Intertwined

(For MSK)

You must have decoded
the compartmentalized flight plan
of M and I
meticulously
while we were busy
re-discovering each other:
M, the Pisces yin,
(my golden lionfish)
to my Gemini yang

Our two spaceships
connected by tenacity and temerity
spinning circles
of opposed directions
within our contained
sparkling Swarovski sea
to a Swing soundtrack
of a live orchestra

Outside our coveted
synchronous dual orbit
safe from the smells of ozone
and sulfur
Catastrophic concussions
abound carrying
cacophonic electronica
with blurred electric guitar riffs
too fast for the human hand
and tribal drum beats

Within our sanctuary
(with my golden lionfish)
harmony is my reward
I am peaceful as a calm sea
predictable as the rising tides
and open without end

But dual-natured I long
to escape outside
of what lies within
my safe silken tether
To breathe in the pollution
for a brief adrenaline rushed
energized, thrilling chaotic holiday

To remind me the galaxy
is a metamorphosing
macrocosm of
eradication and rejuvenation

Cataclysm

the smoke reveals
tiny body parts
scattered across the schoolyard

from a nearby window
a man watches the plume of smoke
finger caressing the detonator in his hand

Cuates

She called them *cuates*, rarely by their given names. It was the one who shared my name who was molested by her "slow," fifteen-year-old brother, the other rescued just in time. How many times has the mother cursed herself for turning away from their girls for the moment it took for their brother to lead them to the laundry room? How many times had her husband cursed her for sharing the story?

Avowal

I went to bat for her 5 years ago,
when she was pregnant with her last baby,
carefully giving her instructions,
advice on how to fight
to get back her three boys from CPS.

She was stronger, then,
a tigress ready to creep
through lava stones to get her babies back.

But now, 5 years later, she's drowning again.
No fiery stones to walk across.
She's just a wet tabby
holding her head under water.

She asked me if I was disappointed in her.
No, I'm not.
She did the best she could—
making decisions that were best for her sons.

Trying to rekindle her roar.

Good Things

Good things come in small packages

I need you to keep it together. Even those who planned for the apocalypse never expected this.

They came in droves, eating everything. First, they ate all of the sprouts; nothing green and growing was safe. Then, they dug up the root veggies. We weren't too sad to see the potatoes go; the last couple of years they'd been pretty to look at, but tasteless. The carrots were to be expected. But the ginger? That was just brutal. How were we going to season all of those dull canned goods without ginger?

We thought the livestock was safe, until the little varmints evolved into carnivores—eating the chickens. The cattle and sheep tried to stomp them down, but the little furry critters just swarmed them.

We were holed up in a makeshift bunker—a cellar, really—pit bulls at our feet, crying like babies.

When they came for us the pit bulls tried to bolt; which would have been funny except that it really wasn't. If the pit bulls were terrified who'd protect us?

We tried to keep our babies safe and off the floor by hanging them in hammocks suspended from the ceiling. So far as we could tell, the little beasts hadn't jumped that far up. Some families weren't taking any chances—putting their precious offspring in elaborate cages to keep out the furry creatures. Toddlers peaking at their parents through the bars.

Though civilization was failing, we still had electricity and cable television. Thank God the flat screen didn't take up too much space with all of us huddled together around the tube. I think someone at the Cartoon Network had a strange sense of humor. They started playing re-runs of Bugs Bunny, Yojimbo and Bunnicula as a joke. We stopped laughing after one of Bugs' friends tried to bite off the baby's finger when he reached out to pet it. How it got past the pit bulls without a sound, we later discovered. Both pits were scooby snacks huddled in the corner of the yard, nothing left of them but bones.

After that, enough was enough. My family decided it was time to take a real offensive. I was not going to live in fear of a zombie bunnies for the rest of my life. Quite by accident we discovered a neighbor with a crazy Pug Chihuahua mixed dog; the kind that had a giant ego, as most small dogs do. That crazy Puggiwah chomped down on any cotton-tail that dared show its twitchy little nose near my neighbor's borders. That Puggiwah had several siblings just as crazy. When word got out that we could win this "battle of the bunnies," we were ready to sell our most prized possessions for one of those little devil dogs. My neighbor made hand-over-fist in currency (strangely money still existed) and bartered items; living like a Palm Springs sheik, breeding Puggiwahs like well... bunnies.

"Bon Marche"

Seattle, Washington

I stare at our hands and remember crossing rainy slippery streets in Seattle on the way to the Bon Marche; where I would take modeling classes every Thursday, after school. The only black child in class, I would learn how to brush straight hair I did not possess and flip imaginary strands outside the collar at the latest fashionable blouses for children.

We would hold hands across the slippery streets of West Seattle; where I would take ballet classes every Wednesday, after school. The madame telling me constantly to tuck in my hips. Until finally, I explained to her that round black hips can't tuck in any further. The only student with no natural coordination.

We would hold hands across the slippery streets of the University of Washington, in downtown Seattle; where I took a children's science class, every Tuesday, after school. After reading "How to Eat Fried Worms," my instructor left the class alone with a tank of mealworms and a burning bare lightbulb inside of a lamp. The first worm I placed on the bulb exploded.

My mother and I would hold hands on the slippery streets of West Seattle; where I would take tap dancing classes every Monday, after school. The only black child in the class.

Key to the Kingdom

I am not the key
nor the lock
nor the door
nor the building

I try to be the foundation
sometimes the street lamp
sometimes the block

I am not the driveway
nor the side walk
though sometimes I am the road
I try to be the freeway

I am sometimes the neighborhood
often, I am the city
today I am the county
tomorrow I will be the state

But for now, I am this chair
at this table
in this room
this pen to this paper
in this 20-year-old recycled military ledger
these new words on its faded pages

I'd be in right relation with

A Cadillac Margarita cocktail at Misty's Lounge near the airport and my usual seat somewhere in the middle towards the back, close to the patio where I can slip out and join the praying smokers. I'd even be okay stumbling into an old lover who just happened to be there on a Thursday night, knowing I'd never darken their doors on weekends. Perhaps we can not discuss my travels over symbolic lovemaking.

But then I'd just as soon drive to Balboa Beach. Saunter the boardwalk to Newport alone by moonlight, watching vacationers try to enjoy the coastal view between TV shows, bonfires and beer.

Or perhaps I'll stay home. Try to resurrect my lost voice on Facebook. These days I only care about posting pictures of my latest culinary creations.

I really have nothing to say about the state of the world. The shootings just leave me shell shocked and fearful of unfamiliar white men. I find myself searching gatherings for brown faces so I don't feel so alone.

I don't know how I feel about the Executive Director from Goodwill. His counterpart never showed me much goodwill when I slaved under her whimsical hoof. But Larry never knew that I went directly into cancer treatment after I left their employ. I just suddenly dropped off the earth. The lingering hug Larry gave me at a nonprofit strategy training strangely felt natural, though we'd never hugged or touched in the past. His embrace felt like home and dying embers in the fireplace. Bitter ashes of memories floating through my "now" of working while dying all over again and trying to hold together three facilities with over 180 staff.

Mornings I'd rather forget my vivid dreams about discarded childhood friends come to haunt me—lurking around department store corners waiting to hear my voice so they can pop out and invade my life once again.

I'm quite sure I won't be bothered with my 30-year high school reunion for any of the four high schools I went to in the three states. I am the only person in the world with my name. My former schoolmates are welcome to "Google" me.

I can still feel the wistfulness in my ex-husband's words typed across the ethernet on Facebook Messenger. Tell me why did I post that collaborative haiku again? I could feel his loneliness like the wedding ring I lost during my recent move.

I want to feel hopeful hearing from my former best friend who left me a quick message in response to my posted haiku. Too many years of silence between us to fill in the gap left by my senseless betrayal. Still after all these years he won't forgive me. Still we remain Facebook friends.

I'm not sure how I feel about this pit and pendulum mood I've been having. Am I hovering on the precipice of menopause so soon? I've nearly split myself in two to keep from saying something sharp on a whim.

I'm certain I really am not fit company for most people these days. On second thought, I'm certain of really nothing these days. Ideas blow through my mind like leaves. No one around to rake them up. I just want I will light the whole batch on fire and say a prayer over the cinders.

I want to plant an orchard on the crisp land instead of a forest. Grow basil and pear trees.

I wasn't feeling
the warmth of your loving touch
said Autumn to sun

Another Elegy

101-year-old James Megellas, the most decorated officer of the famed 82nd. Airborne Division that saw action in the bloodiest battles of World War II always ends
his speeches with "We've got to find a way to stop wars."
Dallas Morning News. Memorial Day, May 28, 2018.

I was a young impressionable student,
newly arrive in the U.S.,
turmoil in every corner of the campus
every drop of rain a revolt against
the brutal storm of indifferent lottery numbers
youthful fragile dreams shattered
by a capricious system.
Students sat on classroom doorsteps,
  quietly
holding friendship hands
  not love
for love is for always.
It was the time of marches
and folk songs
  and a longing for peace.

I studied Tennessee Williams and Arthur Miller
the art of dramatic production, and criticism
hours of creativity and learning crammed into a brimming day
only to come home to the darkness
of an ever present gloom.
On a basic television
that displayed events in black and white
the evening news became a ritual
and at the end there would be a roll call
of American servicemen, some in their teens,

mere children, who had lost their lives
in the remote roiling jungles of Vietnam
and of the enemy dead,
all of whom would never gaze
at the nightly star-streaked sky
or take a single breath again,
and I would cry.

I turned on my large digital television
on November 24, 2016
fifty years later
to learn of the first American serviceman,
a decorated, young father,
killed in combat on the faraway dusty fields
of ancient Syria,
on a festive Thanksgiving day.
He too must have sat wistfully
  beside his beloved
dreaming of a time of peace
surrounded by the voices
of his grown children.

And the screen seems blurry,
wet and stained
filled relentlessly
with what has gone before.

It is May 28, 2018, yet another Memorial Day.
I yearn with the veteran James Megellas
for "a generation when
all young men and young women
of all religions and faiths
can get together...
  to solve our problems
and live together
  peacefully."

There are no flowers in our hair.

Every tree is a poem

A young aspen
mischievously bends
her fair slender trunk
covered with a hundred
shimmering tiny green leaves
shaking like tambourines,
to kiss the passersby.

In great great grandfather
sequoia's canopy
thrive a citadel of living things.
Tree squirrels gracefully leap
from branch to branch,
red tree voles
nibble delicately
on fresh green needles,
legions of ants march
up and down familiar pathways.
Imagine the songs of woodpeckers,
jays, warblers and owls,
wing to fluttering wing.

The elegant plumeria
stands in silhouette
against a jagged rising moon,
gazing affectionately at those
waxen pearly blossoms
that reflect the light,
while obsidian crows
dream among
her silver burnished leaves.

Tall poplars planted all in a row
sway with the wind
dancing in synchrony,
as they whisper their secrets
to the sky.

Juvenile sycamores
stretch out their arms
their five point leaves
embrace each other in camaraderie,
as their barks flake off
to prepare for their
maturity.
They do not know
that they will grow to be a hundred feet,
to casually obscure the pale blue
ethereal sky.

The wind whistles through
the red leaves
of the graceful Japanese maple
so very far from home,
turning over
its pale perishable undersides,
rose madder sprinkled with lacy pink
to resemble a breathtaking
flowering bush.

I cannot cage a dancing rainbow.
Trees, and all their leaves-
curled and rounded
oblong, lacy,
with finger-like ends
and star shaped form,
are sap green with vigor,
gold as they begin to flame
frailbrown towards journey's end,
I know them well.

The autumn of my life
brings me a heaven
heaped with the souls
of all the cherished trees
that have ever lived
and those waiting to be unfurled,
singing their silent songs.

Previously published in *The Weekly Avocet*.

Hope

the eternal mystery,
the perfume of lavender
that lingers
after the flower has faded,
an embryo
that transforms into
womanhood holding
    the seed in her palms,
the yearning for a better something,
many things,
    anything.

It is about the edge of the world
where the precipice
               drops
only
    to be able to float beyond the horizon
when the band stops playing
    and the bright lights extinguish,
the freedom of forgetting
even one's own name.

Hope is an uncluttered universe
where construct merges into abstract,
the desire to shed
the archaeology of the past
while preserving the best of what we were,
with all creation owning
    the right to flourish,
for every birth is mine
    every death is mine.

Hope is the last second of waking
when one knows there may be
    no awakening.
It is a longing for a world
beyond this world
inhabited by the welcoming spirits
of the beloved
    in another eternity.

Commemorating the death of 49 precious individuals at an Orlando nightclub on June 21st. 2016.

This poem was written in response to a prompt provided by Jo Scott – Coe in the 2017 Inlandia Riverside Creative Writing Workshop.

```
            ee
     re    aaaaa
  "K          si
              si
                  si  si"
```

floats your quivering scream,
clearly audible over Mumbai's chaotic city
as you glide in the thermals
in search of food.

Mighty kite wings shuddering
then quietening,
fork tail stilled
distinct dark honeybrown feathers
with rufous markings,
alighting on my windowsill
high up on the eight floor atop a steep hill.

You slowly turn your head to face me,
composed, majestic, in command.

The morning sunlight catches
a sprinkle of powdery blue feathers
above alert eyes
flecks of yellow around your keen nostrils.

I am drawn towards you
mesmerized by dark golden magnetic eyes,
goose bumps springing across my being,
    forgetting
to breathe
my heart strangely stilled
    in peace.

"I know you"
  you cried
an instant recognition of spirits
as I drowned in those orbs
glimpsing a vista of majestic mountain ranges
the millennia of time
over which you have soared
to blend with my heart
  in this mysterious moment.

The Indian kite, "milvus migrans" is a medium-sized bird of prey.

Previously published in *The Weekly Avocet*.

Little gifts of his heart

Earliest of mornings
with eyes barely open
I notice a fine light purple plastic bag
hung on the inside of the bedroom door handle
welcoming my day.
He did not disturb me.

I unscrew the lid
of a fresh milk carton
remove the plastic seal with its attached circlet.
He examines it.
Grandma Deenaz
will you wear it on your finger?
It is uncomfortable...
but I wear it all day
meeting his critical approval,
delighting in his simplest of pleasures.

I am given a kiss
and one of his three remaining small
Easter Hershey bars.
This little one shares his treasures with me.

I struggle with the clasp
of my silver chain.
He offers, unsolicited.
His deft gentle fingers
swiftly complete the task
and he is back beside me
his favorite book
spread open once more upon his lap.

Mortal Meditations

The fog lies thick above the ocean today,
the line between
land and water and sky
obscured by a fine layer of mist
stitched together like a quilt.

The steadfast years of my life too
stretch forward like an undulating sheet
binding the intricate weaves of East and West,
the pain and the passion of living,
its headlong dance not hesitating
at the edge of that delicate mortal tapestry.

Civilizations and nations ebb and flow
as do our lives…

My spirit will continue to evolve after,
to grow in depth of color and breadth
of threads
in richness of being,
a vast continent ahead
to be explored
in another world.

Previously published by Magdalena Rustomji in *Poem of the month–March of 2018*. magdalena_rustomji@hotmail.com

mother

you came to me in my dreams last night,
not as I last remembered,
but a blend of old sepia photographs
from treasured albums

so young, so utterly gentle,
unlined oval face of cream and tinted white
a supple turn of waist a twisted bun of heavy dark hair,
you leaned towards me with intent gaze
drawing deep within my soul,
questioning with bemusement who this woman
from the distant future was

and then I recognized you
startled, with wonder,
for you are a part of my being
my mother of a hundred kisses ago

but you were gone
as suddenly
as you had appeared

The pieces of my heart

A quarter was gifted
a long time ago
to my only beloved.
It travels eagerly
through storm and calm
kisses and coddling
welded deep
within the other
in eternal oneness.

A son graced my being
and took another segment.
How could I have known
the magic of soft skin
sleepless nights
the worry of adolescent trials
would turn into
cherished companionship?
A beloved rock to cling to
in stormy climes.

Then a second babe filled that cradle
and my heart lightened again.
Gentle strength, creativity,
an intuitive understanding
and from early on,
the tightest of loving morning hugs
that washed away the day's anxieties.

The quarter left, rattled in loneliness
for a long while.
The hurry of living

and the worry of the world
covered it with a fine mist
and belied its loneliness.

On a sunny day the mist evaporated
with a dawning infant's cry.
The last bit of heart
flew eagerly, borne on love's currents
and lodged itself
in a grandson's sweet being
and there resides.

Those empty spaces
now are filled.

Semi-Gloss

The man behind the counter in the paint-spattered apron thought he could finally give her what she needed, but then she was off again, groping for just the right word, a far-away stare, a half-smile of urgency on her lips.

"It's like the sky," she said, "just before a rainstorm—you know, when the air is heavy. In the afternoon, when the light is low, and yellow ginkgo trees light up against the sky—it's that sky color. It's the opposite of gingko—it's…."

He focused on her mouth, on how, when she pursed for emphasis, little crevices formed on her upper lip. He wished she would shut up.

"Gray?" he said, whipping out a sheaf of paint chips in various dilutions of India ink.

"No, not really. It's more electrically charged than that. Kind of bruised and melancholy. Like the smell of juniper berries… but not blue, undertones of blue, maybe, and not sweet either. It's more… rueful…."

"Rueful. Rhubarb colored? Lady, that's not even close to…."

"No, *rueful*, like with a just a hint of regret. Think of a three-day old bruise, before it gets that yellow tinge."

A melancholy bruise? He rubbed his hands up and down on his apron and thought about bruises. His own. Other people's. A fresh bruise, a three-day bruise. A bruise that doesn't show. Police photos. A mug shot. The beginning of a bruise on a downy inner thigh. He winced at that image, but once he had it, he couldn't let it go. He could get through a long late shift with that image. *But, the opposite of gingko? What the hell?*

It was times like this that he wished he'd stayed in school. He'd at least be a manager of something instead of mixing paint for the crown-molding-loving, hybrid-driving, gingko-hugging, ironic bruise-savvy crowd.

She leaned forward on the counter scrunching up her crêpey, sunburned chest and pointed at the wall behind him. "This sign here says you'll match any color!"

"Well, yeah, …but you have to actually *give* me a color to match. I'm not a mind reader."

Her stink eye said she didn't doubt that.

She shoved her shopping cart out of the way and started to head for the door. Ten minutes ago, he would have been relieved, but now he couldn't let her get away.

"Look, ma'am, right over there you got your blues," he said, nodding toward the racks of paint chips lining the wall, "and your purples." *Purple and blue—Jeeeezus!* He was being a little too on the money, unsubtle, Ace Hardware instead of Restoration. "Let me help you," he said, coming out from behind the counter and following her to the dark end of the spectrum. He watched her standing under the display lights, her red balsamic hair glistening. Yes, damn it. Red balsamic! He, too, could do specific if he had to. He imagined what her pale skin would look like with a bruise or two. If she paid with a check, he'd have her address. If not, he'd offer his services as a house painter… strictly off the books, of course…deeply discounted.

He stood next to her as she silently scanned the squares of blues and purples fanned out before her, barely breathing, until suddenly she screamed, "That's it! That's the one." She grabbed the swatch and handed it to him, triumphant.

"Aaaah, yes, melancholy, I see it now." Of course, he didn't, but it sounded convincing. She smiled at him and nodded, eyes shining. *This is going to be so easy*, he thought.

Still, he felt a bit off this time, unbalanced. It was odd to feel the regret before instead of after.

Carlos E. Cortés

Fort Leonard Wood

Physical threats made Carlos shudder. This one certainly did.

Ignore the fact that, three years earlier in the spring of 1954, he had won the University of California, Berkeley, middleweight boxing championship. When it came to street fighting, Carlos always remembered his boxer father's warning: "No matter how tough you think you are, sooner or later you'll run into someone tougher."

In May, 1957, Carlos had completed his master's degree at the Columbia Graduate School of Journalism. But September brought his induction into the U.S. Army, military service then being obligatory for young American men. Carlos soon found himself in basic training at Fort Leonard Wood, in the heart of the Missouri Ozarks.

As one of a small group of college graduates in his assigned training company, Carlos soon noticed the target on his back, as other recruits began referring to him and the other college boys as pussies. Moreover, when his platoon sergeant chose Carlos to be his trainee platoon sergeant, it meant that Carlos would be in charge of the platoon every night and weekend after the sergeant had returned home to his family. The only college graduate in his two-story barracks, he alone would have to maintain order among four dozen recruits, many of whom despised his educational status.

Carlos took note of the platoon's deep ethno-racial divisions. There were four cohorts: tough African Americans from places like East St. Louis; tough Puerto Ricans from the island and from New York City; tough working-class whites from places like Detroit and Indianapolis; and possibly tough but more laid-back whites from around the rural mid-west. Out of desperation, he developed a plan of ethnic targeting.

First came the Puerto Ricans, most of whom spoke little English. Thanks to his Mexican father, Carlos could get by in Spanish, so he made a deal with the PRs, as the others derogatorily referred to them. If the PRs would cooperate with him, he would translate for and represent them. Treaty approved.

Next came the African Americans. Carlos identified their de facto leader, a strong, athletic, and charismatic young man named TJ. TJ's obvious native intelligence collided with the fact that he had managed to make it through high school without learning how to read. Now, like all recruits, TJ had to memorize a series of orders and regulations, which he would have to repeat precisely if asked by any officer or sergeant.

So Carlos made a pact with the African Americans. He would personally tutor TJ and drill him until he could repeat the orders verbatim. In return, they would agree to cause no trouble and have his back, if asked. Eager to remain in the Army, TJ convinced the rest of his Black cohort. Two down.

The white recruits presented the most difficult challenge. The rural, small-town whites cooperated from the beginning, but not the city boys, who seemed impervious to reasonable negotiations. They reeked with what today we would call attitude and weren't about to take orders from a college pussy. Carlos' efforts to keep them in line merely led to the threat: this weekend, when the officers and real sergeants were gone, they planned to beat the hell out of him. Since neither courage nor street fighting skill qualified as among Carlos' strongest traits, he took a desperate gamble. He confronted Randy, a broad-shouldered, heavily-muscled dude who appeared to be the city white ring-leader, and challenged him to a one-on-one fight . . . in the ring with boxing gloves at the fort gymnasium.

Obviously not revealing his college boxing background, Carlos proposed a devil's bargain. If Randy beat him badly in a three-round fight, Carlos would resign as trainee platoon sergeant and recommend Randy or whomever else his group wanted. But if Carlos could hold his own for three rounds, Randy and the others would agree not to cause any more trouble. Figuring that this lighter, scrawnier, college-educated pussy was fair game, Randy quickly agreed.

Come Sunday, a good part of the platoon crowded into the dank fort gymnasium—a spare, hollowed-out barracks—to see the showdown. Having a vested interest in Carlos' retaining his position, the African Americans and Puerto Ricans came to cheer him on. Randy's white entourage gathered to enjoy the slaughter.

As they climbed into the ring, Randy looked bigger, stronger, and much more imposing than the fellow Carlos had challenged outside of the platoon barracks. Standing alone, his long skinny arms hanging down limply, Carlos realized he faced a possible beating, followed by a dreadfully uncomfortable conversation with his company commander about why he was resigning his trainee platoon sergeant position. So Carlos drew on brains, not brawn, which he didn't really possess.

Carlos fought defensively, punching and moving, feinting and blocking, while relentlessly working his left jab and ignoring the screams of Randy's entourage that he should stand up and fight like a man. Randy was strong as hell, but while he landed occasionally with Carlos feeling every punch, he lacked the ring finesse to corner and finish off his constantly moving opponent.

When the bell rang ending the third round, Carlos didn't exactly celebrate in triumph, but with feelings of relief, he congratulated Randy on a good fight. Some of Randy's friends argued that Carlos hadn't lived up to his agreement, that he should have gone toe-to-toe with Randy and slugged it out. Fortunately, Randy turned out to be a man of his word, telling his followers that Carlos had shown he was O.K.

From that point on, Carlos carefully monitored and tended the ethnic minefields. The barracks didn't become a grand multicultural love-in, but the four dozen boys from various backgrounds managed to function relatively well as a unit. For the next seven weeks the unofficial ethnic treaties held up, despite a few glitches and close calls. TJ even managed to make it through basic training, although he ultimately became exposed when he had to fill out papers for his next assignment and was politely excused from the Army.

As Carlos headed off for Fort Gordon, Georgia, to be trained as a Signal Corps cryptographer, he bade farewell to his unwanted experience as an acting non-commissioned officer. His showdown with Randy turned out to be the closest he would ever come to wartime duty.

CARLOS E. CORTÉS

Free Throw

As I stepped to the line, the basket seemed higher and farther away than the last time I had shot a free throw. That's not surprising, as it had been nearly forty years since I last tried. I well remember that occasion.

It happened in 1974 during a game of the University of California, Riverside, faculty-graduate student intramural basketball league. Our team, composed of History and Foreign Language professors, was playing Political Science and Philosophy. I had just hit two free throws. Then Poli Sci scored and a Medieval Spanish professor began dribbling up the court. He passed me the ball and I threw it on to a Hitler specialist.

Then everyone stopped. As they stared at me, I spotted my right little pinkie. The ball had hit the tip of my finger, ripping the top two sections out of my knuckle socket and depositing them horizontally on the bottom stub, creating a lop-sided T. Only then did I notice the pain.

Later that night, after he popped my swollen finger back into place, the doctor suggested that I not play basketball for a few weeks. In fact, I never played again. At thirty-nine, I took this as a sign that I had better start acting my age, thankful that I had never suffered a major athletic injury. So by the time of my nephew Adam's October, 2011, Bar Mitzvah in Long Grove, Illinois, about thirty-five miles north of Chicago, I had been a basketball retiree for nearly four decades.

A sports fanatic, Adam decided to hold his Saturday night Bar Mitzvah party at the Libertyville Sports Complex, a sprawling indoor village recreation center. With numerous basketball courts, a soccer field, and a climbing wall among the attractions, Adam and his friends had a blast, while the parents watched and chowed down on pizza and salad served by the complex.

Then one of the dads came up with a bright idea: let's have a basketball game for the adult men on one of the empty courts. A dozen over-aged, over-weight, out-of-shape, testosterone-challenged Michael Jordan wannabees quickly joined up. As they headed for the court, my younger brother, Gary, looked at me.

"Carlos, aren't you going to play?"

I took a couple of steps toward him, then stopped and looked over at my wife, Laurel. Flashing a gentle but mischievous smile, she subtly, almost imperceptibly, shook her head.

Looking back at Gary, I shouted, "No, thanks. Have fun."

The game began, with flabby bodies pushing, shoving, and clomping, seldom leaving the ground. Occasionally the ball would go into the basket, followed by extended intervals of collective bent-over panting and hard swallowing. As I watched, I noticed that there was still one empty basket, so I decided to go out and shoot by myself.

I walked to the free throw line as I had done hundreds of times before, maybe thousands, and took aim. The ball left my hand with a gentle arc and perfect line, only to fall several feet short of the basket. Retrieving the ball, I tried again and again, but my long-lost muscle memory continued to betray me.

Finally, I dribbled to the basket and shot a lay-up. On my third try, the ball went in. Then I spotted Laurel watching me, her subtle smile now a broad and gorgeous grin. She closed her fist and softly pumped her right arm.

Lessons of a Musical Past

Once every three years as we hold our Vermilyea family reunion, I deliver a family history speech at the main dinner event. After one of my offerings, my sister Gloria asked me how I could "put myself out there like that." I answered by reminding her of our musical past.

First, let me say that many memories of my mother involved music. She adored opera; she adored Franco Corelli. She often played our piano, although it barely fit into a two-house compound accommodating a family of ten.

Early on Saturdays and Sundays, Mom turned on the radio to the classical music station. When her favorite programs ended, she put on one of the many opera records that later climbed one wall of the living room. With no other options for storing them, my dad built four levels of shelving with niches for her collection of 78s. Who can forget all of those Italian faces staring at us day and night?

Once or twice a weekend my dad would slip in his favorite record: a scratchy-voiced Enrico Caruso singing "Vesti la giubba" or "La donna é mobile." His wife could stand only so much of that static.

Mom enrolled us in any musical thing that came down the pike. We were always in a chorus (Glo, soprano, I, alto). We played violin in grammar school, taught by one of the many European musicians who took refuge in California during the war—some of the world's finest conductors taught in our coastal schools during wartime.

Of course, we took piano lessons on Saturdays, taught by tall Mrs. Kelly, on the Kelly ranch. When it was one of my sisters' turns (I always liked to be first to get it over with), I went out to the barn to see the owl that sat on a high beam and gave out a hoot once in a while.

And then there came to Carlsbad our music man. Mr. Lloyd Bader opened a music store two blocks from our home (in the Village). My mother sent us right down there, and we came home with our instruments. He needed a trumpet player, so that's what Gloria became. He handed me an alto saxophone, a reed, and a case. The die was cast.

We became prime targets because we could already read music. Mr. Bader was seriously engaged, but not flamboyant like Professor Harold Hill of *The Music Man*. His wife reminded me of First Lady Pat Nixon; omnipresent, kind, smiling, noncommittal, always busy in the background. They had no children, except for the ragtag band kids.

The store furnished our instruments, but we did take lessons. The art of the embouchure, the science of the diaphragm, the maintenance of the instrument and the reed were all new to me. But I was of the age (10 years old) when so many things in life are new, so I took to it as a natural progression of my musical education. (The lessons stood me in good stead when I got to high school, as I traveled from alto sax to the clarinet and on to my beloved bass clarinet.)

Very soon Bader's Band began its sorties into the outer world. We showed up as a fledgling group marching in parades throughout San Diego County. It was fun—the weather was always perfect, it was exercise, and we quickly developed a camaraderie. And then it happened.

Mr. Bader decided that it would be good for us to play for local community gatherings—as individuals! At the age of ten I had never performed individually, except in two or three in-house piano recitals.

After six months on the alto saxophone, I felt ill prepared for what was to come.

I don't know how much you know about the saxophone, but there are four main sizes: First, the straight soprano sax (think Kenny G.), then the curved instruments: the alto sax (my instrument), the tenor sax (favored by most great saxophonists: Charley Parker, John Coltrane, Paul Desmond), and the baritone sax (Gerry Mulligan).

No serious person plays the alto sax! No matter how much control I exerted on it, it voluntarily squeaked every once in a while, just to show me who was boss.

And there I was, a ten-year-old, making public appearances in the summer. I know that my mother volunteered my services, because most of the band members, including my older sister, were "unavailable."

These were mid-week luncheons for The Loyal Order of the Moose, the Elks Club, the Lions Club, The Junior Chamber of Commerce (I guessed the Seniors knew better). Most members had served in one World War or the other—now they were Oceanside or Carlsbad doctors, lawyers, civic leaders; all engaged in community service and charities. They greeted us with unalloyed enthusiasm and appreciation. Sweetie pies.

In my very first appearance I followed Mr. Bader into the Moose Lodge (who had ever even heard of such a place?). Wearing my Mom-made plaid taffeta "dressy dress," and with my pigtails pinned up to the top of my head in the Scandinavian style, I awaited my turn. When it came, I dutifully stood up in front of three dozen men in coats and ties and played on that alto saxophone, to a sea of smiling faces, an excruciating version of "Harbor Lights." (Squeak squeak).

I have always said (as I reminded Glo at the reunion) that it was the kind of experience that has inured me to any further instance of humiliation in my life.

Losted!!

I spent my great childhood at our family home three blocks from the beach in Carlsbad, CA. During WWII, we had to remain close to home and were trained to run for cover if that ear-piercing siren—a half-block away—ever sounded. That alarm meant that the Japanese were on their way to bomb the coastal corridor between San Diego harbor to the south and Camp Pendleton, 8 miles to the north of us.

After the war, there was sweet relief from that stress, and we children were able to roam freely throughout the day. We hiked, biked, skated, body surfed, met in our clubhouse (a former chicken coop), or even walked along the beach to the Oceanside pier, in low tide.

As the fourth of eight children, I knew all of my siblings better than most of them knew each other. In my family there were five daughters, born in Omaha, Nebraska, and three boys, born in Oceanside, California (It's amazing what a little sunshine will do.)

My mother took care of the vast household, while my dad worked. We lived in two houses, with a patio in between them. My folks paid $6,000 for the two-lot property in 1944; my brothers and I were offered $3.2 million for it last year, because it is in the center of Carlsbad Village, and there are 10 developers who need to demolish the houses for their respective projects. We tell them, "IT'S OUR HOME!"

My parents lived in the front house with my little brothers, while we sisters slept in the back house we called the Girls' Dormitory. We were actually all very comfortable.

Cooking for ten people three times a day, washing and ironing every week day, my mother trained her girls, each in turn, to take over these chores. Mom despised cooking for the rest of her life!

My parents were crazy about baseball. Naturally, we formed our own baseball team, and played weekend "batter up" with my dad on the grammar school playground. Our family sometimes hauled food to the beach for family picnics or walked a block and a half to the Carlsbad Theatre, where all of the latest family-oriented movies played: 19 cents for two movies, two cartoons, a newsreel, two previews, and a cowboy short feature—6 cents for the treat.

My dad bought this old 1928 Lincoln Continental, which was the only car in the world that fit us all in comfortably, with its pull-down seats on the back of the front seats. In that car we took Sunday drives out to the country or went to the Triple-A San Diego Padres games. That was the most fun!

We never went out to dinner, except when someone graduated from high school. We were never all invited to anyone's house. But there was always someone to play with and always someone to take your part when trouble arose. Fabulous!

More often than not if we were all going somewhere, we piled into my dad's red company truck, which bore the name, Pacific Pipeline Construction Company. Dad and Mom and the boys sat in the cab, while we five girls crowded into the back of the truck. That was legal then, in the post-war era of low population and scant traffic—when every family was lucky to have one car.

Once every year we went to the Del Mar Fair, fifteen miles from our home down El Camino Real, and it was a beloved treat. We were giddy with anticipation each year and saved our babysitting money for the cotton candy, soda pop and special rides.

In 1948, when I was nine years old, we were enjoying the Fair when my mom said to us, "Where's Scottie?" He wasn't with any of us, so we took off in all directions to find him, checking back from time to time to see if he had turned up. He hadn't.

This three-year-old middle boy, Scottie, was so angelic looking, with the sweetest face in the family: yellow-white hair, blue eyes, a ready smile, he became the only whiny kid my mother had, mainly because we all adored him and spoiled him rotten with hugs and kisses!

My German-Swedish mother was racking her formidable brain to logic the problem out, and soon—in desperation—herded us back to the parking lot. As we approached the truck we saw our Scottie, with his hand on the bumper and his feet squared off, madder than a hornet! Our sweet angel screamed:

"MAMA!! You got losted from ME!!"

Scott has maintained his good looks—if not his hair—into his 70's. At 6'5" he is the tallest of my tall brothers and is now a millionaire who owns a large ranch overlooking the Shasta Valley and out to the Shasta Mountains. He sells timber and natural gas, and still thinks he's the center of the universe.

We should have seen it coming, the signs were there, as we invariably say when we relate this 70-year-old favorite family story to his—and to our own—grandchildren.

Hairy Ode

Oh, hardy hair, honor your courage
Enduring curling irons, torturous flat irons
Holding firm through chemical assaults
Attacked by scissors, razors, clippers
Some of you surrendered
Deserted strands fill brushes
Drains clogged with defeated locks
Gone AWOL from scalps
Only to sprout new places
Immigrant gray follicles
Migrating to upper lips and chins
Hiding in plain sight, uninvited
Warrior stance defying tweezers
Cilia trimmed from nostrils
Shaved and waxed from legs and pits
Electrified, still you persist

Susan and I

crafted our banners
with march messages
VOTES FOR WOMEN
painted on gauzy fabric
sharpied letters on posterboard
I VOTED FOR HER
we met by chance
waiting on court house steps
her purple, white, and gold sash
draped over a worn tweed coat
sensible shoes, broken-down heels
as a crowd formed around us
my apple necklace caught her eye
she said she was a teacher
hey, #metoo
talked about education now and then
how much progress we've made
why we still protest the same inequalities
we chatted more as we walked
surrounded by children in strollers
she wished her friend Elizabeth could see
men carrying signs in support
police directing traffic
she beamed at the sight of a
calm defiant demonstration
not tolerated 100 years ago
back to the steps where we started
I had more questions
but it seemed,
time's up,
so I gave her my Susan B. lucky coin
and a hug of thanks

New Box of 64

We picked at the rainbow of wax
oozing down the white vinyl
on our back seat
for the last 150 miles
of the drive to the Smoky Mountains.
But before that
we woke up when dad slammed
on the brakes, his angry eyes
glaring at "it" in the rear view.
But before that
we curled up for naps
windows rolled down
sweat, sticking to the seat
crayons cooking in the back window.
But before that
we stayed in the lines
of new coloring books
with our pointed crayons
from our brand new box of 64
with built-in sharpener.
But before that
we packed up our very new
1956 two-tone blue Chevy Bel Air
for the annual family vacation.

Black Widow

Come closer, look at my hourglass tattoo
Come closer, I made this web just for you.
Step on it, feel its sticky, messy threads
Get in it, ignore the tiny insect heads.
Come closer, touch my sac of eggs
Just wait there, watch my spindly legs.
Glad you're here, didn't miss our date.
You look good, yummy little mate.
Just relax, enjoy a puncture from my fangs
Delicious, that should quench my hunger pangs.
Thanks so much, I have many mouths to feed
Loved you once, that was really all I need.

NAN FRIEDLEY

Ditto Machine's Demise
(teacher's lament)

I killed it
before the morning bell
office lights still dim
silent workroom.
I have "solvent" on my hands.
I pushed its limits
duplicating fluid-filled drum
100 sheets in the paper tray
math quiz fastened in place
of AB Dick Model 217.
The first few copies
glistened in purple script
crisp, clear problems
waiting to be answered
then bleeding magenta pages
vomited a paper storm
ditto fumes filled the air
incontinent pool spilled
over the work table
then silence.
It was gone.
By now others had arrived
to witness its death
inhaled moist pages
sucking in its last ditto breaths
spirit duplicator in the sky.
No tears were shed.
Some took wet purple souvenirs to sniff later
others stood by the principal's door
inquiring about a Xerox machine

how soon could we get one.
Not much of a funeral.
Custodian carried it to the storage closet
shoved onto a shelf
with other broken office equipment
paper cutter with bent arm
broken-handled die cut
probably the original Mr. Coffee
missing carafe.

DMV

Early renewal by mail.

Check box for donor. $33. check.

Checked mailbox daily.

License never arrived.

So it began.

23 drivers ahead of me formed a line that stretched half the length of the building, then veered right to the entrance. Morning sun at 8:30, already 90 degrees, sweat pooled on backs hunched over cell phone screens. Checked my watch for maybe the 38th time to see how long I'd been there...40 minutes so far. I can almost touch the door.

Two lines form; appointment or "not." 30-minute wait in the "not" line.

Fill out this form and get back in the "not" line...only 20 minutes this time.

Ticket G052 have a seat to join rows of other "waiters" clicking cell phone buttons, dozing awkwardly in stiff black, plastic chairs, zombie driver eyes locked on nearby monitors...now serving B017.

Driving laws and DUI fines spool on a flat screen cycled through five times.

Partway through the sixth, G052 is now being served, report to Window #7.

Paper, temporary license issued; real one should arrive in 10 days.

Come back if it doesn't.

Thanks, I'll bring *War and Peace*.

JANE O'SHIELDS-HAYNER

Thunderdrum:

Excerpt from *The Road to Los Gatos Canyon*

The word "cancer" became a specter. It jumped at me from magazine covers. It floated in my shadow, dodging my gaze, pushing cold fingers into my viscera and squeezing.

I felt abandoned, but by whom? My family and friends supported me in ways that were humbling. Their prayers and sweet words soothed me, like warm bread. I couldn't blame God. The God I knew whirled inside atoms and bent with the sway of trees, yet I had lost dear friends to cancer, friends who died young and were well prayed for. What could I rely on with a God whose intentions are so hard to define?

Illusions of my youth scattered, taking with them my delusions of immortality. They had proven an ill-founded hedge against the passing of days. I felt like processed meat, on a conveyer, riding through biopsies, this scan or that, one medication or another. Was too late? Had I passed my expiration date? I never expected to be colonized by invaders in the middle of my miraculous, ordinary, unfinished life.

I put my friend Paula's CD in my car changer and hit the road. The road is my long-time friend. Tears filled my eyes and mascara-stained rivulets ran down my cheeks. I sang, harmonizing with Paula's smooth, powerful voice, while bass notes, plucked by her fingers, hummed in my bones. I saw her rising from her seat on the front row, singing, as she walked to the stage, with resonance and beauty filling the air.

"Courage my soul, and let me journey on.
The night is dark and I am far from home."

My mind's eye blinked and I saw a Native American drum head, one I had seen in a teaching text book, years ago. The essence of it had stayed with me. A black bird with wings extended flew over the earth. Before it, the ground was parched. Behind it followed a rainstorm.

A drumhead! I would paint on a drum head! My drum would hold the image of the moon. The earth, on another circular form, would lie in the foreground. The sun, on a third disc, would rise behind the moon with flares crowning from its edge. Blue, black and violet clouds would trail the crow's wings, with rain streaking the dark sky. Maybe the wings would become the sea, the holy place my first-born daughter went to sit in the silence.

I would paint the story of my recovery. I scribbled images on any surface in every spare moment. I searched through dusty shelves and found the image of the drum I remembered. I sang the hymn daily, harmonizing as I drove. It became my ceaseless prayer.

> "Billows roll high, and thunder shakes the ground
> Lightnings flash, and tempests are all around...

> But the storm is passing over
> The storm is passing over
> The storm is passing over,
> Hallelujah!"

My journey to Los Gatos Canyon would be delayed and I would begin searching for drum heads.

Credits:

Paula Larke, musician, dramatist, writer and "story-teller / gatherer"

Charles Albert Tindley: *The Storm is Passing Over*

For The Dead in Parkland, And Gun Violence Victims Everywhere

After Wilfred Owen

In warrens of windowless rooms, we sat
Crouched in corners, heads between our knees,
Hands over our ears. Others, huddled in closets,
Hidden behind carts. Louder by degrees,
The sound to us came nearer.

"Active shooter!" the intercom announced,
"Active Shooter!"—not a drill!—
Behind the door, some had gathered,
But the "pop- Pop-Pop" grew louder still—
Ghosts were born, heroes created.

But no grand hallelujahs were heard,
No angels' hands were seen,
To lift or guide us away, no words,
Of hope or comfort had been
Spoken or heard.

Just the sounds, ever louder,
Of footsteps, heavy footsteps, and gunshots—
Blood and brain bits, everywhere—
Princess backpacks and Ramones t-shirts,
Pierced alike; so alike, the blood matted hair.

So alike, the screams and silence,
So alike, this pattern of death, of loss—
From singing to somnolence
Forever silenced, and yet what survived

Was dross, in a trenchcoat, dross.

If you had seen the quarterback,
With half-cracked skull and vacant eyes,
Or the messenger girl caught in the attack
You would not speak that ancient lie,
No modern ears would hear you say,
"Our gun rights matter more than lives,
It is honorable to die this way."

Another Duel

With Apologies to Eugene Field

The shamrock-print dog, and the kelly-co cat,
On opposite ends of the pressroom sat,
With the dog at the lectern, and the cat in the back,
Each on their haunches, prepared for attack.
It was nearly nine, (or so I heard)
And neither one had uttered a word—
The ghosts of James Brady, and ole Jody Powell,
Concurred in opinion, with mutual scowl,
That the morning's event would never end well,
With the dog and cat aiming, the best story to tell,
To finally determine, for once and for all,
Whose public pronouncements, gave greater appall.
(Forgive me if I sound too bitter, I am merely repeating
What I read on Twitter!)

The shamrock-print dog began to howl,
The kelly-co cat cried—foul!—foul!—foul!
And in one leap, was on the stage—
The shamrock-print dog, consumed with rage,
Chased the kelly-co cat around the room,
While all the while, their words of doom,
Their alternative facts, and fake news spewed,
Offered like poisonous coffee brewed,
The acrid scent, wafted throughout the air,
And left all reporters, slumped in their chairs.
(Excuse me if I sound deranged, even Jody's hair
was rearranged!)

Mr. Brady was beside himself—
"Why was there no taser, why was there no shelf
To surreptitiously remove from a wall,
To end this great misery, for once and for all?"
But the shamrock-print dog, and the kelly-co cat,
Intent on more havoc, went this way and that—
Strands of bleached blonde ano-hair,
Were mixed with the fur of a soviet bear—
An amulet worn by the shamrock-print dog,
Given in secret, under cover of fog,
(Don't quote me on this, I only repeat
What was told to me by anonymous Tweet!)

By the end of an hour, the room was in tatters,
The lectern upended, and glass goblets shattered;
The White House picture was on the floor,
The flag barely standing, nothing left of the door,
The room almost empty, the reporters long gone,
Except for one pro, whose work was not done—
It was Mara Liaison, from NPR,
Who gathered the remnants, from near and from far,
Of the dog and the cat, who could not agree,
On who was the best maker of fake history.
"You'd better get used to it", dear Mara said,
As she swept them up, from toe to head.
(Please don't fancy, that I am waxing shady,
I heard that part from Powell and Brady!)

The Petition

Mother's beautiful olive complexion had turned sallow. Father's hazel eyes had darkened. He took off his work boots and threw them across the floor in anger. He shook his head in disbelief, as he discovered that Mr. Jackson, who lived across the street from us, was circulating a petition to keep us out. At age five, I knew that it was not good.

A Hispanic family had never lived in the neighborhood before in Planada in 1949. The neighbors did not welcome them at this time. We found out Mr. Jackson was circulating the petition because he thought that we were the stereotypical Hispanic family with lots of cars and mariachi music.

One neighbor spoke about how dad had fixed her toilet and kept it from flooding the bathroom floor. Dad had bought ice cream cones for her two girls when she recently became a widow and money was tight. Another person mentioned how mom had helped her make flour tortillas.

Mom's cooking had saved the day, as her tortillas were mouth-watering delicious.

In the heat of the matter, Mr. Jackson, even though he had filed the petition, asked dad to take him to the doctor, as his health was deteriorating. Dad took him not once, but several times and without hesitation. We learned to put up with each other and get along as neighbors. I have vivid memories of Mr. Jackson becoming unglued when our ball landed on his front lawn. One day, he stopped raising his voice at us. Perhaps he got used to the noise of the bouncing ball and the screeching laughter that kids make.

The petition was denied, as Mr. Jackson did not have enough of the required signatures to make it valid. Gradually, he came to his senses and realized we were not a threat to the neighborhood, but an asset. When my older brother, Paul, had decided to become a United States citizen, Mr. Jackson became his sponsor and mentor.

My parents resumed their busy lives, ignoring the fact that there was ever a petition. They believed that life was too short to worry about trivial things. Mom was so proud that we were all going to school, except Elisa, who was too young. She reminded us that another reason for coming to America were the good schools.

As time went by, the neighbors began to wonder why we never screamed or raised our voices.

According to them, we were quiet and well-behaved. What they did not know was that our parents rewarded us for doing our homework, doing our chores, and being respectful. They took us to the show, which was only 10 cents, and on warm days bought us ice-cream cones.

What I do know is that basically we are all the same, though we have different skin tones, languages and cultures. When you really think about it, we are more alike than we are different. I am so proud of my parents for how they handled racism. They chose to ignore it and continued living their life. They were determined to live the American dream and that they did. They lived in the same house for 48 years, as they raised and educated seven children, not only to obtain college degrees and be successful, but to be good citizens.

My parents had turned the community around with their kindness and acceptance of others. They were excellent neighbors. Because of their positive influence, people were more willing to accept one another and work together. With perseverance and understanding, most things can be turned around for the better.

Why I Write

There are many reasons why I write, but one of them is to reinvent myself. The rhythm of life runs in cycles. What I was at one time, I no longer am.

From 1967 until 1986, I identified with being "mom" to my children, Natalie and Patrick. I knew who I was. After they grew up and left home, I was still "mom," but not in the same way. I also knew by being dedicated to my teaching career, I was known as "teacher".

The great thing about writing is that I can go back and write about my childhood, my siblings, my hometown and the way things were back then. I spoke Spanish at home and English in school, and soon became bilingual. I grew up making mud pies and swaying on a tire swing dangling from a thick branch of our old walnut tree. Roy Rogers and Dale Evans were my childhood heroes on our new black and white television. I often took the role of a heroin in our make-believe plays. At one time I was Joan of Arc. The young people of today are excited to hear how my generation survived without disposable diapers, cell phones, automatic washers and dryers, microwaves, computers and the Internet.

Today, I am embracing changes in my life. I can now express how I feel about line dancing through my writing. It makes me feel like a shining star, young and carefree, as it removes the worries and stress from my life. It is also fun. In my essays, I can share with others my experiences with my rose garden and my love of nature and herbs.

There are so many things that compel me to write. There are times and events that should never go unnoticed. When I first got married, my husband and I were stationed in Grand Forks, North Dakota, and we were part of the great blizzard of 1966.

That story has been written and rewritten many times. When I retired, I had to learn who I was once again. Retirement hit me like a ton of bricks. It left me vulnerable. I knew I had to do it alone because my husband, Tom, loved his job and had no plans to retire. My first thoughts were what do I do and where do I go? I could not sit at home day after day. A friend told me about the Janet Goeske Center in Riverside. I always wanted to write, but did not take a class right away. Eventually, I enrolled in Rose Y. Monge's memoir writing class where we shared our personal stories on a weekly basis. Several years later, I augmented my writing skills with Celena Bumpus' poetry and creative writing classes. The poetry class is challenging! I had earlier convinced myself that poetry was not for me, but this was not true. I lied to myself. I wrote my best poem the other day. It made me so proud to write it. I submitted it to have it published. I wanted to be an inspiration to others.

Often, I write to give the oppressed a voice. It could be a friend, neighbor, or family member.

These ideas could give someone hope or a fresh start. By writing my poems and stories, they will live on. They will be read by my children and their children. My memory will live on in my stories.

Violet

She came into my life and now she's four
When cookies are offered, she asks for more
In her room, magenta, turquoise and purple are all around
Where laughter, singing and dancing can be found
Her love for me, as she plants a kiss on my cheek, makes me
    smile
It lasts more than a mile
People ask me if she's mine
Even if she's known to whine
Of course, I'm her grandma!
She's won her way to my heart

Fall is in the Air

Fall is lovely with its beauty
Crimson and bronze leaves falling from Liquid Amber trees
Crisp, cool weather
Deep pink sunsets
Days growing shorter
Oh, no here we go again, walking our six-pound Chihuahua in
    the dark
Famished coyotes searching for an evening snack
Oh, my! Fall is in the air!

13 Ways of a Sparrow

High up in the palm trees
Among lush greenery
Was the joyful song of the sparrow
The sparrow gathered twigs with its sharp beak
And pulled silk from the corn in the fields to make a nest
The sparrow shuddered in the warm Santa Ana winds
As the fault line shifts
The nestlings of a sparrow are in sync with its mother
As she shares an earth worm with them
The beauty of the chirping sparrow
Like the Gregorian chant
Purple Jack-O-Rama trees majestically line the streets
Projecting a soft glow throughout the city
Why do you desire the Golden Buddha?
When the sparrow is worth more than its weight in gold
Elvis Presley sang a hymn about the sparrow, that it could fly
For God has his eye on the sparrow
When the sparrow flew away
It outlined the edge of many heavens
In the universe
At the sight of these heavenly creatures
The sparrow flying high in the sky
Even the clouds would cry out to God
For where the sparrow is, I am, up there and free
The sparrow was welcomed everywhere, as he spread love
Perched himself at the right of Jesus
Made himself comfortable
The river is dry
The sparrow searched for spiritual waters
Then the sparrow will fly
Time stood still
The sparrow flew to heaven
Where he basked in the glow of heavenly bodies

GUDELIA VADEN

Flour Sack Dresses

As I pour the flour from the bag, while making pancakes, I notice it is made of heavy and sturdy paper. Quite a contrast when back then flour came in cloth bags. Some of the fabric had flowers, polka dots and stripes. It came with the flour mom used to make tortillas.

I remember Mom, with her long mahogany hair pulled into a ponytail, as we walk to the neighborhood store, only 3 blocks from home. The market smells of oranges, apples and cinnamon. Only this time we are purchasing flour. We reach the baking goods aisle and mom tells me to choose a flour sack. It is my turn for a dress that she will make me from the sack. I pick one that is very bright and colorful. It has orange and red flowers with dainty little green stems I felt so loved at that moment that all I wanted to do was give Mom a big hug. I was not big for my six years of age so the ten-pound sack of flour would do. If not, mom had another one at home.

Mom was quite a seamstress, for the most part of our early childhood, some of my dresses were made from flour sacks. She could sew without a pattern. She first had to put the flour in a container and then wash the flour from the sack. After it dried and she cut the material, she was ready to sew with her black Singer sewing machine. She added different details to my dress, such as matching rick-rack to the collar area and buttons from her button jar. On occasion, she would make matching underwear that looked like shorts. I loved this, as now I could climb the monkey bars without any problem. The finished dress was so lovely; it almost took my breath away. It fit perfectly and she made pockets from a contrasting fabric of stripes and when I wore it, my handkerchief fit just right in one the pockets. Right then and there, I decided that I loved clothes and would do what I could to look fashionable, as time went on.

We were part of this flour sack craze that began as the Great Depression gave way to WWII; when flour sack dresses were not just for impoverished families, but for everyone.

Manufacturers were producing many different patterns and colors. They advertised that they were not only for women and children, but boys and men as well. Once, mom made a shirt for my older brother Paul. It was blue and purple with figures of people on the background.

All of a sudden, he became popular with his high school friends, as his shirt was a topic of conversation. I felt a little envious of that shirt because the colors were so beautiful and it fit him so well.

The onset of WWII, had a great impact on cotton, as it was used to make uniforms for soldiers and people were then willing to give up the fabric in order to support the war effort.

From then on, flour was packaged in paper bags and it has been that way ever since.

Looking back to that era, how creative and resourceful mom could be with a flour sack. She found a way to recycle and reuse material that inspired me to follow in her footsteps. When my sisters and I had outgrown our sack dresses, we took turns helping Mom make a quilt from our dresses and the clothes our siblings had outgrown. When the quilt was finished, my heart swelled with pride. I was so proud of the work that went in to it. The many hours well spent. Mom passed on her creative talents to me. I used recycled materials that became math learning games for my preschool students. I was able to make drums out of discarded oatmeal boxes for my school kids.

Remembering the Stages of my Life

I remember life at ten
Grandpa loved us five
Trips to the movies on weekends
Spoiled rotten to help us forget
A time in the past when Dad had left

I remember life at twelve
Grandpa had now passed
Alone with Mom and Grandma
The projects, our home,
Our future forlorn

I remember life at fourteen
Off I went to the seminary
Three years of camaraderie
Life in a dorm
My future is born

I remember life at twenty-two
The postcard in the mail
You have been chosen
Life in the military
No longer in solitary

I remember life at twenty-six
My bride to be
Chosen by me
A career determined
By a man determined

I remember life at thirty-one
My advanced degree now done
No jobs available in Missouri
My money gone
Off to California forewarned

I remember life at seventy-one
Fifty years have passed
A career is finished
My life a success
I am so blessed

Economy
(a Haiku, a Tanka, a Fibonacci Poem)

Haiku
Economy sucks
It's so hard to make a buck
Return to nature

Tanka
Yosemite is
A wondrous place to visit
A way to escape
From the daily woes of life
Plagued by the economy

Fibonacci Poem
A
Way
To get
What you need
Work hard to achieve
Stay focused on your future goals
Realize your dreams regardless of the economy

An Air Force Experience

Lots of things happened from 1962 thru 1969: JFK was assassinated, the hippie movement flourished, Peter, Paul and Mary played in San Francisco, the astronauts landed on the moon, the internet was born, the Woodstock Festival took place, Righteous Brothers sang, Joan Baez captivated the world. I remember these times vaguely.

I was drafted in 1962 at the age of 22 to support the Vietnam War effort. Instead of taking a chance of ending up on the front lines, in harm's way, I enlisted in the Air Force, having passed their battery of tests with top scores. And I was sent to tech school at Lowry AFB in Denver, CO, where I learned to troubleshoot and repair complex electronic systems. As a leisurely pursuit while there, I took up figure skating and joined the Denver figure skating club, where I learned how to do ice dances. Eventually, I took formal lessons at the Broadmoor World Arena in Colorado Springs and, during my last few weeks, the instructor had me skate a waltz with a young teenage girl, Peggy Fleming. I was 23 and she was 15! Later in life, I learned that Peggy had achieved both Olympic and World champion titles.

While in Denver, I received word from the USO that my brother, Patrick, had joined the marines and drowned while on military maneuvers in Okinawa. His squadron was training in preparation for an upcoming tour in Vietnam. The marines had a choice to either climb a cliff or ford a stream, wearing full backpacks. They decided to ford the stream, and the weight of the backpack pulled him under. The medics tried to revive Patrick by performing a tracheotomy, but it did not work. The USO arranged for the Air Force to fly me to Scott AFB in a Cargo plane so I could attend the military funeral in St. Louis. I did not cry for about two months, I know not why, and then one day I broke down and shed a flood of tears for my loss. I found out later that my brother had taken out an insurance policy when he enlisted, and this was enough to allow my mom to leave the projects and purchase a new home in South St. Louis. My mom is now 97, independent and lives in her own home thanks to my brother's foresight. Out of tragedy and sorrow, pain and suffering often comes some good.

From 1963 thru1965, I repaired Bombing Navigation Systems on B-52s at Castle AFB in Merced, CA. and received an AA degree from Merced Junior College. The college was brand new, with classes held in buildings on the Merced fairgrounds. I met a beautiful young girl while attending classes at the college. She was without doubt the best looking one at the college, and I started dating Delia. We often took trips to Yosemite National Park.

The drive to Yosemite was a chance to relax, to get back to nature, to breathe fresh air, smell the aroma of awesome, enormous pine trees, listen to the ripple of streams and the roar of the Merced River, to camp, to fish, to cook bacon in cast iron pans placed on wood burning stoves, to hike to the top of cliffs soaring high above the valley, to eat wild berries while hiking, to observe bears, antelope, and deer in the high pastures. Yosemite was fun, youthful and romantic. Then one spring day, I proposed to Delia near Yosemite falls, with spectacular sunset views of the granite rocks of El Capitan. I must have swept her off her feet, as she said yes. And then, not that long afterwards, perhaps less than 6 months, to my dismay, I received orders for Grand Forks AFB in North Dakota.

I had to act quickly. I told Delia that we would have to up the wedding date since I would likely not return to California once I transferred to North Dakota. I married Delia in January 1966 and purchased a brand new shiny red Volkswagen for the occasion! We had a wonderful two-week honeymoon, stopped in Vegas for a Righteous Brothers concert, visited my family in St. Louis, and then drove to Grand Forks AFB in North Dakota, where the temperature dipped to 40 degrees below zero on the day we arrived. It was so cold in Grand Forks that I had to buy a special gas heater just to keep the passenger cabin warm. Delia had lived in the San Joaquin Valley for almost her entire life and had no idea what cold weather was like! When the temperature warmed a little, we experienced the "Great Blizzard." While living in a basement apartment, we were snowed in by two-story snow drifts and had to be dug out of our "tomb" when the blizzard ended and life once again stirred. That day, I made a decision that someday in the future, although I knew not when, I would get out of the Air Force and return to live in a nice home in the warm weather of sunny California.

While stationed at Castle AFB, I had applied for an Airman Education and Commissioning Program. The application was rejected due to my poor eyesight and lack of depth perception. I certainly had the ability to get the grades and the education office assured me the surgeon general would provide a waiver, so I re-enlisted early. Unfortunately, the waiver was not granted, and I had another four-year commitment.

I then applied for a special program for enlisted airmen called "Operation Bootstrap"; the Air Force would pay my college tuition and continue providing my full salary and extra living expenses. I carried the paperwork with me from Castle AFB to Grand Forks. At first, the wing commander at the North Dakota base would not approve the orders "because it would look like he did not need the support personnel he had requested." Six months later, the orders were approved, and Delia and I were on our way to Park University, the shiny red Volkswagen loaded with all our belongings, including a new TV we had purchased at Sears, and trunks strapped down on a luggage rack on the roof! There was barely enough room for Delia and me. In some places I had trouble maintaining the minimum speed of 40 mph.

For the next 10 months, I pursued a bachelor's degree in math at Park University in Parkville, MO. In 1967, I transferred to McCoy AFB in Orlando, FL where I continued working on the older B-52 Bombing Navigation systems. My daughter Natalie was born in December, and I actually got to hold her in my arms before I found out that I was heading to Guam on a remote tour, family not allowed!

In 1968 thru 1969, I received TDY orders to Guam (6-month

tour), returned to McCoy for 6 months and then received PCS orders to Thailand (1-year tour). While stationed at U-Tapao Royal Thai Air Force base near Sattahip on the Gulf of Thailand, I provided support for B-52 Stratofortress bombers, also nicknamed BUFFs (Big Ugly Fat Fellows), and as strange as it may sound, while in Thailand, I got orders to go to Guam. I got so busy that I did not keep in touch with my siblings. In those days, we did not have cell phones to communicate, and we corresponded by mail. Mail was so slow that I remember the time my grandmother sent a box of chocolates to me in Thailand; I had gone to Guam *and the candy followed*. When the candy arrived in Guam, I had already returned to Thailand *and the candy followed*. I eventually received a crushed Mavrakos box of melted, moldy chocolate. Ugh!

Little did I know what would take place on my first tour to Guam! I am fond of my youngest brother, Carl. However, I had not spent much time with him growing up, as I attended a seminary far away from my home in St. Louis. What an experience it was the night he showed up in Guam! A booming voice reverberated through the Quonset hut: "Hey! Is there a Vaden in the house?" Three large lockers pushed together formed a room divider that blocked my view of the makeshift hallway. I could not see who was barking the military like command. Surely, I felt I was in serious trouble as I jumped out of my military cast iron bunk bed. He had joined the Air Force, went through nine months of technical training, became an electronic technician for B-52s, and ended up in Guam working in the same Bomb Navigation shop as I. I was only vaguely aware that he had joined the Air Force. I surely did not expect him to show up in Guam!

That night, we went to the enlisted club to catch up on things that happened the last few years, and drank ourselves into oblivion with rum and cokes. We had to crawl back to our Quonset hut, hoping that we would not be discovered by the Air Force police. We definitely were not in any condition to walk, as we surely would have fallen on our faces. Fortunately, we did not suffer much the morning after the night before. We were together for three months, lounged on the beach on weekends, and enjoyed a one-week vacation to Japan. What an experience! As one flies into Guam, the sign above the flight terminal "GUAM IS GOOD" cannot be overlooked.

In Thailand, I will never forget the time the B-52 blew up on the flight line. It was in late July of 1969, and a group of us were in the Bomb/Nav shop. Suddenly, all kinds of chatter cluttered the squawk box: apparently, on take-off a B-52 slid off the departure end of the runway, collapsing on the nose gear and catching fire. The B-52 was part of an Arclight bombing mission to Vietnam, which means it was fully loaded with 500-pound bombs (84 in the bomb bay and 24 on the wing racks) and 300,000 pounds of fuel. I heard that the air speed meters were not consistent. One meter indicated sufficient air speed for take-off, the other did not. They powered down the engines, but were going too fast to stop and skidded into a ditch.

We ran to the door and saw flames about a mile away, at the end of the runway. The cockpit crew had scrambled through overhead escape hatches. I saw a helicopter fly overhead and heard the wing commander say "Get the hell out of there, she is going to blow!" I saw the flash and headed for the hallway. Then the blast hit, shaking our building and shattering the windows. The wing commander had been conversing with a helicopter rescue crew just as the bomb bay detonated. It was a very sad day when I later found out that only one of the four helicopter crew members survived. The impact of the explosion scattered the external bombs located on the wing racks, shutting down the flight line.

Although the work was demanding, 10 hours a day, 6 days a week, I enjoyed good times in Thailand. The Catholic chaplain took us on "retreats" to Chiang Mei, a resort community in the northern part of Thailand. We flew there in Air Force propeller driven aircraft to "rest and recuperate," take in the beauty of misty mountains, tour Buddhist temples, visit the teakwood logging industry, and shop for gifts to send home.

My Air Force experience was about to end. The Vietnam War was winding down and Officer Candidate schools were no longer accepting applicants. I decided that it was time to change paths and applied for a graduate assistantship at the University of Missouri, which was accepted. The only problem was that I had to get a two month early out from Thailand to start in the Fall Semester. I was not sure how to do this, so I went to personnel and talked to an Airman Basic. He said, "Don't worry, I'll take care of everything" … and he did! I received my early out in September of 1969.

I kept my promise, the one I made in Grand Forks. I left the Air Force and pursued a MS degree in mathematics at the University of Missouri. My son was born at the University hospital in 1970. I graduated in 1971—there were no available jobs, the space program was cutting back, and the NASA engineers were laid off. I applied to all 121 Junior Colleges in the State of California and several government agencies with no results.

Once again, I kept my promise!

With no immediate prospects for a career, I asked myself, "Do I want to be poor in Missouri or poor in California?" The decision was easy. I moved my family to California, and when I arrived I had less than $50 to my name; but I had determination, an education, and, thanks to my Air Force career, I was debt free with lots of confidence and a bright future to pursue.

COLTON PUBLIC LIBRARY/COLTON AREA MUSEUM

Led by Jessica Carrillo

Jose Chavez

Bright Morning in Idyllwild 2012

Ponderosa pine nestled together,
like match sticks in a box,
so tall they graze the morning sky,
wind purrs from the west.

Greenish lake reveals gentle ripples,
keeping time with the breeze,
splash of rainbow trout
he scurries off with a gadfly.

Brown squirrel comes to visit,
she sniffs about for my invisible
lunch, chirps at me, and waits;
pickings are slim today.

Slight cocoa-colored lizard,
does his pushups in the sun
no fear of my presence;
he knows where home is.

Crested blue jay arrives calling
loudly from the pine branch,
She sees me & waits for the noisy
reply from the opposite shore.

Thunderheads like cotton balls
at the crest of the mountain,
rapidly swirling from east to west,
gather & later will disappear.

Grey-tipped buzzard appears
riding the thermals like an emperor,
stately wings scarcely move,
glides smoothly, without a sound.

Most visitors come for quiet & solitude,
that won't suffice for me. Trout,
squirrel, blue jay, buzzard, & cloud create
a melodic invitation, calling me to return.

JOSE CHAVEZ

Born in Roswell

There was an alien aircraft that crashed
near Roswell in 1947.

army saw it dozens of eyewitnesses
a body devoid of blood
on a rectangular table
a doctor's report written
in a government hangar
inside Walker Air Force Base

must be a cover-up conspiracy
a nurse saw it all
knew the whole story
understood the drama
the nurse always knows
what the doctor won't say

born in '53 I walked the
streets of Roswell: Second St,
Main, & Van Buren
where abuelita lived
I remember the Chief Theater
on N Main & Safeway
where everyone shopped

my barrio—called Chihuahuita
no aliens there. I once saw
a porcupine & two raccoons
one summer when I was seven

poverty walked the streets with us
broken homes broken trucks
broken cars broken lives
broken people forgotten prayers

no alien museum & restaurant
selling alien burgers
no alien summer festival
no new hotels
no movie sets
no Capt. Kirk
no Mr. Spock
no grainy video. . . so sorry

JOSE CHAVEZ

Comanche Canyon

In the Comanche Canyon near Petaca Peak
Blue Jay lands on Twisted Cedar,
early morning shadows disappear.

Moves to the top of Oak and calls to me.
Before I can answer, flies swiftly
to Piñon Pine across the valley.

Two nearby Magpies cry out, "urraca, urraca."
Like the cool breeze, they tell me to search
elsewhere as Blue Jay has moved on.

I follow them knowing that Wind will soon be warm,
pray for insight and wisdom,
and imagine clouds like eagle feathers.

Past the Comanche Trail of seasons long ago,
Blue Jay stops where Juniper Berries can
be found near Red Canyon Rocks.

A second Blue Jay calls, and together, decide
to stay here. I see Red-Tail Hawk flying
above me and walk east toward Taos Pueblo.

Tío Chuy Gives Directions

My papá wanted to take our family of five to Olvera
St. in downtown LA for a cultural visit & lunch. He
said mamá, who doesn't speak much English, would
remember her little village in Jalisco and be happy.
Tio Chuy came Friday night for tacos and directions.

From Riverside he said to take the 60 Freeway
past the Ontario Airport, but don't stop to watch
the Fed Ex planes because there's too many,
we'll get distracted, and papá might get a ticket.

Pass Corona, and Pomona on the right-hand side until
you pass El Monte—where there's great carne asada
at Taquería El Chango, nobody knows why it's called
that, but don't stop if you want to eat at Calle Olvera.

Get off the 60 to the 110 Freeway or the 101, he said—
couldn't remember which, until you get to Main St,
or maybe it was Alameda. Turn right at the exit. If you
go left you'll end up at Emilio's Llantería where you

can buy some tires if you need them. There's a 7/11
store across the street where you can buy ice cold sodas
in plastic cups and bacon-wrapped hot dogs with onions.
Chuy said his mouth waters whenever he thinks about them.

If you took the wrong exit you can ask the cajero for help.
Tío remembers going to school in nearby south central,
so he used to spend lots of time in downtown LA, when he
had hair, & the chicas were looking fine. He just bought his

first phone, and his third wife, Lolita, is showing him how to use it, but mostly he spends time watching Telemundo to see how Cruz Azul is doing. We got lost the next day—ended up at the Llantería. Since I'm in 8th grade now, I gladly suggested

to papá to use Mapquest on his laptop, or download Google Maps on his iphone, for directions. The lady's voice on the app, will tell you **where** to go and **how** to get there, I told him. Mamá smiled, then laughed after I said that, but I didn't know why.

Two days later, Tio Chuy laughed and said, "*No hay que llegar primero, pero hay que saber llegar.*"

Mr Okeyo

It was 1970 and Ikizu center, ringed by houses with thatched roofs in various stages of disrepair, with a dozen mute, wheel-less and engine-less Land Rover carcasses, was thronged with several thousand excited, eager people. Every dark body celebrated the ten years of Independence from British Protectorate rule clothed with brilliantly colored African kitenge (brightly patterned) cloths. The sun smiled down benevolently from above the equator, bringing out the pungent odor of oil rubbed skin that added ruddiness to Bantu solidarity and strength.

Every tongue praised in mathematically precise constructs of Swahili each celebrant's unique appreciation of the joy and pride welling up in each breast. Each noun, adjective, preposition, and verb intimately united and melded by repeated prefixes, infixes, and suffixes. Every eye focused on the head of a giant of a man clothed in the standard white shirt and black slacks of a self-made professional man, standing head and shoulders above the crowd. His well chiseled face of pure, coal black features, untainted by the universal Bantu brown, revealed the determination to succeed in spite of all odds. He was a self-made man who managed to gain a bachelors' degree education even though such was not readily available to the colonist.

Great drops of sweat emphasized the achievements of this Luo as he stood, the first native Tanzanian principal of the local high school. His uniformed students surrounded him in pride. In his hands Mr. Okeyo held high the Uhuru (Freedom) Torch, acknowledged symbol of Tanzanian freedom and independence that was even then being carried in triumph throughout the land, celebrating the tenth anniversary of independence.

Notes: The Bantu are the predominant race of people in north central Tanzania. They speak one of a collection of languages that have a very complex grammar. They tend to be of a lighter skin color than some of the other races in Tanzania. The Bantu race includes the Kikuyu, family of Jomo Kenyatta, the first president of Kenya to the north, all the way down to the Xhosa, family of Nelson Mandela in South Africa.

The Luo people speak a language unrelated to Bantu languages. They live mainly in southeastern Kenya and north central Tanzania. They have unique customs including one where a male Luo is not regarded as a man until he has sired at least ten sons. As you will quickly deduce, this encourages polygamy. Many of their people have a darker skin color than the Bantu.

Apparently both Mr. and Mrs. Okeyo were carriers of Sickle Cell Disease. It offers immunity against malaria but at a terrible cost of life. Except for their eldest daughter, their numerous children died before they graduated from high school, thus guaranteeing he would not qualify as a real Luo man. Both of them were devout Adventists; consequently, he celebrated strict monogamy. When I met them again at a centenary celebration of Adventism in Tanzania some 35 years after the event I describe here, they were a dignified couple, sadly without the usual accompaniment of grandchildren.

Swahili is the main language of Tanzania. It uses a vocabulary composed of Bantu and Arabic words and developed during the slave trade of the 18th and 19th centuries. It consists of eight different classes of nouns, each requiring all the qualifying words to mirror the class of that noun. Verbs are extremely regular, making them easy to learn and use. It does not distinguish between genders, so is an ideal gender-neutral language.

The derelict Land Rovers would typically come to life at least once a month in the pursuit of the village source of income: animals poached from the nearby game reserve. They were kept in this form to divert any suspicious police or park rangers.

By Bus to Dar es Salaam

An opportunity to attend a math teaching workshop presented itself at the end of the 1968 school year. Our principal, George Dunder, urged me to go. As usual the school had no money for such things, but the government was willing to pay teachers to attend, so I applied and was accepted. Since there was no extra money for transport, I couldn't fly down to Dar es Salaam, and the school even refused to provide a train ticket. We didn't own a car, so I rode the bus. The trip was about 850 miles one way. This would take us at least two days and the intervening night.

The trip was my baptism by fire into Tanzanian life.

When I caught the bus at Nyamuswa, it was only about half-full. Everyone was sitting near the front of the bus. Since I was going to be on it for a long time, I went to a seat near the rear of the bus, pulled out a book, and started to read. I enjoyed the ride and the view, but the view didn't change that much, so I enjoyed reading. The driver drove as fast as he dared. He passed other busses in order to pick up fares before the other driver got there.

It hadn't been an hour when we struck a really nasty washout on the road. The driver made no attempt to slow down. The back of the bus bounced high into the air. I flew up off the seat and smacked my head really hard on the steel luggage rack overhead. The proverbial stars that I had never really seen in any previous experience flew in every direction. My head hurt and my neck felt as though it had been broken. As my body slammed back into the seat, I put my head down onto my knees moaning from the pain. Instantly I flew off the seat a second time and smashed the back of my head on the rails above. A new set of stars exploded with fresh fireworks in front of the first set. My body crumpled back onto the seat. This time I grabbed the bottom of the seat with both hands and hung on desperately as the rear end of the bus continued to bounce completely out of control.

I looked at the people in front of me. None of them seemed to have bounced very far, and none of them so much as gave me a sideways glance. With my head and neck screaming in pain, I began to do some math. It didn't take me long to figure out that the further back I sat behind the rear wheels of the bus the higher I would bounce. When we found a relatively smooth part of the road again, I moved up as close as possible to the other passengers. The rest of the trip was much less painful.

None of the roads during those years were paved except the 110 mile stretch from Morogoro to Dar es Salaam. The non-paved roads were fairly smooth gravel, much of the time. They were graded to have a high crown with edges curved on down into gullies three or more feet deep on each side. Since December is the midst of the short rainy season, we got the usual afternoon tropical downpour. The wet roads were very slippery, much of the time. In order not to slide into a gully, the driver drove straight down the middle of the road.

People walked up and down the roads, especially near any settlement. When they saw a bus coming, they would scurry to one side or the other. Had they not done so, the bus driver would have simply driven right over them. Any car or pickup on the road would slow down and pull over as far to the left as possible, its driver hoping not to slide into the gully nor get struck by the bus. We learned this on our first day in Tanzania, Fritz Martinsen picked us up at the airport. A bus came by as we were driving from Musoma to Ikizu. Fritz pulled over to let it pass, and on the wet surface we slid off into the gully, striking the vertical edge of the road with a thud that added several new dents to his already well dented Ford Zodiac.

At the beginning of the trip not too far south-east of Mwanza, it rained, making the road very slippery. Our bus was moving much too fast for safety. Cars slid over into the ditch on either side of the road to get out of our way. Suddenly, the passengers all jumped up, chattering wildly. My Swahili was still rudimentary and knowledge of local languages nil, so I didn't understand what had excited them. I stood up and looked anxiously forward. The sky was dark from the thunder storm we were driving through. Ahead of us vague lights showed the form of another bus coming straight at us. He, too, was driving straight down the crown of the road. Our driver blew his horn desperately and swore fluently in whatever language. But he blankly refused to move over and give the other bus right of way.

Finally, our driver realized that the other bus wasn't going to move over, either. He hit the brakes with both feet. We fishtailed wildly left and right along the road. Every passenger stood as tall as possible. Some screamed, some swore, and all were yelling at the top of their lungs. It appeared a crash was inevitable. "Sit down and hold on," I yelled, but they had panicked and probably didn't understand much English. I sat down and hooked my legs and arms around the steel supports of the bench. It became obvious to me why bus crashes in Tanzania usually had so many casualties.

I couldn't help straining my neck to try and catch a glimpse of what was going to happen.

Both busses had their lights on, and both were wildly blowing their horns. We were indeed slowing down but not quickly enough. Weaving madly, we headed towards our inevitable doom.

I prayed fervently for our salvation. Finally, our bus came to a complete stop. The other bus had also managed to stop. The front bumpers of the two busses were so close together that no one could walk between them. Everyone jumped off the bus and formed a circle around the two drivers. At first it appeared that the drivers were going to beat each other up. However, all they did was yell and scream at each other.

Eventually, after a lot of shouting, cursing, and yelling, everyone got back onto his or her bus. The passengers were totally silent as they realized how close they had come to dying that evening. The busses backed up far enough so that each one could move over to its left. Then they inched by each other at a distance that an extra coat of paint would have prevented. Total silence reigned. We were all afraid. As soon as the busses got past each other, they pulled back onto the crown and raced off down the road as madly as they had been doing before our near death.

Those busses were in far worse condition than any rickety school bus you've ever seen. The seats were hard and often broken. Occasionally along the way a crowd of vendors would greet us. We would stop briefly. The vendors had chapattis (unleavened flatbread), boiled eggs, roasted meat, live chickens, bananas, or mangos for sale. Travelers would lean out of the windows dickering loudly for some item they wanted.

These busses had no toilets, so soon a large enough percentage of the riders demanded that the driver stop. The driver found a flat, slightly grassy area with no trees or rocks nearby. As soon as we stopped, everyone got off and formed a large circle around the bus. Facing outwards, they took care of their bathroom needs before boarding again. The first time this happened I was so steeped in western privacy norms that I stayed on the bus, figuring that I would use a restroom at the bus station in the next town. However, there were no bus stations in any of these towns and definitely no public restrooms.

A couple of hours later, I needed to go so badly that I was almost blowing bubbles. Again, everyone got off, and I joined the large circle. Relief flooded my body, and I climbed back into the bus. I asked why they stopped where there were no trees or rocks to hide behind. They looked at this green-horn mzungu (white man) and laughed. Could anyone be so stupid as to not know the reason? Yes, I was that stupid. Well, they were all afraid of lions and snakes. And in this flat area with practically no grass they could see that there were no lions or snakes. As for modesty...? That is an expendable commodity when they grow up in one room homes where not only cooking and sleeping take place but also the changing of clothes and procreating. Toilet needs are taken care of outside on the edge of the cleared area around the house. Dogs clear up the human manure, so the place doesn't smell.

We finally arrived at the bus station in downtown Dar es Salaam. I inquired as to where I could catch the city bus to take me the eight miles out of town to the University College of Dar es Salaam. I was pointed to a particular bus sign and told which bus to catch. There was a large but manageable crowd collected at the sign. When the bus pulled in, everyone shoved forward as hard as they could, elbowing each other out of the way. I considered myself too dignified to fight for my seat, and soon every place was taken. Most of the people had gotten on the bus, and I took heart that I would clearly make it onto the next bus in about twenty minutes.

In due course the next bus rolled in, and the scene was repeated. I was rudely shoved away by everybody else's elbows and again found myself standing outside and looking in. I guess I'm slow to learn because the scene repeated itself after another twenty minutes. This time I had a little silent talk with myself and determined to get on the next bus. My elbows were just as effective as everyone else's. Indeed, I got a lovely window seat in the front half of the bus where I wouldn't again bang my still sore head. Nobody got mad at me. The good old British idea of standing in a well-behaved queue for everything had never caught on there.

My understanding of Tanzania travel had been vastly increased. My principal was delighted that the workshop freely provided me with a box of brand-new math textbooks sufficient for me and my students. The trip itself was practically routine, and when the bus dropped me off in Nyamuswa about two o'clock in the morning, I had only about two miles to walk home guided only by the starlight. Thinking of the possible presence of elephants or leopards on this rural dirt track leant wings to my feet.

Suikerbosrand

What many may know about the Suikerbosrand is that it is a mountain range that in English translation is called Sugar-Bush Reef. It has no gold but is a sister range to the Witwatersrand (White-Waters Reef) that hides perhaps the richest store of gold in the world. Running southeast from Johannesburg, the largest city in southern Africa, the Suikerbosrand derived its name from the colloquial name for South Africa's national flower, the protea or sugar bush. In its heart lies the very popular Suikerbosrand Nature Reserve that sports over 200 species of birds, some zebra, springbuck, springhare, hyena and, if one is very lucky, a leopard. Near its center stands Kaalkop, a peak practically devoid of vegetation that is often crowned with snow in wintertime. On the edge of the nature reserve a beautiful dam provides home to many water birds.

But what I know about this dam and the Suikerbosrand in general comes from my experience when I was a student near there. We called this the Big Dam that, long before anyone dreamed of a nature reserve, was built to supply water to my school, rural Sedaven High School, a Seventh-day Adventist boarding school for white students during South Africa's apartheid days. Now it is open to all students wanting a Christ-centered education.

Saturdays at Sedaven consisted of Sabbath school and worship service in the morning. These were often interesting but as often simply endured. After lunch we usually took a walk. As in almost everything else, girls were allowed to walk in one direction and boys in the opposite direction.

On one occasion, four of my friends and I decided to walk north up the canyon that ends at the Big Dam. We forgot that this was the week that boys were supposed to walk south and girls north.

We hiked the mile and a quarter up the canyon and found ourselves standing on the earthenware dam wall. Michael stripped his clothes off and quoted Christ when he said during his great temptations, "Get thee behind me, Satan."* As he jumped into the water he shouted, "Satan got behind me and pushed me in!" We all followed suit. You should know that swimming on Sabbath, under any circumstances, was regarded as a serious sin.

It was autumn and the water cool. We swam around gleefully until someone said, "There come the girls!" Sure enough, there were at least twenty girls coming down the road to the dam. They walked out on the dam wall and stood near our clothes. We began an animated conversation that lasted for at least half an hour. By this time, we boys were all very cold, as we had been forced to stay in the deep water to hide our nakedness.

Suddenly, both of my legs cramped up in extreme pain. I knew that people often died in the water from cramps, so I fully expected to die. However, I was not about to get out of the water naked with all those girls standing next to our clothes.

Finally, we heard the first supper bell ring. The girls turned and walked back up the road. As they disappeared from sight, we hauled ourselves from the frigid water, pulled pants and shirts onto our wet bodies, and dashed back down the canyon, arriving just before they locked the dining room doors.

On another Sabbath afternoon about 10 of us boys started out on a hike—in the correct direction this time. We hiked along the southeast facing side of the rand in the general direction of the closest town, Heidelberg. We walked across the first valley, which had the Big Dam at its head, and up past the English teacher's home.

Our English teacher, Stanley Edwards, did his best to come across as a friendly, good-natured teacher with a number of sports interests, especially cricket. I had known Mr. Edwards for several years before I went to Sedaven, and I liked him. I think most of the students really liked him, especially the English-speaking group. Sedaven was founded as a bilingual school where all classes were taught in both official languages, English and Afrikaans. Language teachers were expected to teach exclusively in their lan-

---

* *Luke 4:8*

guage. I don't believe I ever heard him speak Afrikaans, which tended to alienate him somewhat from that group. Of course, to us high-school students, anyone who was a teacher represented authority and was thus always under suspicion.

Most of the rand is fairly arid, so we blazed our own trail. We climbed up over the ridges and down across two or three smaller canyons. Along the way we would tear open the dark grey termite mounds we encountered in search of a scorpion or a snake. In one of these I caught a small night adder. It was not even a foot long, but it was related to the deadly puff adder and so elicited a lot of excitement. Its poison fangs were located far back in its mouth, and because of its small size, it couldn't open its mouth to actually deliver the poison unless someone was stupid enough to get a little fold of skin inside the mouth. I stuck it in my shirt pocket where it remained contentedly for the rest of the hike.

An hour or more after setting out, we came to a large and deep canyon where a dry river watercourse had cut vertical sides making its crossing quite difficult. We found a large flat rock on the edge of the canyon that allowed us to stand and stare into its deep, dark depths. The guys were soon each bragging about their own lack of fear and prowess in face of such a scary height. Suddenly the rock we were standing on started to tip noticeably into the canyon. Bravado forgotten, we yelled with one accord. Turning around, we all dashed madly towards the safe edge of the canyon. We leapt wildly onto the rocky soil and scrambled away from the edge. Amazingly, providentially, we all made it without knocking each other down after the plunging rock. It bounced back and forth on the cliff faces as it tumbled some fifty feet into the canyon. We watched its progress in silent awe.

The distant ringing of the supper bell snapped us out of our various reveries, and we dashed pell-mell back to supper. Sitting at table in the dining room, we told of our narrow escapes to our wide-eyed table mates. Suddenly, a girl pointed to my shirt and screamed. The tiny night adder had warmed up enough to peek out of my pocket. It lived in my dorm drawer for the rest of the school term, but that's another story.

Berries and My Plum Thicket

Where I grew up in southwestern Washington State, the weather consisted of drizzle and occasional sun showers. I learned to take advantage of the latter to get outdoors. Our green shake house sat on a hillside below the road and vibrated to the rumble of logging trucks. The living room and downstairs bedroom windows faced the road, one through a bush where we once watched a nest of baby Robins grow up. The front room windows looked across feathery grass, which Daddy tried to tame with a small hand sickle, and some violets that grew wild on the bank.

Both front and back doors faced the driveway that sloped down to our garage that housed our car and a small woodshed across from the back porch. Looking across the driveway from either door, we could see the garden and an old milk house beyond the huge butternut tree at the far corner of the garage.

On some dry days I remember taking a book, like Sam Campbell's *Looney Coon* or Youngberg's *Miracle of the Song*, and heading to the row of apple trees that marched from the blackberry bushes below the road halfway to the cedars along Cedar Creek. Stepping through the tall grass behind our house, I'd climb up into an apple tree. When I found a secure place against one of the rough branches, I'd open my book and read until Mother called or discomfort dislodged me.

Sometimes, however, on a gray day without drizzle, I wanted to be alone, so I traipsed along the path beside the garden and beyond to where I could crawl into my secret hiding place—my plum thicket. I discovered this tightly bunched group of small trees once when I went past the garden looking for blackberries. (In spite of their thorns, I love picking blackberries.)

I found the berries near an old fallen-down barn, and when I explored the area beyond them to my left, I spied what became my plum thicket. Tall grass, nettles, and burdock shielded this dense patch from the house and garden. To the north and west the vine covered grey barn ruins and trees with thick undergrowth hid it. Blackberry bushes blocked any view of it from the road on the uphill side. It was truly secret.

Wriggling my way between the one to two-and-a-half inch trunks, I reached an opening where I could sit, legs bent. Okay, I'm hiding. Now what? I studied the leaves on the miniature trees around me. Not much difference. Pretty much all the same.

Then I tried to imagine the spaces between the trunks as rooms in a house. There's a bedroom. This space could be the kitchen.

(Pause.)

Oka-a-ay—but I can't get into them! So I imagined myself as tiny as Alice in a forest of giant trees. That didn't last long. Humph! If I were like Alice, I'd be walking, exploring—not just sitting.

So I pushed my way out of my hiding place to find something to DO.

Guess I never took my little sister Elvina to the plum thicket because—well, I barely had room to sit in it myself. With so many drizzly days and a sister and neighbors Monte and Loren to play with on sunny non-school days, I probably only visited my thicket two or three times in the five years we lived at Cedar Creek. Besides, sitting still for a long time with no room to move and nothing to do has never been my style!

Picking berries, on the other hand, is my style. Even now when Wil and I travel through berry country—black, blue, or straw—if I spy some near the road, I holler, "Stop! I want to pick some berries." He usually pulls over, smiling and shaking his head at a wife who wants to brave insect bites, thorns, and stains just to eat berries. As I mentioned, picking berries, even blackberries, is my style. Besides, I just might find another secret place like my plum thicket.

Heidi's Good Idea: A Children's Story

"Do we have to move?" Seven-year-old Heidi just heard Dad say they must all—Dad, Mom, Heidi, and her three brothers—pack up and get ready to move to another city.

"Yes, I have a new job," Dad smiled down at Heidi, "and it's not near here, so we will move closer to where my work is." Both Dad and Mom looked happy.

"But I don't know anyone there," Heidi frowned. "I'll miss all my friends from church."

A tear escaped her eye.

"What about us?" her older brothers grumbled. "We don't either. We'll have to go to school without our friends."

"I understand. We will miss our friends, too," Dad told them. "But I promise, when we get there, we will look for a new church where we can make new friends."

As he promised, once the family got settled in their new city, Dad looked online for a church near them. "Look, kids, this church is only a few miles from us. Let's try it this weekend, okay?"

When they visited the new church, Heidi looked around and whispered, "Daddy, these people are old. They have gray hair." After the service, she saw some using canes or walkers to get around. "Where are the families with children that can be our friends?" Heidi wondered.

When they got home after church, Mom and Dad looked at each other and shook their heads. "That church has all old people in it. We have children," they said, "and we need a church that has children in it. Maybe we should find a different church." That's when Heidi spoke up. "No, Mommy, Daddy. This church needs us! It needs children. Maybe God sent us to this church because it needs children."

So Dad asked, "Well, boys, what do you think? Shall we keep going to this church like Heidi suggested?"

"I guess so." "Sure," they answered.

"We can always go somewhere else if it doesn't work out," the oldest observed.

The next weekend Heidi skipped to the church door ahead of her family and chirped, "Happy Sabbath" to the surprised lady there. As Dad, Mom, the boys, and Heidi filed in and filled a pew, friendly smiles and nods welcomed them.

After the service, the members surrounded Heidi and her family. "We didn't think you'd come back, but here you are!" one member said joyfully.

Patting Heidi's shoulder, another remarked, "I'm so glad you came again."

"Won't you join us every week?" one man invited. Others smiled and nodded, agreeing. So they stayed. Week after week Heidi's family worshipped there. "Oh look!" Heidi tugged at Mom's dress one week. "Grandma Grady brought two little girls with her!" Heidi's excitement sparkled in her eyes. "Maybe they can be my friends," she whispered.

"Can they be my friends, too, Mommy?" Little Brother asked.

"I'm sure they can," Mom smiled down at him.

Soon Heidi's whole family was helping at church. Heidi and Little Brother said   "Hi, what's your name?" to the new girls and made friends. Dad and her older brothers kept the sound system working. Mom sang, her beautiful voice leading the congregation or bringing special music. She also told stories especially for the children.

And they all made new friends—thanks to Heidi's good idea when she said, "This church needs us! Maybe God sent us here."

Sylvia Nelson Clarke

I Want to Be

I Want to Be

Balanced

Achieving

Listening

Loving

Heading toward the Goal

SYLVIA NELSON CLARKE

Quote from a Friend

"My House Calls to Me"
Dirty windows distract and distress
Garden growth greets and grates
A bounty of books beg and beckon
Piles of paper reproduce and pollute
Stuff stacks, scatters on surfaces
Time ticks by, taunts and teases
I NEED to
simplify!

Suborder Lacertilia

I see you slink
little Skink
Have you a gizzard
limber Lizard
What about a sauna
spiny Iguana
Does your chirp echo
small pink Gecko
Ever seen an impala
black Chuckwalla
What's the deal-a
Mister Gila
I'll open the door
for you, Monitor
Where's your wagon
Komodo Dragon
Your best suit's on
Sir Chameleon
Your tail's at risk
bright Basilisk
Is this the right road
happy Horned Toad

You look like your mama
Mwanza Agama

Two Blocks, Mommy,
can I ride 'round two please?
My fourth birthday Bob-O-Cycle out,
I'm ready for new territory.
Was it a nod or "okay" made me
think it was a go-ahead?

Push, pull, push, pull,
up, down, up, down, I bob
on my seat along the dirt street,
past Jimmy's house and
across the second-long street
of our little town.

Oh, Look! Slide, swings—
here's the school!
Climb! Whoosh! Climb up,
slide down—three times!
Legs out, legs in I start to swing
again and again, 'til I fly

higher and higher and
catch a glimpse of
my home, that big
brick hotel over there.
Slow down, jump out,
and run back to the slide.

I'm at the top when a big boy
rides up, leans his bike
against the schoolyard fence.
"Hey, Sylvia, your Dad's looking
for you!" Uh-O! Trouble!
Not safe to stop and enjoy.

Push pull, push pull,
up down, up down I hurry
back toward home.
Two blocks is long.
Mommy's waiting on the porch.
"Wait 'til your Daddy gets here!"

SYLVIA NELSON CLARKE

Winter of My Life

When snowflakes show up
on my head,
and cold seeps deep in
to my bones,
it's harder to rise
from my bed
and learn to deal with
these "smart" phones,
I guess it's the Winter of my life.

I often awake
with some pain
or really don't sleep
well at all.
I no longer dance
in the rain
or walk without care
lest I fall.
This comes with the Winter of my life?

But make no mistake:
I still love;
a warm heart inside
still beats strong.
I smile at cooing
of a dove
and often break out
into song.
So what if it's Winter in my life!

A slower pace now
is just great—
More time to enjoy
what I've missed:
Listen to children
laugh, debate,
Appreciate just
being kissed—
These gifts in the Winter of my life.

Wounded Bird

I have a guilt groove in my gizzard
into which I often fall;
I carry rocks inside my crop
that weigh me down or form a wall.
How can I fill that groove so deep
where I continue sliding in?
Could those useless rocks I keep
stop me from distrustful sin?
No! Only the Maker, I've found,
can heal that groove, remove the rocks.
He gently lifts me from the ground
and breathes love in me when He talks.
"Remember, Child, I took your guilt
and paid for it with my own blood."
So I no longer need to wilt:
Let praises flow out like a flood!

The Waiting Room

She sat in the straight wooden chair in the tiny office, reading her book without noticing. When the clock on the table chimed the eleventh hour, she closed her book, checked her wristwatch and walked out the door, letting it slam behind her.

Startled by the loud sound, the sleeping, old man, sitting in the corner, jumped up, pointed his walking came at the door and screamed, "Step one foot in here! You're a dead man!"

"Sir," the nurse said, as she touched his arm. "It's only the door."

Turning to his wife, he said, "Let's go home."

DEBORAH DYBOWSKI

dismal (haiku)

dim, dark and dismal
expanse for hope diminished
without a window

Summer

Summer
Picnics
under shady trees
invite hungry ants to dine,
watermelon seeds

DEBORAH DYBOWSKI

Morning's come (tanka)

Appreciate life,
all that it has to offer,
for there's good and bad.
Find the good and cherish it.
Let the bad wither away.

Last

All along it was a fever,
a dreadful burning inside;
too hot to handle,
but, too hard to let go.
Clinging with total strength,
she held on;
hoping to make it right,
Straining to maintain control
or all would be lost forever
'til it was.
Time ran out.
No more to be done.
No more strength to give.
Lost in a sea of water
all that she had,
would ever have;
gone for all time.
No more hugs and giggles.
No more tickling toes.
No more snuggles at bedtime.
Where would she go?

TESOROS DE CUENTOS AT CASA BLANCA PUBLIC LIBRARY

Led by Frances J. Vasquez and Rose Y. Monge

My First Guitar

It was 1957 and I was 10 years old and in the fifth grade, when we moved to Emerald St. Our new house was right behind the Casa Blanca Elementary School. We now had new neighbors. There were kids across the street, up the street and down the street. As a kid I was excited!

One of our new neighbors was Richard Maldonado. He was tall and handsome, *muy guapo*! My mom and dad became friends with Richard and his wife, Lupe, whose family lived across the street. Richard could play the guitar and sing. He was great! I just gazed at how he held his fingers on the guitar neck and moved them around, back and forth, like a tarantula crawling up and down the neck. He made that guitar sing! He sounded like he should be on TV, he was good!

I knew right there and then, "I wanted to play the guitar and sing!" Not like him, but like Elvis!

I asked my mom for a guitar and she said "Ok, but you will have so some work around the yard. I will make a list and when you are done we will get you a guitar."

"Great!" I started working pulling weeds, mowing the grass, trimming trees, trimming bushes, watering the plants, raking leaves, painting old furniture, etc., etc., etc. Every day for weeks. It seemed like two months. Maybe it was one month, because both my parents got paid once a month. Finally, my mom and dad came home with a guitar. It was beautiful! It was dark on the edges and lighter in the center. Not too big and not a guitar made for kids. Like Goldilocks "It was just right!"

I started to strum it over and over. It sounded great! But after a while it got out of tune and it didn't sound good. In fact, it sounded bad!

Robert, my new friend across the street, got a guitar too and his brother, Arthur, could tune up our guitars. So, together we started playing the guitar. Our friend, Henry from down the street, also got a guitar. Now we were a trio! Man, when we all got together holding our guitars, we looked great!

I bought some books and charts to read. I learned and practiced with them. Soon, I was able to play some songs. But the guitar books had old songs like the cowboys used to sing. Songs like "Home, Home On The Range," "Sweet Clementine" and "My Bonnie Lies Over The Ocean." Who wants to play that? Not me! I want to play Rock n Roll!

So I, as self-appointed leader of this trio, picked up a record by The Frogmen called "Underwater." It was an instrumental. All guitars. I learned all the parts, the rhythm, the bass and the lead. I played the lead. I taught Robert the rhythm and Henry the bass. And when we played all our parts together, "it was magic!" We sounded just like the song, "Underwater" by The Frogmen! I was amazed!

That's how a band works. By each person playing his part!

Those were the days. Kids having fun, learning to play the guitar. Each day was new. Each day we learned something. We never knew what the next day would bring. Who could imagine, that this experience, years later, would lead to forming the band **The Emperors!**

DORALBA HARMON

¿Milagro? O Simplemente Fe Y Fortaleza?

Naci en Colombia el 19 de diciembre de 1939 y fui la primera hija de mi padres y el más Preciado regálo de Navidad llegaron siete hermanos y hermanas a enriquecer mi vida. Cuando tenia yo más o menos 13 años de edad—y a pesar de que nadie en mi casa leia—llego a mis manos un libro *El Poder Del Pensamiento Tenaz* de Norman Vincent Peale. Lei que mi destino estaba totalmente en mis manos y que a travez de mi mente, tenia control total de mi vida. Me parecio incredible y hasta absurdo pero entre más leia, más razonable y maravilloso me parecia.

Termine creyendo en él totalmente y mi madre continuo comprandome los libros del autor que se anunciaban en la ultima pagina del libro. Creci y segui comprando libros acerca del mismo tema, que he leido con mucha fe y passion durante 65 años sin parar. Hoy tengo dos clubs de lectura, este es el unico tema que tratamos, pero que incluye muchas facetas. A continuacion, les contaré una de las tragedias más traumaticas, y a la vez la lección que me ha dejado la experiencia más maravillosa de mi vida.

Vivia en Puerto Rico con mi hijo y una tarde a las 6:30 p.m. Sali a la esquina a comprar leche y deje a mi hijo de seiz años en su cama, pero sin cobijarse porque era verano. Al regresar, y querer abrir la puerta del edificio, senti que alguien puso un objeto en mi espalda. Un hombre dijo, "Habra y no grite porque este revolver tiene silenciador y la mato de inmediato. ¿Quien esta en su apartamento?" Él pregunto. "Mi esposo." Respondi, tratando de amedrentarlo. "Siga," ordeno. El abrir la puerta del apartamento fue uno de los momentos más dificiles para mi. Se iba a dar cuenta el bandido de que solo mi niño estaba ahi, y que al verlo a mi hijo, se pondria a gritar y entonces nos haria daño a los dos.

Al llegar a la cama vi que mi hijo se habia cubierto de pies a cabeza. El bandido vio solo un bulto. Me tomo del brazo y me saco a la calle donde otro hombre lo esperaba en un carro. Me quitaron una bufanda que tenia yo al cuello, me vendadon los ojos y me tiraron al suelo en la parte trascera del carro. No sé por cuanto manejaron y al detenerse el carro, me saco y me llevo a una casa destartalada y sola. Me quito la venda de los ojos. Pude ver que habia un solo hombre. Trato de violarme, pero gracias a Dios no logro tener una erección. Después de molestarme sexualmente, de un brazo me saco otra vez al carro.

Yo crei que me iba a dejar en cualquier parte de la ciudad, pero lo que hizo fue sentarse al volante, sacar su revolver y decirme, "Esto es para que no me chotee." Disparo trés veces a boca de jarro y yo recibi las trés balas en mi estómago. Él arrancó en su carro, y yo cai al suelo. Trate de levantarme, pero no pude porque mi pierna izquierda pesaba como si fuera de cemento.

A mi lado derecho habia un matorral y a la distancia podia yo ver edificios y pense arrastrarme hasta alli para pedir ayuda. Luego pense que el esfuerzo haria que me desangrara más rapidamente y sin alcanzar mi meta. La carretera en donde estaba no era pavimentada, pero aun asi decidi arrastrarme a traves de ella porque a lo lejos veia luces y carros que cruzaban. Al poco tiempo, cai en un charco de agua y me senti muy bien, porque dentro de mi sentia un fuerte ardor como fuego. Me voltie de espaldas y mirando al cielo dije, "Dios mio, si en tus manos esta que muera, así sera, pero lucharé por vivir porque tengo un hijo que me necesita."

De repente óigo las sirena de una ambulancia y entonces dije, "Gracias, gracias Dios mio." Los paramedicos me ponen en una Camilla, se suben a la ambulancia y empiezan a preguntar: "¿Quien hizo esto? Porque? Lo conoce? Coopere, Señora." Y todavia en el hospital seguian preguntando, hasta que les dije que no fueran estupidos, que él que trató de asesinarme no se había identificado. Y, por caridad les pedí que fueran a ayudar a mi hijo de seiz años. Más tarde me enteré de que nunca fueron a buscarlo.

Me anastesciaron para operarme y sacar las balas entre en coma durante trés semanas. Al despertar inmediatamente llega a mi mente la imagen de mi hijo. *¡Quiero hablar! ¡Quiero gritar! ¡Qui-*

ero saber como esta mi hijo! Pero en mi boca hay un aparato que me impide hablar. Quise bajarme de esa cama, correr y averiguar como esta mi hijo, pero no me puedo mover y mis brazos estan atados al barandal de la cama. Tengo sondas por todas partes y entonces muevo mis brazos tan fuerte como puedo para hacer ruido y llamar la atención.

Aparece una enfermera, que al mirarme tuvo que ver la desesperación en mis ojos y dijo, "Voy a llamar al medico." Llego el medico y dijo, "Voy a sacarle lo que tiene en la boca." Lo hicieron, y trate de hablar para preguntar por mi hijo, pero no salio de mi boca ningun sonido. Me desamarraron la mano derecha y me trajeron lapiz y papel. Anote el nombre y teléfono de mi ex-marido. Lo llamaron y cuando llego al hospital, lo primero que me dijo fue que mi hijo estaba bien y con la esposa de su socio. Yo quedé feliz. No me importaba nada más y me volvio el alma al cuerpo. Vino una enfermera a limpiarme y pude ver que mis intestinos estaban afuera en una bolsa plastica para su cicatrización. Los medicos tuvieron que botar la mitad de ellos, porque las trés balas fueron recibidas en el estómago. Luego vino el medico y me dijo, "Siento mucho decirle Señora, pero usted no podra volver a caminar, porque los nervios de su pierna izquierda estan completamente atrofiados." A lo cual yo le respondi: "Respeto su opinion, doctor. Usted es el professional, pero no la comparto. Yo voy a caminar. No se como, ni cuando, pero lo voy a hacer porque tengo un hijo que me necesita y no precisamente invalida."

El doctor salio del cuarto sin decir una sola palabra y probablemente pensando, pobre mujer no quiere aceptar la realidad. Si hubiese habido más gente alli, seguramente hubiesen pensado, *¿Quien se cree esta mujer que es? Dios, que puede hacer Milagros?* Durante mi estadia en el hospital nunca me quisieron hacer terápia a pesar de mis suplicas, porque el doctor no lo ordenaba. Sali del hospital y pedi la opinion de otros tres medicos, he implore que me hicieran terápia, pero todos al mirar las radiografias y la historia clinica, decian lo mismo: "Usted no podra volver a caminar. Acepte la realidad, Señora." A lo cual yo respondia, "No lo acepto porque esta no es mi realidad."

Desde el primer dia que el medico en el hospital me explico la situacion, yo empece a visualizarme, con la misma fe, pasion y emosion de 25 años atras, cuando decidi creer en el poder de mi mente, y en que yo podia controlar mi vida. Me veia corriendo, jugando en el parque con mi hijo, patinando, esquiando en las montañas, nadando y bailando que ha sido siempre uno de mis mayores placeres en la vida. Daba gracias a Dios y al universo, porque para mi lo que veia en mi mente era real.

EL MILAGRO SE HIZO. Me tomo dos años y medio en sillsa de ruedas, caminando con muletas y más tarde con un bastón, pero nunca perdi la fe de que lo lograria y hoy estoy convencida de que este es el secreto—Creer que puedes. Ahora comprenderan porque de una experiencia tan traumatica, pude aprender la leccion más maravillosa de mi vida. Antes solo por fe creia en el poder de mi mente y Fortaleza interior. Ahora creo por conviccion, he vivido una realidad, que aunque escrita con sangre, fortalecio mi fe en la capacidad de mi mente y en el inagotable potencial de mi Fortaleza interior. Sumado esto a mi actitud cien por ciento positiva, he logrado hacer de mi vida un Eden lleno de Paz, Armonia y Felicidad. Pude comprobar en lo más profundo del invierno, que habia en mi un invensible verano—que nada, ni nadie logrará nunca perturbar. Asi me ciento maravillosamente imperfecta y escandalosamente feliz.

Como Las Tragedias Nos Pueden Traer Bendiciones

He perdido a mi hijo, mi único hijo y quiero desahogarme escribiendo, expresando lo que siento, porque lo que llevo dentro me carcome el alma y destroza el corazón. Soy consciente de que no lo lograre, porque no hay palabras en ningún idioma que puedan expresar el dolor, la desesperación, la angustia, la rabia y la impotencia para entender porque se fue.

Es ley de la naturaleza que yo me vaya primero. Solo puedo decir que no hay tragedia mayor que una mujer pueda vivir en la tierra, esta es la única en mi vida que me ha tirado al suelo, revolcado en el polvo y hecho comer tierra. Mi desasosiego era tal, que no podía estar sentada o acostada, solo caminaba dando golpes en las paredes, gritando, llorando, maldiciendo contra Dios y el mundo entero. No comía, ni dormía hasta que el cansancio y la debilidad me tumbaban por cortos periodos de tiempo y entonces despertaba a vivir el mismo infierno.

En diez días quede convertida en un esqueleto humano; tuve que ir al médico y por primera vez en mi vida tome tranquilizantes y pastillas para dormir. Decidí irme a Cuernavaca a buscar el apoyo de mi hermano, y llore durante todo el viaje. Llegue a casa de mi hermano llorando. Me desahogue con él y su esposa, y los dos me acogieron con amor y compartieron mi dolor. En ningún momento dijeron una palabra, lo cual agradecí. No existe una palabra en ningún idioma que pueda brindar consuelo o amortiguar el dolor. En un momento así, todas las palabras suenan huecas, vacías y hasta ofensivas.

Mi hijo había sido secuestrado en Santo Domingo y una amiga suya me llamo para decirme que hacia tres días que había desaparecido. Empecé a prepararme con el efectivo para una recompensa, pero nunca nadie llamo a pedirla. El investigador privado que busque, me dijo que seguramente estaban esperando que todo se calmara. Yo empecé a hacer lo que siempre hago en momentos difíciles, visualizar mi anhelo hecho realidad y dar gracias.

No deje de trabajar, pero todo el día entre cliente y cliente en mi trabajo de vendedora de muebles, ahí estaba yo meditando y orando. Lo veía en casa de mi hermano en Cuernavaca, porque eran los planes que teníamos. Me visualizaba bailando con él; compartiendo con todos en el comedor y conversando acerca de nuestra filosofía de vida que era igual. En ese avión llendo a Cuernavaca, llore tanto porque sabía que mi hijo no me estaría esperando en el aeropuerto—ni en ningún otro lugar del mundo—como lo hicimos antes tantas veces en nuestros viajes. No recibiría más sus bellas tarjetas de día de madres, de cumpleaños, de navidad, de día de las secretarias, de aniversario. Y otras para simplemente decirme, estoy pensando en ti mami y te quiero hasta el cielo, o gracias porque tu amor y tu dolor me dieron la vida, o gracias por las nalgadas legalmente merecidas, o gracias por ser como eres. Podría pasar días recordado sus mensajes de amor y agradecimiento.

Durante mes y medio estuve orando y visualizando a mi hijo que regresaba bien a mi lado y con una fe y una certeza tan grande que así seria, que en mí no cabía ni la más mínima duda. Con esta técnica de la fe, yo ya había vivido un milagro. Así que cuando supe la realidad, el golpe fue tan fuerte, que poco falto para que me destruyera. Pedía a Dios con toda mi alma la locura, porque así no tendría que enfrentar la realidad. Las pastillas para dormir y los tranquilizantes empezaron a hacer su efecto. Así que al lograr un poco de calma empecé a analizar y me dije: "¿Y ahora qué?" No voy a suicidarme porque de cobarde no tengo un pelo, no voy a vivir amargada el resto de mi vida porque simplemente no lo acepto. Yo nací para ser feliz. ¿Qué me queda entonces? Aprender a vivir sin él y sin amarguras de ninguna índole. Y como a estas alturas del paseo [tenia 69 años], ya tengo un poco de control mental y emocional, la paz y armonía empezó a llegar a mi corazón.

Otro tipo de milagro se realizó. Invitaron a mi hermano a una gran fiesta. Él me dijo, "Vamos," yo le dije "No estoy para fiestas."

Él me dijo "Tienes que empezar a vivir hermana." Así que fuimos y al poco rato de estar en el salón, me puse a pensar que mi hijo debería de estar allí bailando conmigo. Me salí al jardín a llorar, al rato mi hermano me encontró, yo no podía parar de llorar. Al fin lo logre y regresamos al salón. Al poco rato ya estaba bailando. Le dije, "¿Que hace que no podía contener mi llanto y ahora estoy bailando?"

Esto fue mes y medio después de su partida y fue la última vez que llore. Así que como el ave fénix que se levanta de las cenizas, abre sus alas y remonta el vuelo en busca de nuevos horizontes, yo me levante del suelo. Abrí las puertas de mi corazón y un caudal de ternura y amor se desbordo hacia los seres más necesitados. El dolor vivido hizo estremecer las fibras más sensibles de mi corazón para poder ver y sentir el dolor ajeno.

Buscando a quien dar y ayudar, encontré niños huérfanos con hambre de amor y pan. Encontre una mujer con cuatro hijos inválidos viviendo de las limosnas, y un grupo de inválidos— necesitados de una mano amiga que les ayudara a recorrer el difícil camino de la vida con sus cuerpos quebrantados. Y fue sublime el descubrir que al querer yo dar y ayudar, fui yo quien más recibió. Mi dolor y amargura se tornaron en felicidad, porque con lo poco que daba podía hacer una diferencia enorme en sus vidas. El amor y agradecimiento que recibo, trae más bendiciones y alegría a mi vida.   Hoy entiendo que esta es la verdadera felicidad, sale de lo más profundo de mi corazón y nunca nadie me la podrá arrebatar. La felicidad que brindan las cosas materiales, viajes, joyas, casas lujosas, son placeres que van y vienen. Esta otra felicidad es la única riqueza que me llevo al dejar este planeta y ni los alti-bajos de la bolsa en N.Y., la pueden tocar. El haber descubierto esto se lo debo a la partida de mi hijo. No digo muerte porque no creo en la muerte. Para mi es simplemente un cambio de vida. Él ha de estar feliz al ver como su madre se prepara deliciosas limonadas de los limones que le da la vida. Pude verificar una vez mas y que siempre después de la tempestad viene la calma y en lo más oscuro y profundo del invierno, comprobar otra vez, que hay en mi un invencible verano.

Hablando de Actitud

Acabo de cumplir mis 79 años de edad y soy inmensamente feliz, con una felicidad, real, intensa y duradera que sale de lo más profundo de mi Corazón, mi alma y mi mente. Es una felicidad muy distinta de la que proviene de las cosas materiales—de tener mucho dinero, que es lo que la mayoria de la gente entiende por felicidad. En mi opinion, es un eror, porque si fuese asi, no moririan tantos millonarios por sobre dosis de drogas.

Mi felicidad proviene de mi alma, porque soy capaz de apreciar y agradecer en su justo valor tantas bendiciones. Proviene de mi alrededor y de mi Corazón porque soy capaz de dar y compartir todos esos dones y bendiciones recibidos. Y, proviene de mi mente, porque a traves del maravilloso don de Creer que tengo en mis manos, el poder de dirigir mi vida como yo quiera y la madurez suficiente para hacer de ella la major obra de arte de mi existencia.

Al envejecer, no siento que mi cuerpo se encoge—al contrario—crece, a travez de las multiples experiencias vividas durante casi ocho decadas. Experiencias tan maravillosas algunas, como intensas y tragicas otras, pero estas ultimas son precisamente las que despues de tirarme al suelo, revolcarme en el polvo y hacerme comer tierra, sacaron a flote la inagotable Fortaleza que hay en mi. El dolor transforma el egoismo en amor y por eso hoy, en vez de decir, "¿Porque me pasa esto a mi, Dios mio?" Quiero decir que puedo hacer por los demas aprovechando mis vivencias de dolor, tragedia y felicidad. Si no fuse porque he pasado 66 años de mi vida leyendo libros hacerca del poder de la mente, imposible me fuse vivir una vida tan rica y plena, sin Dolores de ninguna indole, ni fisicos y de los otros... no estres, no amarguras, no envidias, no miedos, no frustraciones—con plena confianza, paz, amor y serenidad y asi me visualizo a mis 100 años de edad. Los años vividos me han traido madurez y seguridad, cambiaron la incertidumbre por la experiencia. Me gusta sentir que las cosas que antes me atemorizaban, ahora me resultan familiares. Ya no me averguenza admitir mi ignorancia y preguntar lo que no se. Me identifico con la frase de Socrates: "Solo se que nada se."

Tengo una mente habierta y puedo escuchar sin escandalizarme, ideas opuestas a las mias y respetarlas sin aceptarlas. Habia cosas a las que me parecia imposible poder sobrevivir, pero ahora que he sobrevivido a mas de una tragedia en mi vida, he podido comprobar que despues de un infierno de tristeza surge la paz y la felicidad. Que siempre tras la tempestad viene la calma y en lo mas crudo del invierno aprendi al fin, que habia en mi un invencible verano.

Puede ser que mis 79 hayan llegado con algunas canas y hasta arrugas incipientes en mi piel, pero como no es exactamente ni el color del pelo o la textura de la piel, lo que define la felicidad, mientras no se me arrugue el alma, y mi mente siga ansiosa por aprender, viajando por todo el mundo, conociendo tantas culturas y disfrutando tantas maravillas, bailando donde quiera que voy y compartiendo mis ideas. A mis 100 años de edad, sere joven, sana y escandalosamente feliz.

Mi futuro en este presente es tan maravilloso que disfruto intensamente cada dia como si fuese el ultimo de mi vida. Aqui me identifico con Amado Nervo cuando dijo: "Muy cerca de mi ocaso yo te bendigo vida, porque veo al final de mi camino que yo fui el arquitecto de mi propio destino. Cuando plante rosales, coseche siempre rosas. Ame y fui amada, el sol acaricio mi faz."

VIDA NADA ME DEBES…. VIDA ESTAMOS EN PAZ. Y feliz ascenderá mi alma a otro nivel de conciencia, porque vivi plena y intensamente y sin remordimientos porque mis erores me dejaron grandes enseñanzas, y mis aciertos grandes satisfacciones.

Musings about Mental Health Empowerment in Riverside

I was thrilled to be there. It was the *Alternatives Conference* of 2016 in San Diego. The conference was originally organized in 1985 by people with mental health challenges who were advocating alternative views on mental health issues. This was my second *Alternatives* conference. Usually, I am unable to attend, so I was trying to take in everything. A woman sitting next to me looked around, then looked at me and said in a hushed voice, "I don't want to share this with most people here, but I'm a social worker. I understand the anger at mental health workers, but we're not all bad. I'm also a peer."

I guess some people might find that amusing or perplexing, but to me it underscored some of the reasons for the conference. There is some animosity between peers and people who work in mental health. When peers call themselves survivors, they often mean they are survivors of the mental health system. Stigma and lack of understanding is found among more than a few clinicians. But most of them really want their clients and patients to get better and have better lives. Still, it's hard for people, including professional or families without these challenges to truly understand, even for the so-called minor mental health challenges like depression and anxiety. Some say, "If they just tried harder. Everyone gets depressed. Everyone gets scared."

Have you ever lost a loved one? Do you know how it feels those first few days when the shock wears off for a few minutes and the indescribable despair and hopelessness overtakes you? That's what depression often feels like. I know about half a dozen people who ended their lives. They all struggled with "just depression."

I have been involved in mental health empowerment in Riverside for several years. *Peer* is the word we use to refer to people with mental health challenges, people with interrupted lives. People with mental health challenges have been misunderstood, ridiculed, and persecuted throughout history, but have also been responsible for some of the world's most extraordinary creations as the advocacy group-Icarus reminds us. I had been teaching a class to train people with mental health challenges to become peer support specialists for ten years, only stopping a few months before the conference.

Peers are wounded healers with an insider's perspective, trying to help other peers who are early in their recovery journey. They are reframing their experiences; reconnecting with themselves and significant others; finding meaning and purpose; and expanding their sense of possibility.

People become peers for different reasons. Some have been struggling all their lives since childhood or adolescence, some since infancy. Some had very successful lives, until some tragedy blew them out of the water. Others were on the verge of starting careers or families when they were sidelined by illness, trauma, or life.

The mental health empowerment movement is all about people learning to reclaim their lives after major emotional devastation and upheaval. I have worked with very different kinds of people who sought answers in different quarters. But they were all hurting with lives that fell apart. Some had been in prison, some had lived on the street, some had been in gangs, and some were ex-Nazis. Others were proper and straight-laced, but for one reason or another their lives fell apart. When peers came to my classes or workshops, they were in a different place. They were risking to hope again.

I often run into former students at various places around town. Sometimes out of nowhere, as I am picking bananas at Trader Joe's, someone grabs me and gives me a huge bear hug. A bit startled, I stare at the grinning hugger, trying to remember. "Hi. Do you remember me? I was one of your students. I wanted you to know that I have been working for several years now as a mental health peer support specialist. I'm a success. Thank you." Their success is very gratifying to me. Some have returned to school and gotten their degrees, even advanced degrees.

But some are still struggling, but not giving up. They tell me they haven't forgotten what they learned in class about self-acceptance, hope, and redemption. "Even though I have done things in my life I'm not proud of," some tell me, "you taught me not to give up and that I still have something to offer."

Peer support is difficult work. It is more of an art than a science. People in emotional distress need love, support, and community. Their stories need to be heard without judgment and other people's agendas. Like everyone else, they also need adequate healthcare, a decent home, good schools, and meaningful jobs. It is not rocket science.

Although I am not teaching politics in college anymore, I like to think that over the ten years, I have taught over 1,000 students. I continue making a difference in some people's lives. I know they certainly made a difference in mine.

Victorio Mendoza—My Grandfather

My grandfather on my father's side of my family was named Victorio Mendoza. He was a small man about 5 ft. 6 inches tall. He was of Mexican blood: Indian and Spanish mix. He was born in the Mexican state of Michoacán. Michoacán was at the time populated by the Tarascan nation of Indians. I was told that in Mexico, he was a merchant by trade.

At the time when he left Mexico, the Mexican Revolution of the early 1900s was just beginning. He wanted no part of it.

I heard different stories about how he came to California. In one story he paid 5 cents to enter into the United States. In another story he crossed the border by working on the railroad. Either way, he finally settled in the city of Riverside. He made trips to the city of Anaheim for whatever reason. I think he met my Grandmother Lala there before they married. He purchased property on Evans Street near the Santa Fe Railroad line, which included a house where he and my Grandmother lived and raised a Family. They lived at that address the rest of their lives.

My Grandfather was quite a businessman. He bought a storefront on Madison Street in which he operated a grocery store for over 50 years. He also rented part of the storefront to the U.S. Post Office. Additionally, he rented another part of the building for a barbershop.

He also ran a nightclub for a short time in the city of Colton. It was called the club 66 or 99. He also bought several houses on Evans Street in Casa Blanca, which, at first, he rented to his three sons. All of his Family at one time had their First homes on Evans Street. Grandfather was a hard worker. He worked every day from 7 a.m. in the morning to 7 p.m. at night.

My Grandfather had two Daughters. My Aunt Mary (Santos) was the oldest of the Family. And my Aunt Annie was the youngest of the Family. He had another Daughter named Ruth, who died in an accident at an early age—about five years old.

Along with his three Daughters he also had three Sons. Milton was the oldest, my Father Morris, and my Uncle Tony was the youngest. I think I had heard that my Grandfather had two other Sons, who died in the influenza epidemic of the early 1900s.

I do not want to forget my Grandmother Lala, his lifelong wife. She stood with him in good times and in bad times.

Susie Sanchez My Friend

I have been taking Holy Communion to Susie Sanchez, an old friend of mine for a number of years, as she is wheelchair bound, now.

I got to know Susie by attending 5:30 p.m. Mass at St. Anthony's Catholic Church in Casa Blanca a long time ago when my kids were altar servers.

Susie Sanchez is a former Casa Blanca resident who turned 100 years old last December 2017. Susie should be remembered as a champion for her beloved St. Anthony's Church. She was the God Daughter of Angelita Castro Wells, one of the founders of St. Anthony's Church.

During her life time Susie helped raise funds for the Church which included a yearly Fiesta. At one point in time when the building plans for a new Church in Casa Blanca were being developed, no bell tower was included in the design plans, even though the church had a bell. So, she along with Mr. Theo Medina organized a second church fiesta to raise funds to build the church's bell tower.

Because Susie would always ask people for money for her Church and the Priest, people would call her the beggar woman, but, I would refer to her as a Lady of Charity. When she could drive, she would visit the sick in their homes. She also collected food to feed the hungry, and help the poor. Growing up during the Great Depression, she personally experienced what it's like to be hungry. Yes, Susie is quite a Christian Woman. She would often say that she was not perfect. But maybe without her knowing it, she was helping to make her parish and the ministries of St. Anthony's of Casa Blanca a better place for the community.

Susie can no longer get out to go to Church services. It makes her sad and sometimes angry that she cannot fight for her Church and some of its changes, but, she still prays the Rosary, and she holds it up in her hands and says with emotion, "This is powerful!" I would only wish that she finds peace in her heart and mind. I know God loves her and Susie will be in His arms one day.

A Time to Dance

Yoli, stop fidgeting, and stand still, Mami admonishes me. I can't help myself for I am so excited. Next week, I'll be dancing in the Fiestas Patrias in front of the entire town of Agua Prieta. Well, maybe not the entire town but lots of people. The Fiestas Patrias, or Mexico's Independence Day, is the biggest holiday next to Christmas and the celebration is a community affair.

Almost done, m'ija... pacienca, I just need to pin the hem on the dress, Mami says. We can't afford the colorful "chinas poblanas"— the traditional sequined dancing ensemble, so Mami improvises by making ours out of sturdy, durable crepe paper—the type used for paper flowers sold in fiestas. Her trusty foot-pedal Singer sewing machine will make the interfacing out of cloth. She will spend hours hand-stitching it to the delicate crepe paper. My dress is scarlet red and older sister Trini's dress is vibrant yellow.

Trini is nonchalant since she danced last year in the fiesta. At the time, you begin school at 6 years old in Mexico. Why can't I go to school with Trini, I beg Mami. You're too young, m'ija. I see Trini getting dressed in the morning, picking up her little wooden chair and walking to the school 4 blocks away. Every day she tells how fun it is to draw and paint and have a little garden all her own. I beg and whine every morning and I just don't understand why I have to wait. Once, I try sneaking out and follow Trini but the teachers send me home. After weeks of tantrums, Mami informs me that I can go to school with my sister. I jump for joy! How did that happen? Mami tells me that if Trini will supervise me, I can attend if I behave.

As expected, Trini throws a fit. I promise her that I won't give her any problems. Eventually, she accepts it since we're never in the same classroom. The school is actually a large department store building which was donated by a businessman who left Mexico to live in Douglas, Arizona. The school has six classrooms on the first floor. Each of the six classrooms represents a grade level. The second floor is used for storage of some kind.

We have a month to get ready for the fiesta. Our teacher asks us to raise our hand if we know what the national dance of Mexico is. Nobody raises their hands. Have any of you heard of the *Jarabe Tapatío*, she asks. Everybody raises their hand. Niños, she tells us with a smile, the *Jarabe Tapatío*, is the national dance of Mexico. Do any of you know the steps for the dance? Again, nobody raises their hand. Well, niños by September 16, all of you will be professional *Jarabe Tapatío dancers*! Everyone claps their hands in delight. Practice during lunch she tells us and see if your parents will help you in the evening.

I can't wait to practice! Trini is dancing *La Raspa* which seems to be a much easier dance but she's willing to give me a few pointers. We try to get my brother Javier to be our partner but he would have nothing to do with us. Baby Rodo is a toddler and not much help but he giggles and stomps his legs as Trini and I twirl and sway away. Sometimes, Mami and Papi join in the fun by spinning us around and dancing to the music on the radio.

The big day arrives! The plaza in front of the Catholic Church looks magical with papel picado strung from tree to tree with shiny lights peeking through. There's an electric energy from the food stands offering savory offerings. Hungry children and parents line up to buy tamales, carne asada, tacos, grilled corn, churros and other tasty treats. I'm starving but don't dare eat a bite since I'm too excited while carrying my dress gingerly with both hands.

My dress is fragile and can damage easily, so Trini and I wait until the last minute to change inside the church. I love my beautiful frock! My blouse has two layers of ruffles; a full wide skirt with a bottom ruffle. I stand as still as I can, waiting to get on stage. They finally announce our class to come forward. I'm giddy as I twirl my skirt to-and-fro dancing the *Jarabe Tapatío*. It's a long dance and my chubby legs are getting wobbly. Loud applause greets us getting off the raised platform.

And now, I can relax. Papi buys us tacos and horchata (a re-freshing sweet rice and cinnamon beverage). We gather around a wooden bench to enjoy the performers. Soon, my tummy is full and I'm content. The evening ends with fireworks which leave me breathless. The vivid, fiery lights punctuated by thunderous booms illuminate the plaza sporadically. Cascades of sulfur-coated ashes trickle down the plaza. When I get home, I can't sleep, reliving the day's events.

The next day, Mami finds burn singe marks on our outfits which find new life as paper flowers for the family altar and as memen-tos of my dancing debut. Sadly, this is my only 16th of September, or Mexico's Independence Day, celebration and Mami has no oc-casion again to make us those fabulous crepe paper dresses.

A Time to Work

Where am I? I'm groggy and disoriented. I yawn; struggle to stretch my arms but the pain is horrible. Why does every bone on my body throb out in pain? And then I remember. The first day of picking is always the worst. I feel like I've been flattened by a cement truck. Every step I take is excruciating but I know that in time my body will adjust. Looking around me, I realize this railroad box car is our home for the summer. I sit on the edge of the makeshift bed made from wooden pallets with assorted blankets used as mattresses. The rustic beds are lined up against the walls and take up the entire expanse of the box car. It's still dark outside. The aroma of percolating coffee permeates the tiny living quarters giving me a shot of adrenaline.

At the far end of the cubicle sectioned as the "kitchen," Mami cooks oatmeal on the two-burner Coleman propane stove for our morning breakfast. Brothers Javier and Rodolfo bundled up from head to toe, snore in unison. Older sister Trini tends to baby Magdalena who is cooing incoherently. I step gingerly around the pallets and head over to help Mami with the morning chores. Buenos días, m'ija. Did you sleep well? I mumble something about my body hurting. Please cut up the potatoes for me, she tells me. I oblige in silence and then sauté the potatoes with green onions and eggs on the other burner of the stove. Afterwards, I spoon the potato filling inside the flour tortilla, rolling it tightly with a sheet of wax paper. I place them in paper sacks for us to eat later for lunch.

I hear a car door slam outside. It's Papi who's always awake before everyone getting his old trusty Ford station wagon in running order. He steps inside. He smiles at Mami and tells her he's ready for a cup of coffee. Mami lovingly brings him the steaming cup as Papi kisses her on the cheek. A few minutes later, brothers Javier and Rodolfo are wide awake and rush out stepping over each other on their way to the port-a- potty. It's always a competition of who's going to get there first. Once we have breakfast, we're ready to go, for we sleep in our work clothes for extra warmth and to speed up our morning ritual before heading to the fields or orchards. A bowl or cup of oatmeal blended with evaporated milk, water and a little sugar is our usual breakfast. I savor the warm and sweet concoction, knowing it would be hours before we eat again. Rays of sunshine trickle inside the box car and it's time to leave. A plastic crate holds our burritos, jugs of water and oranges, bananas or apples to snack on during the day. The boys jump into to the back of the car while Trini and I take the middle seats. Papi takes the drivers' seat as Mami holds Magdalena on her lap. Another grueling work day is ahead of us as I open the window and feel the crispness of the Fresno morning. Little did I know then that a similar morning scene would be repeated over the years in the migrant circuit.

What is it about the migrant years that makes me feel nostalgic? I don't miss the aches and pains of picking figs, grapes or plums, or living in tents, abandoned barns or dilapidated box cars. But in spite of this, something extraordinary happens. It's the only time where life is simple, uncomplicated and I feel safe as long as the family's together. We hurt, sweat and laugh together.

Often the aroma of home-made tortillas connects me to my migrant years. I close my eyes and I see Mami in front of a make-shift pit or comal forming the flour tortillas into shape in the evening coolness. Papi holds court with the other camp fathers reminiscing about his life in Mexico. They in turn share their stories uttering occasional profanities which embarrasses Mami. Trini and I stay close to Mami keeping an eye on our brothers. The camp kids read comic books, play jacks, jump rope or chase each other under the twilight stars. It makes the daily toil tolerable.

Would I change anything? In hindsight, yes. I should have listened more carefully to Papi's stories and written down Mami's recipes. When I tell stories about the migrant work to the five siblings who are born in the United States, they look at me with wide-eyed wonder. They are too young to remember. The five of us who are born in Mexico and experience it, will never forget.

A Time to Say Good-bye

The classroom is tingling with anticipation. All eyes are fixed upon the clock that is slowing ticking off the seconds: 5, 4, 3, 2, and then 1. The school bell mingles with the explosion of celebratory yells and laughter as the students make a bee-line towards the narrow door. Mrs. Byrd, my 7th grade teacher sighs audibly and tells the kids to have a great summer. I doubt if anyone hears her. It's the end of another school year at Jurupa Jr. High.

I back away from the commotion. For me, school has always been my refuge. Leaving Mrs. Byrd saddens me for she has made this year so special. She's more than my Language Arts teacher for she takes me under her wings and showers me with kindness. She's beautiful with her short, dark, curly hair and blue eyes reminding me of Elizabeth Taylor. She never gets flustered even when the kids get rowdy. All she needs is her stern "teacher" look followed by her warm, friendly smile to keep them in line.

In a few days, I will be in Fresno with the family picking figs in the sweltering heat. No, I don't want to leave. I want a few more moments with Mrs. Byrd to say good-bye and thank her for her gentle guidance throughout the year. You don't have to stay to help me today, she says. I'll be coming back tomorrow to clean up the classroom. Dad won't be here for a while and I already have cleaned my locker, I respond. Ok, she answers but let sit down and visit. Would you like a Sno-Ball? My mouth starts watering.

Mrs. Byrd sometimes rewards me with oranges, apples and sweet treats when I clean the blackboard, straighten out the desks and stack books on the bookcases after school. But the best treat is the occasional Hostess Sno Balls! The pink, round, spongy, marsh-mellowy, cream-filled, chocolate confections are delicious. She opens one of the drawers from her desk and takes out the cellophane-wrapped treat. She hands it to me and takes another for herself. I thank her and she asks me to bring a chair next to her desk.

Go ahead and eat, she tells me. As I savor the gooey treat, my mind drifts back to the beginning of my first year in junior high. Things are much easier in elementary school with only one teacher. Here, having six classes with six different teachers is intimidating. I try to be invisible and keep pretty much to myself. My sister Mary doesn't have any classes with me but we get together at lunch to eat our brown-bag lunches away from the cafeteria. She's always been more gregarious so she's not fazed by her schedule.

Some people come into your life for a reason. Early in the school year as I wait outside the library for Dad to pick us up, Mrs. Byrd stops by and invites me to wait in her classroom to get out of the heat. I walk beside her as she speaks. You're doing very well in my class, Rosie, she tells me. Thank you, I respond. You are an excellent student but you're very quiet and don't volunteer much, she adds. What can I say? She's right. She notices my silence. Do you like your other classes, she asks. I don't like P.E and Math much, I tell her. But the other classes are ok. What is your favorite class? Yours, I respond quickly. I like learning new words, I add.

She asks questions about my parents, my siblings and stories about the migrant circuit. I detect a sincere interest on her part and from that day forward, being a 7th grader becomes a little easier. As the year continues, we grow comfortable with each other and become friends. I'm having problems distinguishing the **sh** sound from the **ch** sound in English since I hear no difference between them. She drills me with vocabulary words having these sounds. In return, I teach her conversational Spanish.

I look around the classroom for the last time wishing the year could start over. What are your plans for summer, she asks me. I tell her that family leaves in a few days to pick figs in Fresno. I'm also going away for the summer, she says. My husband is being transferred to Lackland Air Force Base in Texas. We leave in a few weeks. I'm stunned. I knew that she wouldn't be my Language Arts teacher next year, but to never see her again is devastating. I assume that I could continue visiting her every once in a while. I begin to tear up unable to speak. She notices my distress and comes around and gives me a big hug. You'll do fine without me, she adds. I hold on to her for a second as Mary comes into the room. Dad is waiting for us, she tells me. I wipe a tear and only whisper *adios* unable to tell her how much I care for her. I leave quietly with Mary but I can still see Mrs. Byrd smiling and waving good-bye to me.

CASA BLANCA EN HUELGA

In Casa Blanca, there are thousands of forgotten, neglected
TESOROS
1946 CASA BLANCA WARD SIX ELECTION
RIVERSIDE, CALIFORNIA POPULATION: 48,228

In the 1940s, the Casa Blanca community was a part of Arlington's Ward Six. During that time, Mr. Jesse Rathgeber was the incumbent Councilman representing Ward Six. He was also a rancher who owned and managed twelve acres of orange groves in his ward. He hired laborers from Casa Blanca to harvest the oranges.

In 1946, Mr. Rathgeber ran for re-election. During that same year, a labor dispute developed between Mr. Rathgeber and his employees from Casa Blanca. Apparently, Mr. Rathgeber and the Casa Blanca orange pickers' representatives were not able to reach a mutually beneficial agreement.

In 1946, the contracted wages for a full box of oranges was 0.7 cents per box. There were some exceptionally fast orange pickers who were able to fill 100 boxes a day—which would earn them $7.00 a day before deductions and taxes. Those pickers were known as cieneros. Despite good-faith negotiations on the part of the pickers, and seeing no other alternative available to them, the orange pickers decided to go on strike.

Huelga

It's not known for how long the strike lasted. Mr. Rathgeber was not a happy man—by taking into account his behavior and vindictive actions. The dispute started as a personal labor issue between Mr. Rathgeber the rancher and the employees. However, Mr.

Rathgeber chose to make the issue political. He tried to use his City of Riverside Ward Six office as a weapon to retaliate against the strikers and punish their families—and all the residents of the Casa Blanca community. He compounded the problem by refusing to attend meetings, or to discuss any other issues regarding the needs and wellbeing of his Ward's constituency in the Casa Blanca community.

By taking that type of negative reaction, Mr. Rathgeber created a much bigger problematic issue—beyond that of a labor dispute in his private business enterprise. He made it personal. The issue was no longer a labor dispute between a rancher and his employees, but one that involved and impacted every single person residing in Casa Blanca.

The residents knew they had a serious problem on their hands. They were very concerned and worried because Casa Blanca did not have a representative in City Hall who supported their causes or who would lobby on their behalf. They had to find a solution. Soon!

In 1946 the Mexican American population in Riverside, like all other Barrios in the Southwest, had very few options available to them. Discrimination towards Mexicans and Blacks was the norm. For example, the Riverside Daily Press Newspaper reported on July 12, 1946, that the Riverside City Council defeated "An ordinance which would have prohibited the display of signs discriminating against race, color or religion.... The ordinance would have prohibited display of the sign 'We cater to white trade only'" Keep in mind this action was just three years after the so-called Zoot Suit Riots of 1943 that began in Los Angeles.

Reflecting on the 75th anniversary of the Zoot Suit Riots, The Riverside Press-Enterprise reported on Saturday, June 2, 2018 with the headline, "THE ZOOT SUIT RIOTS OF 1943 MARK A DARK PERIOD IN SOUTHERN CALIFORNIA HISTORY: SOME EXPERTS SEE PARALLELS TO TODAY'S ANTI-IMMIGRATION SENTIMENTS."

Back in the 1940s, war was raging in Europe and the United States entered World War II after the bombing of Pearl Harbor,

Hawaii. During this period in Germany, Adolf Hitler had his "Brown Shirts," the S.S., and the Gestapo, who arrested people and killed with impunity anyone who did not support the Nazis. In addition, he had his "good German Nazi citizens" to terrorize their victims and separate mothers from their babies, and other inhumane acts that only deviant monsters are capable of committing.

Is Nazi History Repeating?

In 2017 and 2018 in the U.S., Trump has his "Green Shirts" KKK, Neo-Nazis, Skinheads, racist rednecks, Red Caps, the invisible "white pointed hats" and other Trump "good, honorable Christian citizens" who sanction and justify the inhumane policies of the Trump administration of separating children from their mothers and putting children in cages in Federal detention centers (prisons). Their justification of these policies is that they are enforcing the law.

There are no laws that allow for the abuse and torture of children. Those justifications are similar to the ones used by the Nazis in 1946 before people were executed for crimes against humanity. Never forget that evil men will always lie to justify atrocities. Evil will triumph while good men do nothing.

Belltown

Back to the 1940s—to Belltown, an unincorporated Riverside Barrio of predominantly Black and Mexican residents—and about ten miles from Casa Blanca, the residents were having problems with the Riverside Unified School District. Residents were concerned about the District's discriminatory and unfair policies regarding the distribution of school funds. They needed advice and they needed it quickly.

Somehow, they were able to contact Mr. Fred Ross, a legendary community organizer from Los Angeles. They persuaded him to come to Belltown to help organize for community action. Mr. Ross agreed and helped the residents of Belltown to resolve their concerns regarding the unfair school funding issues with the school district.

As the wind blows, apparently somebody from el Barrio Casa Blanca spoke with Mr. Ross regarding their problems with the orange grower's unfair labor practices and low wages. They also talked to him about their councilman's intentional neglect of his civic responsibilities to his Casa Blanca constituents.

Fred Ross took interest in their concerns and went to Casa Blanca to meet with a group of community leaders. After a speaking with them, he found that the people were very upset with Councilman Rathgeber and were anxious to dump him. Fred Ross explained to the group about the importance of the BALANCE OF POWER.

Ward Six City Council Election

Fred Ross learned that it was an election year in Casa Blanca's Ward Six. He went to the Registrar of Voters office and counted the number of registered voters with Spanish surnames. He discovered that less than ten percent of Mexican names were registered in Casa Blanca's Precincts 59 and 60.

Promptly, Fred Ross engaged Mr. Mabra Madden, Principal of the Casa Blanca Elementary School, and Mr. Joe Park, Commander of Casa Blanca American Legion Post (who also worked as a supervisor at the Arlington Packinghouse known as La Prenda where many Casa Blanca men and women were employed). He also engaged Mrs. Lillyus Stowers, President of the Casa Blanca Operation Bootstraps Committee, Mrs. Georgetta White and Mrs. Belen Reyes, President of the Casa Blanca Unity League, Mrs. E. L. Vargas, Mrs. Mattie Ponder, and others whose names were not recorded in history.

The concerned citizens understood the urgency of the situation and decided to immediately organize a voter registration drive in Casa Blanca. *Note: to be eligible to vote in 1946, a person had to be at least 21 years old—born in 1925 or before. A person born in 1925 would be 93 years old in 2018.

Mr. Park's American Legionnaires and other people spread out throughout the Barrio, knocking on every door enticing and explaining to residents how important this election was for Casa Blanca. Everybody already knew about the registration drive and was anxiously waiting to register to vote. Most of the people welcomed the help they were getting to register. However, as it happens with some people, there are always those who are negative and declined to register—they will use any pretext not to get involved. **They do not comprehend that when there is a problem, the worst thing they can do, is to do nothing.**

The plan was: if the people all threw their votes one way that is the way the election would go. On Monday, 16 de September 1946, a meeting was held to ensure that everything was in order. Casa Blanca was ready and anxiously anticipated the arrival of their most deserved triumph.

On Tuesday, September 17, 1946, el Barrio Casa Blanca was alive with excitement. There was much movement. Mr. Parks, as always was energetic and enthusiastic—driving on all the streets del Barrio in his truck with speakers installed on top of the roof. Joe Park was blaring out enticing, encouraging words to the people to come out and vote. Casa Blanca walked or drove to their Precinct 59 polling place at the Casa Blanca Elementary School located at 3020 Madison Street—the same school that was a result of unified community action taken 34 years earlier when in July 11, 1911 two Casa Blanca women delivered a petition to the school board signed by eighty residents to demand that the Riverside School District erect a neighborhood school in Casa Blanca for their children—another recorded historically victorious event.

Never before or after the 1911 school board petition had Casa Blancans experienced such stimulation by creating a huge turnout of united people, putting aside their personal differences and grudges—acting only in the best interests of their beloved Barrio Casa Blanca. By doing the right thing. By working together.

The Balance of Power

As planned, Casa Blanca voted in one solid bloc. All voted for Mr. Rathgeber's opponent, **Mr. Zollie Hair**. After the voting was completed and the polling places closed, the only thing left to do was wait for the final tabulation of the votes.

At the beginning, Rathgeber held the lead throughout the early returns. His supporters and people from the other precincts were cheering and felt sure that Mr. Rathgeber was going to win re-election.

Then, the last returns started to come in from Casa Blanca Precincts 59 and 60. Gradually, but steadily, Mr. Zollie started to catch up. When all the Ward Six Precinct votes were counted, the final tabulation totaled **244** (Zollie = 193 votes; Rathgeber = 47 votes). The total for all Ward Six Precincts: Zollie = 665; Rathgeber = 602. Zollie Hair won the election by 63 votes.

In the Ward Six election of 1946, of all the precincts, Casa Blanca's Precinct 59 polled the heaviest, thus earning Casa Blanca the distinction of holding the BALANCE OF POWER in determining the election results.

Commitment, tenacity, unity, hard work, wisdom, and respect for Casa Blanca, will always produce fruitful rewards.

Casa Blanca's success in stopping Mr. Rathgeber's re-election for the Ward Six City Council seat was a huge victory for Casa Blanca. On September 26 at the next Council meeting following the soured loser's defeat, Mr. Rathgeber announced that he was going to challenge the results of Casa Blanca Precinct 59 votes.

Riverside Mayor Walter Davidson and City Clerk Albert Mills informed Rathgeber that it would be necessary for him to file suit in the County court. He never filed! Perhaps he did not want to suffer another defeat at the hands of **Casa Blanca's organizing power**—SI SE PUDO <> SI SE PUEDE!

1950 Casa Blanca—Four Years After the 1946 Election

Between the years of 1946 and 1950, Casa Blanca was very active working on various community improvement projects. Since its establishment in the late 1800s, Casa Blanca has suffered from discrimination and neglect by elected members of the Riverside

City Council.

Several civic groups emerged before and after the victorious election in 1946. There was the Casa Blanca Welfare League and its offshoot, the Casa Blanca Health Council with Peter Vargas as President. The Casa Blanca Unity League led by President Belen Reyes advocated for their students.

The very active American Legion Post was led by Joe Park (of which everyone was a member) and Mrs. Lillyus Stowers' Operation Bootstraps Association. These two groups were responsible for organizing petitions in Casa Blanca to present to the City for infrastructure improvements like sewers and paved streets. Until 1950, every home in Casa Blanca still had an outhouse—there was no other alternative.

While most of the city's residents enjoyed the right to have sewer lines connected to their homes and paved, lighted streets and sidewalks, Casa Blanca taxpaying residents suffered from not having the rightful comforts others enjoyed. In the years from 1945 to 1950, Mrs. Stowers' Operation Bootstraps Association—in collaboration with Joe Park's American Legion Post—together stirred a successful renovation spirit in Casa Blanca.

Casa Blanca 1950 Population: 46,764

In the 1950 Riverside City Council election for the Sixth Ward, defeated ex-councilman Jesse Rathgeber for the past four years could not accept the fact that he had been defeated in 1946 by the people del Barrio Casa Blanca (who voted for his opponent, then current Councilman, Mr. Zollie Hair). After four long years of enduring the suffering of his humiliating defeat in 1946 at the hands of the Casa Blanca residents, Rathgeber decided to enter the race again for the seat of Ward Six in the 1950 City Council election. He was confident that this time, with a new and better campaign strategy, he would be able to defeat Mr. Hair and the people of Casa Blanca.

When the people of Casa Blanca heard the news that a possible new campaign against Mr. Rathgeber was probable, they knew that a hard struggle lay ahead. The residents of Casa Blanca's Precinct 59—including all the other nine precincts of Ward Six—understood the seriousness of the announced message. The resilient people of Casa Blanca had other ideas and got ready to meet the challenge. Drawing from their experience of the 1946 campaign (even without the advice of Mr. Fred Ross), they knew what they had to do.

Once again, the Casa Blanca community mobilized the AMERICAN LEGION POST headed by Mr. Joe Park, Mr. Mabra Madden, Mr. Leo Baca, Mrs. Lillyus Stowers' OPERATION BOOTSTRAPS, Mrs. Belen Reyes' CASA BLANCA COMMUNITY LEAGUE, Mrs. Pauline de la Hoya, and Mrs. Clara Benzor—they all got busy organizing in the community to get out the vote.

Casa Blanca duplicated the task of four years before in 1946. Multitudes of people went to the Casa Blanca School to cast their votes overwhelmingly for Mr. Hair. Again, Casa Blanca's bloc vote turned the tide in Mr. Hair's favor. The election was very close: **993 for Hair** <> 967 for Rathgeber. ANOTHER GREAT VICTORY FOR CASA BLANCA. VIVA CASA BLANCA! **CASA BLANCA RIFA C/S.**

Mr. Madden's name was frequently mentioned in bad light by Mr. Rathgeber in the Riverside Daily Press Newspaper. Critics who opposed Mr. Hair and Casa Blanca were often bitter in their remarks. On September 20, 1950 in the Riverside Daily Press, Mr. Madden answered his critics, "We may have had in the past many wonderful Councils. But, when those Councils neglect a District as they have neglected Casa Blanca, then it is no wonder the community will vote for the councilman that helps it."

So, beware of strangers bearing shining false gifts!

CINDI NEISINGER

Shicken and Ships

In the evening, before guests arrive, the aroma of hot peppers for salsa being charred on the comal*, wafting through the air making your eyes water and grabbing your throat till you cough.

Later, I hear my mother yell from the kitchen, "Put the ships and salsa on the table, Mija. The Shicken is almost ready." I wouldn't dare correct her accent. Would you? The chancla** is real, people! She greets a distant great aunt/tia at the door. Hugs and more hugs, then our beautiful Spanish language flows from both women. That's when it happens…. I greet her with "Pleasure to meet you." Then the look! My mother looking very embarrassed, looks at me, then her, and sheepishly explains "*No habla Español.*"

Speaking more or less, Spanish does not measure how Mexican I am. I am proud to be of Mexican heritage. Recently, at a book fair, I had a conversation with an author of a bilingual children's book. I told him about a book I want to write, the genre, woman's fiction. The protagonist is a proud Mexican/American woman. Not unique, but she is not bilingual. What? She doesn't speak Spanish. In my story she shows the conundrum of losing our mother language. And there are many of us. I am proud to be American, but, with much love and loyalty, I still incorporate traditions to honor my Mexican heritage.

I am a second-generation American, my uncles and cousins have served in the Armed Forces and pledged to serve and protect our great country. As a child, my divorced mother worked long hours in her beauty shop called Dorita's Hair Fashions. We lived in a suburban area of San Gabriel Valley and I was submerged

---

* *Comal: A flat surface cooking grill used for charring and heating spices and peppers and heating tortillas.*
** *Chancla: A flip-flop used by a Mexican female to discipline their child or husband for doing or saying something that angers her.*

into an American/Anglo culture. Sometimes my friends would invite me to dinner and strangely, served bread and butter in the middle of the table. No Tortillas!

The mother language disappeared for me around this time. I can show you an exact timeline of this unfortunate loss. My grandparents one from Spain, one from Mexico, both spoke only Spanish, but they were well-educated and had what America is built on: huge entrepreneurial spirits. After coming to America, they became dual citizens, during the Great Depression. Soon after their arrival they opened a neighborhood market in the Los Angeles area. They saved and lived frugally, even making undergarments out of flour sacks that were boiled to make the material softer, then grandmother would add lace that was sewn on for a cute trim. A few years later, the government proclaimed Eminent Domain on their property and they read in the newspaper of plans for something called a "Freeway" that would be going through their market and surrounding areas to make transportation faster. (Faster? Well, if they only knew in the future about the 91 Freeway? LoL!)

This so-called progress was a huge blow. However, with the money the government offered, it was possible to purchase another market and two houses. A blessing in disguise.... With their good fortune and money saved, they prospered, paid their taxes and thrived. Also, helping the community with running tabs for food, when money and jobs were scarce, until the war was over. They lived with the ideals of the American dream for which our country was founded on.

They had five children, my loving Mother Dora, the youngest, Aunt Helen, Aunt Patty, Aunt Mary and my hero Uncle Ray—who served in the Army—fighting with his comrades in the Battle of Normandy, forcing the Germans to retreat into France. All of them graduated from Garfield High school in Los Angeles, and were bilingual.

My mother, married and had her first child, my older Sister Isabel, who only spoke Spanish until she entered elementary school, learning English there and becoming bilingual. I was born as my sister entered elementary school. Sadly, around this time, my parents divorced and my mother brought Spanish-speaking babysitters/nannies from Mexico to take care of us while she worked.

Here is where things change and the mother language was lost for me…. From the time I was born, my big sis Isabel *translated* for me!

At school, we were only allowed to speak English. Spanish wasn't an option. At home my sister translated with the nannies. English became my primary language. The neighborhood I lived in was mostly Caucasian. Soon, I was a "Coconut." Brown on the outside and white on the inside! As a teen, I listened to rock n roll and wore the styles of that generation: bellbottoms, wallabees, cords, fringe vest. Also, sometimes with cousins, I would cruise Whittier Boulevard in a low rider and listen to oldies. Then with friends, cruise Valley Boulevard in a high rise, souped-up GTO. Very confusing time, "Stairway to Heaven" vs. "I do love you." But, at home, we always had tortillas, beans and large servings of Spanglish. We still had traditions of making tamales before Christmas with the family setup like an assembly line. I had worked my way up to masa spreader, with the back of a tablespoon, I carefully pressed the thick masa on the wet corn husk. If I didn't do it right it was returned. Another tradition and home comfort food that was anticipated yearly… was the smell of cinnamon and a warm Capirotada (bread pudding) during the Lenten season—always served with a cup of hot Ibarra Mexican Chocolate. My brother and I would go looking for that sugary round bar and eat it, when we could find it. Good food memories… love.

Being a Mexican/American that doesn't speak Spanish is frowned on at times by our own culture. Sometimes rudely. There is a slang word used, "pocha*" meaning Americanized with very limited Spanish. I recall a situation at work when a customer looked at me for help to translate for her. I said, "I don't speak Spanish." She responded in Spanish, "*eres demasiada morena para no hablar Español!*" Translation: "You are too brown not speak to Spanish!"

---

* *Pocha: Stereotypically, is a Latina that speaks English and lacks fluency in Spanish.*

Because I wanted to keep my job.... I didn't reply. Although I wanted to ask, "Why don't you learn English?" Also, at home during holidays, sometimes with visitors and relatives, *that look...* they give you when you say *"poquito Spanish."* Then, my mother sadly, starts to apologize for not teaching me properly. And just recently at a Museum Gala, a handsome, distinguished Hispanic gentleman walked up to me with a big smile, (I'm single so I was trying to remember my flirty skills) telling me in Spanish that I remind him of a famous singer, ... soon his smile disappeared, as I said, *"No hablo muy bien Español."* That look again! Ugh! No hook-up there.

That author with a bilingual children's book, told me that when he does promotions in Mexico, it is frowned upon if you don't speak proper Spanish. My mom agrees with this and gave me an instance of this happening to her. She is bilingual, but while visiting family in Mexico. She said, *"Voy a agarrar un bus."* in Spanish it means, "I'm going to catch a bus," but the correct way to say this is *"Voy a tomar un bus."* "I'm going to take a bus." Family laughed at her improper language skills and gently explained that she just said she was going to catch a bus the way you catch a ball. Even she was a victim to the *fluency police.*

Recently, I was taken aback by the many responses I received when I posted my feelings about this subject on my FB page. I deleted it because I thought it was still too taboo. But, the stubborn Latina, Chingona that I am! I reposted it! And I waited. Soon I heard from many, with similar and validating experiences. Yes, I think we all agree.

My conclusion is that fluency of language does not define you in ethnicity or race. It is not a measurement of how Mexican we are. I rightfully proclaim my Mexican heritage and roots! Spanish Lesson: Soy orgullosa de ser Mexicana! (I am proud to be Mexican!).

I Remember

During the summer of 2018, I attended the second half of the Casa Blanca Tesoros de Cuentos Writing Program. I was very excited! I looked forward to attending these sessions in the coming weeks at the Salvador J. Lara Casa Blanca Library. I learned writing skills and how to input my story on a computer. I was also happy to see Frances and Rosa and my writing friends again after a short break. One of the prompts given in class was to write about childhood memories living in Casa Blanca. Here are some of my stories.

I remember Grandma Lupe babysitting us cousins at her home on Railroad Street in Casa Blanca. She was patient and caring, and her delicious mole, caldo de pollo and homemade flour tortillas were the best I ever ate. The flavor and the aroma of her tortillas will stay with me forever. She grew a variety of plants in her herbal garden: chamomile, mint, cilantro, oregano, and rue—herbs that she used for healing teas and in her dishes.

I remember Grandpa Zeferino tending his vegetable garden where he grew chiles, corn, tomatoes, and nopales. I shared pencas from the nopal with my other cousins and my sister. He also grew fruit trees, including apples, plums, peaches, figs, and apricots. The fruit was delicious—organic: no pesticides and fresh. Both Grandma and Grandpa had a chicken coop where they raised different types of hens and roosters for eggs and chicken soup and mole.

I remember Grandpa attending night school to learn English and U.S. History to become a U.S. Citizen. I am proud that he attained his citizenship after working hard all day, picking oranges. Growing up in Casa Blanca was an enriching experience. What makes Casa Blanca so unique is the people who live there. Now, I am impressed by the diverse cultures of the people who lived there growing up: Mexican, Japanese, Italian, and Black. Some of the residents have either moved away or attended college to better themselves and some have returned to our community.

One of my most vivid memories is the Victoria Packing House. I remember the aroma of the oranges as my older sister, Evangeline and I walked to Casa Blanca Elementary School along the railroad tracks. Some of the labor workers would throw us an orange or two. During recess at school, we ate those sweet-tasting oranges. The sounds coming from the packing house engines and sorting machines were very loud. I'm sure it affected the hearing of the packing house workers.

Grace Bailon—Casa Blanca's Beloved Librarian

Grace Bailon was the first librarian in Casa Blanca and served for 35 years from 1957 to 1992. I was five years old when I first met Grace. She was very strict, and I was afraid of her, but she had a kind face so my fear of her quickly went away. I was fascinated by the way she read stories to those of us who could not read yet. The following year, I was in first grade at Casa Blanca Elementary School and was taught to read by Mrs. Jean Grier.

Learning to read was one of my valued treasures. I loved going every day to the library located on Madison Street, the main street in Casa Blanca. And… it was just around the corner from my house on Peters Street! Grace taught me to put life in my words as I read and to change voices for different characters in the story. She was my mentor. She encouraged me and hundreds of others to read constantly, to continue our education, and to go to college. She always said "Leer Es Poder" which translated to English means "Reading is Power." She always made me feel special over the years, and we became great friends.

Grace was originally from San Bernardino but eventually made Casa Blanca her home. She was named Grace because she was born on Thanksgiving Day. Like myself, she was blessed with only one child. His name was Espee and I went to school with him. Grace always had a way with children but I wanted to be a teacher, not a librarian. I used to gather the neighborhood kids to play school almost daily with me. Our recess was held in the back yard of my Granma who lived next door to me. We had swings and a tetherball pole and ball. We would drag boxes around pretending they were wagons. Both boys and girls played together with jacks, marbles and hopscotch.

With Grace's encouragement, I was able to travel to places by reading. I could never go to these places in "real life" such as India, England, Spain, etc. I loved to read to the neighborhood kids and

I pretended to be Grace when I read.

During high school, I became interested in *New Age* books. I always wanted to know everything and was very open-minded. Grace used to set these books aside just for me. She would call me to let me know when a new book came in. She taught me how to take care of my books, not to tear or fold the pages and to respect books as treasures. I always cherished the books which I purchased with my own money and re-read each one every year. Even though I now have hundreds of books, I don't read as much as I used to. I lost my concentration due to a major depression, but I still read every day.

After my daughter Erika was born, I took her regularly to the library. When Erika was four years old, she received her first library card from Grace. Erika even signed the card herself. She attended first grade at Washington Elementary School and her teacher was Mr. Yeager. She would have attended Casa Blanca Elementary School but the school was burned down by arson in the 1960s.

One day when I was in my 20s, Grace left me an important phone message. She had recommended me to the Riverside Unified School District as a preschool teacher. The district needed a bilingual teacher. I was still attending Riverside City College, now Community College, majoring in the Early Childhood Education Program. I was trying to realize my dream of becoming a teacher. Grace convinced the RUSD that I was the perfect candidate. I was completely bilingual and as a special bonus, I was born and raised in Casa Blanca. Everyone in Casa Blanca knows and loves me.

I went to the job interview feeling quite nervous because I hadn't finished the program at RCC and also, I was a divorcee with a two-year old daughter. Grace encouraged me with these words: "Sí Se Puede" which In English means "Yes You Can." I love Grace very much and she has become a true friend.

Over the past year, I started a petition to rename the Casa Blanca Library Garden in Grace's honor before we lose her. I am trying to get the people of Casa Blanca to recognize her as a valuable contribution to this community. I plan to submit the petition to the City of Riverside and the Main Library. I am both saddened and angered that this library was not named for Grace Bailon.

God is Love

GOD. Who is GOD? GOD is LOVE. I prefer to call GOD, LOVE. God is neither male nor female, but Spirit. LOVE.... just is.

Now, I really understand what the singer Marvin Gaye meant when he wrote the song "God is Love." It was through my relationship with Marvin Gaye's music that I became more aware of LOVE. LOVE spoke to me through Marvin's music. Finally, I returned to LOVE, after being sooo lost in the darkness of this world. I thought LOVE had forgotten me and deserted me, but LOVE was always with me in the darkness, all along... LOVE dwells in my heart. LOVE will never abandon me, not ever!

The Indians spoke of THE GREAT SPIRIT, whom we call GOD. They knew who they were speaking of. LOVE is spirit and is always available to ALL. I don't believe in the devil. I know evil exists in the world because of man. Man invented the devil to have someone to blame for the evil they do in order to avoid taking responsibility for their own sins. LOVE aka GOD does not punish us. It is sin that is its own Punishment.

FRANCES J. VÁSQUEZ

Teachings of La Nana Pancha

Two hundred years before Christ a Nahuatl-speaking culture... In their magic books, 'the picture books' the Náhua recorded the sacred happenings... folded sheets of paper made from the bark of the amatl, a wild fig tree, or from deerskin or maguey.

~ Toni de Gerez, Author and Librarian

Breaking news—The Department of Antiquities at the University of México City announced a major archaeological discovery. On September 9, 2066, acclaimed professor of archaeology Marcos Hernández Vásquez announced the discovery of three ancient pre-historic scrolls, called *Amoxtli*, securely sealed inside a large pre-Náhua era ceramic jar. Archaeologists, anthropologists and historians of Mesoamerican studies from around the world expressed their delight about this unprecedented discovery. Scientists are eager to conduct basic research on the new discoveries of the ancient civilizations that settled in Mesoamerica prior to the magnificent Olmeca and Náhua cultures.

The large four-foot tall by three-foot wide, exquisitely hand-crafted ceramic jar was uncovered in the wall of a subterranean chamber in Teotihuacan between the Pyramid of the Moon and the Pyramid of the Sun along the Avenue of the Dead. The massive earthquake that struck México City in March 2066 exposed an opening to the tunnel leading to the discovery of the chamber. Professor Hernández Vásquez was thrilled to report that scientific testing of the *Amoxtli* scrolls using Instrumental Neutron Activation Analysis authenticated them to be over 4500 years old and made of *Amatl* fiber, the processed bark of a fig tree native to a region the *Náhua* called *Tlatilco*, a place that flourished along the banks of long-extinct Lake Texcoco in the Valle de los Mexica.

The Hernández Vásquez research team determined the provenance of the ancient jar is also from *Tlatilco* and is at least 4500 years old. Renowned scholar of ancient languages, Natalie Dunham Hernández deciphered the exquisitely written glyphs inscribed on the well-preserved *amatl* scrolls. All three *Amoxtli* are written in a hieroglyphic-type language remarkably similar to the *Nahuatl* language of the Náhua civilization that ensued over 3000 years later. She has meticulously transcribed one of the *Amoxtli* scrolls, and named it *Ichtaca Providencia I*—Providence Reference Book I. The ancient scroll explained previously unknown historical facts of the matriarchal Tlatilco civilization and revealed secrets of their mysterious migration patterns in the Western Hemisphere. Maestra Dunham Hernández' transcript of the *Ichtaca Providencia I* scroll describes the traditional matrilineal teachings of a *Tlatilco* grandmother named Pancha to her young granddaughter, named Nelli. Below is a transcript of the Dunham Hernández *Ichtaca Providencia I* scroll:

Beloved granddaughter, flesh of my flesh. My adored necklace of precious stones, as your old *Cihtli*, the nana who nurtures you, I implore you to pay attention. Now that you, Nelli are a bright seven-year-old *cihuaton*—a little woman—Listen carefully, for it is my duty to teach you the ways of our ancestors. For, in just two years you shall proceed to the *Telpochalli* education center soon after your ninth birthday. There, you will be given instruction on basic *Tlatilco* history, arts and culture.

Now listen! You are a cherished tesoro. You are green jade, our most precious treasure, a gift from Mother Earth. You are my color—the rich hue of la tierra. Your inheritance is derived from the majestic legacies of celestial deities and magnificent tribu Mexicatl.

Nelli, you are noble. You are precious. You are of the stars. Your ancestors are magical people endowed with wisdom, artistry, and sharp intellect. You will learn their wise teachings as recorded on the revered *amoxtli* texts— our official sources of learning.

You must learn by heart about who and what you/we are—and memorize the stories of our origins; how we, the Mexicatl are endowed with the essence and teachings of magical beings who descended on Mother Earth thousands of moons ago. Our ancestors were an elite celestial tribu who journeyed from the most luminous star in the heavens—*Citlalli Luna*. The mother of all the gods, *Coatlicue* led the expedition with an assembly of the smartest, most knowledgeable scribes, teachers, artists and architects that her heavenly tribe produced.

The *Citlalli Luna* explorers came to *Mexicatl* in peace and friendship as good-will ambassadors. They wanted to learn about our humanity here on Mother Earth. In the spirit of reciprocity, they eagerly shared with the Earthlings their advanced cosmic and spiritual powers, and inherent technical skills. The celestial ambassadors were fantastic craftswomen, revered astronomers, and skilled architectural engineers. The artistas who accompanied them were held in high esteem for their creativity and ability to transport their powerful psychic energy that generated the *focol* of our culture. They taught us to create objects that transmit a vital supernatural force that unites animate beings: humanity, animals, plants, the elements, planets, and the stars. The essence of our origins from *Citlalli Luna* is and shall always be imparted in our people and in our works.

We, the *Mexicatl* learned about the divine inter-connectivity of Tierra Madre with the stars, moons, suns, and planets of the Universe. The *Mexicatl* are a chosen people—blessed by the mother of all gods to be specially selected to learn and safeguard the divine knowledge and wonderful secrets of our genesis from the heavens.

Mija, you are *Citlalli Luna* and *Tlatilco* and *Olmeca*. You must study the divine ways of our ancestors: their teachings and their art. Do not dishonor them. Learn how to be like the diosas, the goddesses. The four most important diosas for you to emulate are: *Ixchel*, the goddess of the earth, moon, and medicine; *Tonalnan*, luminous mother of light; *Citlalli*, a shimmering bright star in the sky; and, *Coatlicue*, grande madre of all the gods. You are noble. You are precious. You are my blood. You are *Citlalli Luna*.

My cherished child, know and understand that you have been shaped by the divine: your noble character and upbringing, and your beautiful visage is a mirror image of *Tonalnan*—bearing the clarity of light. During infancy, from the venerated day you were born, I carefully applied wooden planks on your regal baby head and gradually, week-by-week, month-by-month, I tightened the cords of the planks to shape and form your small, pliable cranium to resemble those of the graceful elongated heads of the original *Citlalli Luna* settlers. For your information and knowledge, graceful adolescent girls, like your Tia Vanesalli, who are destined to be dancers, will have their teeth filed and decorated with precious gems and sea shells to resemble those of the iconic *Citlalli Luna* danza performers.

Education is the key to truth and knowledge.

The first professors of higher education were individually selected by *Coatlicue* herself to help the *Mexicatl* elders develop our excellent schools—the centers of learning for the older youth. The wise professors enhanced our higher education system to instruct the brightest Mexicatl youth. Inspired, the wise elders created sacred *Amoxtli*, literary texts made from *amatl*, the processed bark of a special fig tree that flourishes in our fertile valley. These *amoxtli* texts were used to record important occasions like the death of a queen or king or the birth of a royal child. They recorded the election of a new governor and documented the ceremonies of special events. The elders inscribed sage advice—words of wisdom for our daughters and sons, their parents—all our people.

Hundreds of *amoxtli* were housed in the sacred temples, in the schools, and at the civic centers.

Our *divine Coatlicue* prescribed that the education of children begins in the home where the mothers and fathers teach consejos to their own children and recite Mexicatl moral and spiritual principles for the first seven years of life. Remember, my Nelli, in our advanced culture, to be a well-educated child, you must always be courteous and show respect to your parents, grandparents and all the elders. Now that you have attained seven years, I, Pancha, your loving *Cihtli* will tutor you for the next two years until you reach the age of nine. I will prepare you to advance to the *Telpochalli*, our eminent education centers where you and other clever nine-year old youth will be taught various life skills based on your own personal aptitudes and abilities.

Erudite Mexicatl elders teach that at about the age of nine, it is understood that you will have attained the age of reason, and will therefore have the aptitude and comprehension to attend the *Telpochalli*. There, you will memorize by heart our beautiful ancient hymns and sacred praise songs. You will learn to read the inspired glyphs of words and songs of praise written on large folded pages of *amatl*. You will learn to memorize the special happenings and historical events of our society. You will be given lessons about the meaning of dreams and how to apply the interpretations and ideas imparted by your sueños to help guide your decisions and life choices. You will be taught astronomy and the secrets of the Universe, and how to count the moons and years.

Nelli, at adolescence, only the smartest, enlightened youth shall be promoted to the elite *Colmecac* for specialized higher education. Depending on their aptitude and abilities, these select students will be taught and mentored by the sagest of elders to become caciques, curanderas, teachers and master artistas. With all my heart, I pray that you, my special jade mija, will attain entry to the houses of the *Colmecac* and make your family proud by following in my own chosen profession as a *curandera de patli*, a respected medicine woman, yo tu Nana Pancha.

Remember this! The *caciques*, our high priestesses prophesized and wrote in the divine *Amoxtli*—the sacred sources of learning—that thousands of moons from now, in this verdant valley of Lake Texcoco, our celestial people will give birth to a mighty civilization that shall be called *Náhua*. They will establish an expansive empire that will rule this valley and beyond. We will also give rise to other future enlightened civilizations who will rule in each of the Four Directions: the mystical Maya to the South; the indefatigable Yaqui and tenacious Tarahumara cultures to the North. The colossal Olmeca to the East, and the industrious, artistic Zapoteca to the West. The *caciques* prophesized that these future *Mexicatl* civilizations shall rise and fall like the seasons of our years come and go. They will produce the *yocol*—the fruit of our own madre civilization. The *Cihtli*, our sage grandmothers, were destined to transmit the keys to *Mexicatl* sacred knowledge. The *caciques*, blessed keepers of the cosmic secrets shall inscribe their knowledge in the *Amoxtli* to be kept in the libraries of the acclaimed *Colmecac* School of Philosophy and Theology.

* * *

The Hernández Vásquez research team led by Marcos Hernández Vásquez and Natalie Dunham Hernández plan to convene an international conference of Mesoamerican scholars in 2067 at the University of Ciudad Obregón in Sonora They plan to report on imminent research findings related to the amazing *Amoxtli* scrolls. It is highly anticipated that the other two scrolls will have been transcribed and its findings will be the major topic of scholarly research.

* * *

Glossary of Nahuatl Terms

Amatl	Paper text
Amoxtli	Books as sources
Chalchiuitl	Jade
Cihtli	Grandmother
Cihuaton	Little women
Citlalli	Star
Coatlicue	Mother of gods
Colmecac	Higher education centers
Ichtaca	Secret
Ixchel	Goddess of the earth, moon, and medicine
Metzli	Moon
Mexica	Mexico
Mexicatl	Mexican
Nelli	Truth
Patli	Medicine
Telpochalli	Education centers
Tonalnan	Mother of light
Yocol	Fruit of...

* *Citlalli Luna* means star moon

Frances was inspired to write this short story by an exhibition of Tlatilco artifacts from ancient Mexico, curated by Catharina E. Santasilia, at the Riverside Art Museum in collaboration with Riverside Metropolitan Museum. She thanks Jessica Carrillo of the Colton workshop for reviewing a first draft of this part one of a trilogy in progress.

Civility ~ No Más

Civility's death caught us all off guard. We were shocked! The killers attacked like thieves in the night. We were aware of the frequent assaults by the disgruntled Alt-Right and their adversaries, particularly Fear, Rude, Insolence, and, Misogyny. In the past, Civility prevailed over brazen onslaughts, due in large part to her association with Esprit de Corps and open Dialogue. She flourished by working in the background. Consequently, the brutal, covert assassination of Civility on November 8, 2016 was staggering, and dealt a severe blow to Unity and the nation's collective consciousness.

White Supremacy has taken credit for the demise of Civility. Their horde of assassins has been assured unlimited Coors on tap in Paradise. Their mission is to ply the art of the Rude Deal, and replace Democracy with Authoritarianism as the rule of law. Guardedly, amicable Discourse has gone underground.

Civility is survived and mourned by her loving family: Courtesy, Diplomacy, Grace, Promise, Purpose, Empathy, and Respect. She was the esteemed daughter of Humanity and Intellect. Civility was a model student of Miss Good Manners from the prestigious International School of Respectability, which has established a memorial scholarship in her name.

Civility mattered for proponents of egalitarian incumbents of Democracy's highest civic offices. For consolation, Civilitarians inebriated their stunned bodies with wine and spirits. Any substance at hand was indulged by the grieving offspring of Humanity and Intellect—seeking to dull their anguish, which had gripped their sensibilities.

The Media spawned a generation of News Junkies who reveled in fomenting and Tweeting rude stories, and spinning real news to their own liking. Some Junkies resorted to generating fake news rather than engaging in Civil Discourse. "Civility never existed," proclaimed the Alt-Rude Dealese.

Illustrious Pall bearers solemnly carried Civility's shrouded body into the Temple for a state funeral. These included: Grace, Purpose, Respect, Reason, Hope, and Promise. Social Justice delivered an evocative eulogy that examined in Socratic method, "What was Civility like?" Some posited that she resembled an articulate Libertè. Others imagined her as an eloquent Amazon. A few likened her to Fiat Lux. Ms. Justice commended Civility's affinity for books: Prose, Poetry, Textbooks, and other tomes. Hardbacks, Soft Covers, eBooks and Kindle. Civility wrote brilliantly—Literacy made all the difference—she had mastered the elusive art of persuasive, credible, well-crafted communications. Civility had based her genteel composure and transactions on the teachings of Knowledge and Wisdom—acquired by her prodigious readings, solid education, and adherence to the Golden Rule.

Ms. Justice warned about the sordid implications of Civility's major foes: Fear, Rudeness, Racism, Misogyny, Myopia, Insolence, and the notions of White Supremacy. Buoyed by Hope, she concluded her tribute with a bit of levity and veiled derision by mocking the "Y tu mamá también" movement.

The imminent reincarnation of Civility is highly anticipated by the Moral authority of the world. They eagerly await her return to uplift and illuminate Civil Discourse. Civility's family, friends and allies, meanwhile vow to immortalize Civility and keep her precepts viable by modeling and illustrating how she once reigned supreme in a cultured, civilized society.

Frances wrote this essay after J. David Stevens, "THE DEATH OF THE SHORT STORY" and reviewed in Inlandia's creative writing workshop led by Jo Scott-Coe in Riverside.

FRANCES J. VASQUEZ

Tesoros de Cuentos

The Inland region is enriched with a treasure trove of diverse cultures: the valuable gems in people's customs, traditions, music, cuisine, dance and stories. How do we preserve these tesoros? Inspiration came from Juan Felipe Herrera when he was California State Poet Laureate. During a spirited Unity Poetry event on the Main Street Mall in Riverside, he encouraged an enthused crowd to, "Value our parents' and grandparents' stories... Value your own stories, and most of all, your voices... celebrate your voice when you make enchiladas and tamales. Celebrate your beautiful voices. Share your voices." I was enthused to help the Mexican American community express their beautiful literary voices—their unique experiences. A litany of ideas ruminated in my imagination, as I visualized bilingual, bicultural writing workshops to chronicle the wealth of stories held in the hearts and memories of "our gente".

I recruited Rose Y. Monge, a gifted bilingual memoir teacher to help me facilitate a writing workshop in the Barrio. Together, we developed lesson plans and conducted our cuentos writing group in Casa Blanca. Our goal was to help workshop participants discover their beautiful literary voices.

We conducted a spring six-week series of workshops at the SST. Salvador J. Lara Casa Blanca Library, located in the heart of Riverside's oldest, predominantly Latino neighborhood. This past summer, through special arrangements with the library, we convened in the Mabra Madden Computer Lab for a series of six-weekly workshops that also included lessons in basic computer skills—culminating with their submission of wonderful stories to this anthology.

We encouraged participants to chronicle what life was like, back in the day. We aspired to help them give voice to their unique stories about family, school, and their community. A treasure trove of sweet and sour recollections unraveled as they reflected on abuelitas' favorite dichos: those wise sayings that taught us life lessons. We revisited childhood memories of grandma's delicious tortillas; of days working at grandpa's store; gripping accounts of tragedy and loss and an uplifting journey to happiness (in Spanish); of Casa Blanca's beloved librarian; of a citrus workers' strike that unified the community... and changed everything. These and more stories are shared here.

It took the village of Casa Blanca to give literary voice to the stories that were crafted as a result of our cuentos workshops. Thanks, and appreciation to the Casa Blanca Community Action Group for allowing me time on their meeting agenda to discuss the workshops and invite participation. Gracias del corazón to Anthony Rivera, Morris Mendoza, and Roberto Murillo for their wisdom and support. Thank you to the efficient, friendly staff at SST. Salvador J. Lara Casa Blanca Library for providing a comfortable, welcoming place to learn and write. Heartfelt thanks and gratitude to Daryl Bird who provided expert and patient technical support in the library's Mabra Madden Computer Lab.

We are especially grateful to the Inlandia Institute for a pivotal partnership. Mil gracias to my co-facilitator, Rose Y. Monge (and kindred Sonorense) for her generous contributions. Most of all, special appreciation to the cuentistas who shored up the courage to express their beautiful literary voices. For some in our group, they composed on a computer for the first time. These emerging writers gave much to share—their diligence and tesoros de cuentos (and many more stories waiting to be written). Aplausos to: **Ernie Benzor, Doralba Harmon, Maria Jaquez, Morris F. Mendoza, Roberto Murillo, Cindi Neisinger, Lillian R. Solorio, and Scharlett Stowers Vai.**

Como dice el dicho: "*Las palabras vuelan; los escritos quedan*".

ROWE BRANCH OF THE SAN BERNARDINO PUBLIC LIBRARY

Led by Romaine Washington

From A to Z

"A, B, C, D, E, F..." Recite again. "A, B, C, D, E, F..." Again. "A, B, C, D, E, F..." Over and over and over again, recite until it stops.

She mentally reels off the alphabet to drown out the sounds of the creaking bed as it hits the dented wall of her bedroom. His grunts and groans that sound in her ears fade to background noise as she repeats the letters again. She waits for him to finish, and as always, he kisses her forehead—the way a father tells his daughter goodnight—before whispering a small 'Happy Birthday' and returning back to his room he shares with his wife, her foster mom.

When the silence of the early morning hours hit and she knows he is asleep she slowly gets out of bed. Careful to be quiet, she puts fresh jeans and a T-shirt on and kneels on the floor. She sticks her hand under her bed, rummaging around until she pulls out the suit-case she packed that morning. It holds everything she would need—money, clothes, non-perishable foods, and her iPod that he bought her in request of her silence. This is the night of her eighteenth birthday, the legal mark of freedom—a freedom she intends to take full advantage of—immediately.

* * *

Dust flies in the air when she opens the door to her room at the 'Rose Hill Motel'. What an exciting name, she thinks as she rolls her eyes and drops her bag on the bed in the middle of the room. It isn't much, but it is affordable and safe.

A fresh shower later and she is out walking around and breathing in her new surroundings. The sun is bright and there is a slight spring breeze in the air that lifts her long, crimson hair and lets it flow into her face. There are no flashing lights, no casinos, and no hookers on every corner—just a serene, peaceful, and bird chirping neighborhood with the occasional graphitized wall.

Her eyes dance over a diner called Paul's nearly a block away.

Her stomach growls, which reminds her that she hasn't eaten since dinner last night and she makes a bee-line.

The door opens with an annoying ring when she steps in and she is greeted with a girl's voice calling out, "Take a seat anywhere you can find!" Scarlet glances around the small, worn diner. The walls are painted a bright blue with paint ball like splashes of red, yellow, orange, and green. Though the walls seem like a fresh blast from the past, the floor's linoleum is peeling up and stained and the booths could be redone.

She finds a seat near the back with a menu on the table and opens it. A few moments later Scarlet looks out of the window across from her and tries to take in what she's done. "I'm Kat, what can I get for you?" A girl in her early twenties looks at Scarlet expectantly with the pen clicked open.

Scarlet's eyes flash up from the window to the waitress and she closes the menu. "Just a short stack of pancakes and a water, please."

"I haven't seen you around here before, are you new?"

"Yeah," Scarlet pauses, unsure of what to say before continuing, „I just got here today. I'm looking for a fresh start, somewhere new to be."

The waitress nods. "Nowhere better than Rose Hill for such a mission." She smiles. "I noticed you looking at the ‚for hire‘ sign in the window." Kat nods her head in the direction of the window. "Do you need a job? We're looking for someone." Kat flicks her long, brown hair behind her shoulder and out of her face as her light brown eyes gaze down at Scarlet.

Scarlet scrunches her eyebrows before she realizes that there was, indeed, a 'for hire' sign in the window she had been looking out of. She takes in Kat's expression—the never ceasing smile on her face and the honest to God cheeriness behind it. She isn't used to anyone being so positive and it sets her back for a second. "A job wouldn't hurt. I'm going to have to do something to stay alive." She smiles slightly, a small quirk of her lips.

"I'm Scarlet." Kat's smile grows nearly ten-fold. "After you eat, I'll tell Jed we found someone."

* * *

"How long are you going to stay in that motel," Kat asks as they lock the diner door and step out into the night air.

"I've been thinking about getting a roommate." She shrugs before she continues, "I mean I have a two-bedroom apartment and no roommate, just me." She finishes before they look to cross the street.

Scarlet kicks a rock before she sighs out. "I don't know... I hadn't really thought about it much," she says with a light shrug of her shoulders. "How much would the rent be?" Kat smiles. "Four fifty. It's half. What do you say?" She nudges her shoulder into Scarlet's.

* * *

Scarlet walks in right behind Kat, not two days later. She holds her single duffle bag tight in her hand as she looks around. She lets her mind wander on to the sheer dumb luck she's had since she has arrived.

"Well, this is home sweet home." Kat swings her hands out as if she is holding the whole world in her arms at that very moment, and she is—to Scarlet anyway. Home. Security. No more motels for Scarlet.

By lunch time Kat has managed to show Scarlet every square inch of what she will now call home. The place is decorated in typical Kat fashion—bright colors and everything perfectly organized, not a stray book anywhere. However, even with Kat's wonderful sense of style the walls remain the mandatory white.

"I really appreciate all that you're doing for me. I don't know where I would be if I hadn't met you here. I've never had someone hand me anything and I don't know what else to say other than thank you so much."

"Don't think of it as a hand out, besides, you're doing the dishes," Kat jokes before she playfully punches Scarlet in the arm. "Oh, and my laundry next week!"

Scarlet laughs. "Deal."

A week later the laundry is done and Kat and Scarlet are binging on T.V. Kat turns her attention from the screen to Scarlet. "So, what's up with you? You've been all smile-y and quiet since you got home." She watches Scarlet shake her head and focus on the show. "Oh, come on. Tell me," Kat begs for Scarlet to gush on what has her all happy so suddenly.

Scarlet's lips turn up without her permission and she quickly covers her face with both hands. Kat chants, "Tell me! Tell me! Tell me!" She pokes Scarlet in her ribs.

She moves her hands form her face and turns to Kat and in a single breath tells her, "I met this really, really cute guy at the Laundromat. His name is Adam and he gave me a quarter and he's just really cute! He was, like, tall and had these really nice brown eyes and long brown hair to his shoulders! And he was built! Ah!" She screams and covers her blushing face.

"Did you get his number," Kat yells, excitement making her words squeak.

She drops her hands once again and looks at Kat. "I didn't think about that." She sighs a quiet dammit under her breath.

* * *

Leaves begin to fall from the trees and the wind begins to pick up when Scarlet hurries into work fifteen minutes late. She runs behind the counter to quickly pull on her apron. "I'm sorry I'm late!" Jed calls out from the kitchen, "Don't let it happen again."

Scarlet nods and makes her way to one of her tables. The morning looks as though it's been slow and she figures it's the reason Jed isn't too upset. She's thankful; that is until lunch hour hits and the diner begins to fill and customer demands become more frequent. Her head is spinning as her hand speeds across her note pad writing down each order as soon as she can before rushing it to Jed to fill.

Kat is just as busy, balancing five different plates at once. Both Scarlet and Kat are running around like chickens with their heads cut off. They barely make it out of lunch hour alive and are quick to take their breaks shortly after.

"So why were you late this morning?" Kat asks as she sits next to Scarlet at the counter.

"I would have waited for you but I couldn't. Sorry," she finishes.

Scarlet shakes her head before she takes a sip of Coke. "I just woke up late."

The day passes in a blur and before long it's nearly closing. Chimes from the door fill the diner when a male walks in. Kat wipes down another table before she looks up and smiles at him. "Hey stranger, what're you doing here," she asks.

The man shrugs his shoulder and mimics her smile.

"What? I can't visit my little sister at work?" He sits at the bar counter and spins around once before he turns to look at Kat again but jerks his head behind him when he hears someone yell from the other direction.

"Kat! Where's the mop?!" Scarlet yells while she looks around the back supply closet. She's been looking for nearly ten minutes and there isn't a corner she hasn't looked in already. She places her hands on her hips and sighs. This is stupid! She thinks.

Kat yells back, "It's out here! I already got it!" Scarlet glares at an empty wall before she walks out of the supply closet and back out to the main floor. She stops mid-step when she notices who Kat is talking to. Her mind spins just as fast as she has frozen. What is he doing here? How do they know each other? Oh my God, are they together? ...Kat never mentioned a boyfriend! Is he here to take his quarter back? Wait, wait! Slow down Scarlet. Maybe he's here for a late-night snack... or maybe he's just a friend. Yeah, friend.

Scarlet snaps back into focus when she hears Kat ask her if she's okay. Scarlet shakes her head. "Yeah, yeah, I'm fine." She forces a smile. Kat's eyes squint in concern. "Are you sure? You've been a little off all day."

"Yup, fine." Scarlet keeps the false smile on her lips to keep Kat from pushing further. She switches her view to the man next to Kat and swallows back the worry-lump in her throat. "Adam, right?" She worries her bottom lip between her teeth and scuffles her right foot against the peeling tile of the floor.

He beams a sixty watt smile her way. "Yeah, and you're Scarlet. Nice to see you again," he says, "I didn't know you worked here."

A cheeky grin ghosts over Kat's face as she puts two and two together. Laundromat boy, he must be, Kat laughs to herself.

Scarlet and Adam whip their heads towards her.

"What?" they ask in unison. Kat immediately stops laughing, but keeps her smile.

"Scarlet, Adam is my brother. Adam, Scarlet is my roommate and bestie. As for me, Kat, I am a third wheel here." She prances off with the mop leaving the two of them to stare awkwardly at each other.

* * *

Each day that passes Scarlet worries her lip and bites her nails more. Kat, Adam, and she have bonded quickly in the last few days. Inside jokes run together seamlessly, laughs drown out the sounds of the howling wind, and smiles stretch their lips like taffy. With all that is good, the lip worrying and nail biting should fall back and disappear. Time flies when you're having fun, but it stretches when you have something knotting your stomach.

* * *

The door chimes in the diner as a customer walks through the door, his cologne permeating the air. Oh no! No, no, no! Scarlet shakes her head screaming internally not to let it happen—it happens. Vomit. Vomit everywhere. She feels the burn in the back of her throat as her breakfast slops against the old floors.

Jed forces Scarlet to sit and drink a 7Up until her stomach calms down. He doesn't need customers running out because she killed their appetites. Scarlet feels fine, the smell just caught her by surprise is all. The day flows like any other after that. She feels fine.

* * *

Every day that week is the same. Kat is concerned. Scarlet is scared—she knows what's wrong. Just because she knows what's wrong doesn't mean she wants to admit it. If she admits it, she will get nowhere with Adam, she will get nowhere in her adventure of a happy world. Admitting what's wrong, even to just herself, will mean she will be back where she started. Square one. She denies it until one day she can't button her pants all the way. She stays home that day.

Scarlets stops joking, stops laughing, stops smiling. It's over. Kat pesters her, waiting for answers.

Kat isn't stupid. She notices the lack of disappearing feminine products, the lack of fitting clothes, and the lack of caffeine intake. Kat is sitting next to Scarlet on the couch that night, watching *Family Feud*. Commercials are rolling and Kat mutes the T.V. as she looks at her friend. "Scarlet?"

"Yeah," Scarlet keeps her eyes glued to the screen.

Kat sighs, "You know I know, right?"

A lump builds in Scarlet's throat, as she looks at her. "You know what?" Beads of sweat build across her hairline despite the cool air in the room.

"Have you gone to see a doctor? You both are going to need care," Kat tells her, knowing that she hasn't, in fact, seen a doctor.

Tears line the waterlines of Scarlet's eyes and begin to spill over. She looks away quickly wiping her eyes. She whispers a quiet, "I know." She takes in a deep breath, a weight lifted off her chest. She hadn't realized how it would feel to have someone in on the secret. "I don't know what to do, Kat." Her eyes dart to Kat in hopes that she will have all the answers. The only answer she gets is a tight hug. Tomorrow will be another day with a fresh mind.

* * *

"Hurry up! We're going to be late," Kat shouts through the bedroom door at Scarlet. They are on their way to the salon for a day of beauty. Scarlet has been feeling frumpy with all the weight gain and baggy clothes that Kat decided she needs a day to feel like a girl again instead of some human incubator.

Scarlet is sitting in the chair with a drape wrapped around her neck, accentuating the weight she has gained in her face. She hates it. Rather than focus on the mirror she flips through a magazine when the hairdresser begins. Smooth, cold metal glides along her neck as the stylist slips the hair between the blades of her shears. The snipping sound infiltrates her ears as she feels the lock of hair slip down her back and hit the floor. She feels the comb slide against her scalp, sectioning off her hair. Her heart flutters, the reality of her snap decision registering. She's going to look like someone new, someone ten pounds lighter. She's going to be someone new, someone different. The stylist may be cutting simple strands, but Scarlet is cutting him off. She doesn't need him or her hair. Did she think ten pounds lighter? She meant one hundred sixty-five pounds lighter. Each strand is a string attached to her that he pulled like a puppet master, a string that he used to parade her around with. Each string is severed.

TO BE CONTINUED...

Trifecta

Trail Ride

My horse and I are in the hills
The sun shines hot, releasing the earthy aroma of oiled leather
There are scurrying noises in the near-by chaparral
And the cry of a hawk in the distance.
My spine moves in sync with the horse's back
My horse and I move as one

The Jump

Walking my horse in the wash,
I feel him tense underneath me,
Arching his neck and pricking his ears forward
He is staring at a log; he wants to jump it.
I give him permission, by standing in my stirrups
Leaning over his shoulders, loosening the rein
And squeezing his sides with my legs.
He takes off, not a foot on the ground;
My horse and I take wing.

The Lesson

In the arena, coming down the center line
The instructor says, "leg yield."
This is a movement when the horse goes sideways as well as forward;
He will transverse from the center of the arena to the outside rail.
I lower my weight into my outside seat bone,
Turn the horse's head slightly to the inside,
Tap lightly with my leg by the inside girth.
I feel him lifting himself up and moving to the rail;
My horse and I are dancing.

Remember

Remember the wireless weather station we had?
Remember how it told temperature, humidity and wind
    velocity?
It forecast the weather with icons of suns, clouds, and rain drops.
I don't remember if you brought it home or I did
But you were crazy about it, you would check it several times a
    day
We would argue with the TV weatherman,
based on our weather station.
We took it to the new house when we moved.
Remember we had an argument about where it should go?
We ultimately settled for the front yard
After you died, when I looked at it, I would remember you
And how much you enjoyed it.
Remember the weather station?
It broke a week ago.
I couldn't let go of it until today.

Four Scenes with a Horse

The Gift

"You must leave here," the voice boomed through the canyons and forests in the garden. A man and woman stood under a tree, heads bowed, not looking up. "However, before you leave," the voice said, "I have a gift for you." Out of the flowering meadow stepped a magical creature. His coat was gold like the sun and the hair on his neck and his tail were silver like the moon. He was athletic and graceful, with large liquid kind eyes. The stentorian voice said, "Because of your foolishness, you will now have many burdens. This creature, called a horse, can be useful to you. Be kind to him and he will help you. Now leave." Adam moved to the horse and took up the rope around the horse's neck. With his wife, they left the beautiful valley and stated down the dirt track into the desert.

The Burden

Adam walked between his pregnant wife and the horse, who was now covered in the dust of the road. Adam's head was bowed, his shoulders stooped. His steps were shuffling and his mind slow and sluggish. He felt devoid of light and happiness. He had sinned and now he would pay the price. He was responsible for the feeding and safety of his wife, his coming child and now this stupid horse. What could this horse do?" It was just one more thing he had to take care of, another payment for his sin. The horse matched his steps to the tired man. Then the horse smelled water and gently stepping forward and led the tired group to a spring next to the road, where they all drank their fill. The man began reappraising his attitude toward the horse.

The Respite

Eve was heavily pregnant, tired, sore and unhappy. She did not know how long Adam planned to walk today. They weren't talking much these days. She was not sure how much longer she could go on, and telling him that was sure to bring on another scolding and blaming argument.

She eyed the horse walking beside her. He seemed a mild enough creature as he plodded with them, seemingly content with their company. She looked at his broad back and had an idea.

"Adam, do you think I could climb on the horse's back and he could carry me? We would make much better time if I could." Adam looked at her with dull eyes and said, "Do what you like."

Yet he held the horse, while she got on. They did make better time and Eve, quite liked the view from the horse's back. The concept of riding the horse opened up new possibilities to her.

The Helper

The goats and sheep had broken out of the pen, again. Now, he needed to round them up, stupid creatures. Abel gathered the horse and climbed on his back. He and the horse made quick work of gathering the herds and bringing them back to the homestead. They had developed a partnership in this round-up activity. It had been his parents who had told him how useful the horse could be. Now he would be able to meet his brother and help build the fire for the sacrifice.

Cindi's Question

Was that my Mother's Spirit brushing my back and shoulders
    while I was watching her in the home movies?
MY Answer:
There was a time I wasn't aware

But, we two were one
I was safe in her body
Our hearts beat in rhythm

I could hear her voice
I thought things would never change

But change they did
One became two

Our identities became separate
But the connection stood

She is gone now
But still part of me

I still hear her voice in my head
Smell her perfume in my dreams

Why would she not be here
Touching my hair in memory

Brushing my memories in photographs
Touching my soul with love

Love does not die when people are gone
Love survives in the hearts of those left behind

And sometimes in connections
That defy normality.

Red Lulu

He was in love. He was older now, and had several love affairs behind him, but this was for real and would last a long time. They had been in love for a few years. However, time had not dimmed his fascination with her. She was a beautiful redhead and he called her Red Lulu. They were on an outing today, and had gone to the local county fair, where he could show her off and be proud to be seen with her.

It was a summer day. He could feel the sun on her skin as he ran his hands lightly down her sides. She felt warm and comforting and made him shiver with appreciation.

The scents of popcorn, cotton candy, and meat grilling wafted in in the air. He could practically taste the Philly Cheesesteak, dripping with juice and the cold beer, he would have for lunch.

The shrieks of the losers at the arcade made him grimace, while the yells and laughter of children on the carnival rides in the distance made him smile. The day was ending and the reds and orange of the setting sun shimmered on the pond on the midway, and on her skin, casting a warm glow on her features.

"Well, Lulu, should we go home?" She didn't disagree, so he climbed into the driver's seat of Red Lulu and drove his cherry red '57 Chevrolet home proudly. Patting her on the dashboard he said, "I love you Red Lulu," as "Little Deuce Coupe" played on the radio.

S. J. PERRY

Lazarus

I didn't ask to be brought back to life.
I had made peace with my sickness.
I was just getting used to the idea
that all my suffering was over.

Four days in the tomb, decomposing,
and then a sliver of light, then a stream.
The stone rumbled away.
Then a shout: "Lazarus, come out!"

When I stumbled, blinking, out of the tomb,
my sisters and neighbors cringed, gasping.
No one even wanted to touch me,
let alone unwrap me as the rabbi ordered.

What am I supposed to do now?
I have willed away my inheritance.
I can fit all that's left in my ossuary.
I didn't ask to be brought back to life.

S. J. PERRY

My Corvid Curse

Caw! Caw!
I'm a goddamned crow!

I'll eat
any damned thing.
I can't help it.

I'll float
on a thermal,
scanning
for fruit,
bugs,
worms,
nuts,
mice,
trash,
roadkill.

I'll spot something
and swoop down,
clamp my beak on that shit,
tip my anvil head back,
shake,
gulp,
and let my craw work.

Sometimes
I'll stack bread
or pizza
or dog food
in my beak
and carry it
to my cache.

Sometimes I'll share
a bit
with my local murder.
We caw
about this feed
or our last feed
or our next feed.

Hunger
is our consciousness,
our existence,
our damnation.

Maybe in spring
we feel other urges
briefly, a quick tussle,
then hunger.

Hunger is
all there is
until
a raptor rips me,
shredded,
from the sky,
or sickness saps me
from inside.

From the moment
I hatch
until I die,
I carry
my corvid curse.

I'm.
So.
Goddamned.
Hungry.

Splash!

Shimmering turquoise
sunlight tangos flits, dazzles
dappled water lilts

azure oasis
promises velvet immersion
breathless surrender

hot cement stings feet
scurry, toes curl catapult
splash! coolness soothes soles

gelatinous depths
embalm bobbing body, glide
in pool's perfect peace

drips lurch around limbs
a damp, cool aura cocoons
chilled space between heat

breeze drifts, careens over skin
whisked droplets return to clouds

dry, tightening flesh
warm rosy blush, sticks to chair
ah! plunge in again

Little Lacquer Box

Little lacquer box
hewn from nature's art
reveals a tree's life
red and amber, aroma of cedar

a girl's first treasure chest
cradles coveted pre-teen jewelry
azure crystal necklace, oxidized chain
faux pearls crimped along a string

memento of Niagara Falls
carries home travel keepsakes
photos fit snugly
waterfall mist blurs smiles beneath black ponchos

sanctuary for grease-stained recipe cards
my mother's handwritten, elegant cursive
a lump of butter, pinch of salt

catchall for trinkets
Mardi Gras beads, emerald and magenta
mismatched dice, green and blue marbles, rusted jacks

sacred shrine
clasp locked, dangling heart-shaped tag engraved
pet's cremains stacked with six others
never to be opened or buried;
makeshift mausoleum

A Special Treat

MY EYES MEZMERIZED
BY THE RAIN
A STEADY DOWNPOUR
CREATING PUDDLES
EACH DROP
LEAVING RINGS
IN MOTION
A RAIN DANCE
TURNS ME
INTO A DREAMER
WRAPPED UP
IN A WARM BLANKET
OR
THE URGE
TO TAKE A WALK
AND FEEL, HEAR, AND LOOK AT
THE RAIN
TO VISUALIZE
NATURE REVIVING
THAT'S A SPECIAL TREAT.

HELGA VROOM

Phases of Swimming

Rendezvous in a pool

Standing at the edge of the pool
Letting one's body down into waters cool
The skin wakes up
Water becomes lover's touch
Swimming fast
Let it last
The crescendo of water's touch
From feet to head above.
Smooth, swift and light
Water and body unite.

Spiritual endeavor

Rolling over and facing the sky
Grateful I am, my soul can fly
Swimming along
Filling with a song
The sky deep blue
Clouds dancing only a few
I moved out of life's cage
No baggage at this stage
And learned to die
While much alive

Salty (Sestina)

his big voice charm wraps around my waist.
his big hand grab right where I fit
when I hold my breath, to make me small
enough to be sucked inside his puckered lips,
but then flicked away like a bead of sweat,
a memory of the taste of salt.

the night is gargling hot water salt
without a throat. confusion chokes my waist.
he evaporates like the sweat
on my bed, where lonely think she fit
laughin' at the tear dripping off my lip.
lonely just another name for desperate and small.

limp I sit, soaking up the small
memory of margarita salt
dancing on the tip of his lips,
his boisterous laugh tickling my waist
as though this is where we supposed to fit
into the same sweet bead of sweat.

pheromones bathe us in frantic sweat
but time shrinks me into a small
corner of his life, where he wants me to fit,
a side dish, a dessert, a pinch of pink salt,
a cinched belt of hope around my waist.
I gleefully pucker up my lips

to kiss the air where his lips
used to lie so fast, he'd break a sweat,
his boisterous smile calling my waist.

but I can't make myself that small
anymore. want to be more than a grain of salt
on the tip of a memory where I don't fit.

not desperate enough to fit
on the tip of a narcissist lip
where lonely is a pinch of salt
wrung from the stench of mildewed sweat.
cannot allow myself to shrink that small
again. to wait inside my waist

for salty hope dipped in sweat
where parched lips sit unfit too small
for self-respect to waste.

Nook and Knobs

If the wood on top of the dresser was made of skin it would be one long scab with dried cracks and layers of flesh threatening to roll away from bone. Gashes in the scab are longing to be peeled, but peeling it would mean the skin would never look the same again. The color would always be too light and there is the threat of creating an eyesore of a scar so damaged as to be unsalvageable. The threat of gangrene and the need to amputate the top would leave me with a headless dresser. Better to hold onto the scab crusted skin for as long as possible—put a bandage over it... in this case, the dresser top is hidden underneath a slab of white marble with grey veins running through it. The marble almost sits perfectly on top though the cut is different and just the corners of the dresser peek out—not enough to expose the scab, just enough to hint at something resembling antique.

The back of the dresser is covered with a brocade cloth of dusty brown, wood hues and emerald green with a repeating theme of a Japanese styled house and garden. It is cut and edged perfectly and is the most beautiful part of the dresser. I dare not remove the cloth to expose the wood beneath; I have no idea the condition but since it is covered, I imagine something similar to the top, warped and ruggedly worn. Knowing my mom took time to find this material, glue and hammer it onto the back is an imagined memory I cherish. It is as though she brought a lost puppy home to nurse it back to health, or as much health as possible.

I don't know what the dresser looked like when she bought it, what made her buy it and why she decided to keep it and bandage it up. It served as storage for her linen napkins and hand-laced table cloths, so it more than earned the patch job it sports. Besides the damaged top and hidden back, the dresser has another ailment. It has four feet to support it and the front two are wounded. The dresser perpetually leans forward on these two sorrowful feet.

This was an easy fix; I found furniture pads and I stack them on top of each other to balance the front with the back.

In addition to the stacked foot pads, shelving paper was needed to line the inside, where there was a gap between the drawer bottoms and the front of the drawers. It looks rather nice. Finally, there are the key holes in the front of the dresser, impractical for everyday use, if that is possible. In my imagination, it can be used regularly, as long as it is handled with care. I found three regal knobs to compliment the antique, seen-too-much relic that compliment it well. I have found the perfect nook for the dresser where it sits content with its hidden top and back, propped front feet, lined drawers to cover a gap, and keyhole replacement knobs.

This marginally functional dresser in the spare bedroom conjures memories of my mother. Her desire to salvage and make beautiful every-thing and everyone she came in contact with, including me, a remnant of a girl, birthed and left to be adopted. And there it is, her hands salvaging rejects, and me enshrining an imagined perfection of who she was and trying to whittle a space in a nook of acceptance where I can be as content as the warped dresser.

Warped is a good word to describe the aches of aging, a patch here, a bandage there, major and minor operations to give the appearance of being optimally functional, but obviously dated and wounded.

My son tries to persuade me to throw out the dresser. He says, "This is not your style, buy something more modern, something that doesn't need to be handled with delicate care." I wonder if he senses the mirrored connection between me and the dresser and wants to preserve the idea of a younger me in his mind, one that doesn't need so much help.

The more he works to persuade me of the dresser's uselessness and lack of style, the more he convinces me that this nook needs the dresser as much as the dresser needs the nook. It serves as a reminder that I, like the dresser, can be reclaimed, patched up and useful, can tell a story of love and care, just by its very presence.

OVITT FAMILY COMMUNITY LIBRARY IN ONTARIO

Led by Tim Hatch

Tim Hatch

When I Die

Cremate me.   Scatter my memory where
memory is sweetest. Take me to Morro Bay
at sunset, when sky and seawater meet
in a gradient kiss, and know that I never saw myself

until you saw me. As the reflection
of the rock fades with the light, tell me
you love me and let me go

to the breeze. Let only gulls
cry as I'm carried away and give me
the smile you gave me each day.
When you return, as you will, breathe

deep, take me inside, and remember
I love you, constant as the tide.

the wind loves the lost

there is a boy   lost
in the Santa Anas   wailing
through a lifetime   there are many boys

one is a river
bending through hard country

one is obsidian
beautiful, empty

one is a shore crab
sideways clacking circles in the surf

one is a bloated red sun
ancient and haunted by every mistake

all of them are liars
cringing behind the heavy
curtain of a belly laugh

one is a pleading drunk, hands
stuck together
praying in the crawlspace between enlightenment
and wakefulness   where   god
drums distant constellations
sings   to his   children

but the wind is closer than God
and howls without end

Tim Hatch

Hilltop Sunset (Father's Day, 1985)

Last warmth dies on closed eyes
    tilted toward a shiver. A breeze

sifts through a cluster
    of manzanitas, growing off

the hillside and up, reaching for
    sunlight, like a beggar, whispers

there is no "deserve" in a language
    older than God. The sky is a battle:

sun rings halo thunderheads
    billowy monuments to the absurdity

of struggle. A pill bug, exhausted
    with conflict, curls away from

the dinner light clawing through
    windows below. Refuses to go home.

Boulevard Summer

Late-night neon snakes writhe up the hood of my 77 'chero
windshield lit up like a heat-wave Christmas
by the vacant glow of traffic lights. The road, itself

a faded star, refuses to age with grace, blind
to its own beautiful, beat up dignity. The shooting
star of my cigarette, lands in gutters filled with crushed

dreams and cracked hypos that can't be unseen as we roll
past a manic gallery of fashionable junkies and the tragically
hip, milling about The Roxy, black-leather ghosts, waiting to happen.

TIM HATCH

Bill Speaks

I'm sitting in a chapel, listening to the pastor
who came with the plan speak kind words about a man

he never met. He asks us to bow our heads and run
through a prayer. The repetition of "Lord" always makes me smile

(not my nicest smile): "Lord, bless this gathering
Lord, as we come together Lord, to celebrate the life of Bill Lord,

and we ask that you look after him Lord,"
and he goes on. If he was saying "Steve" instead of "Lord"

("Bless this gathering Steve, as we come together
Steve, to celebrate the life of Bill Steve"),

everyone would assume he was attempting
a mnemonic he'd read in a self-help book.

My morning was two hours of failing to get students
to participate in class discussion followed by traffic

followed by grading interrupted by an email wanting me
to know I'm not getting an interview

at one of the schools I've applied to followed by traffic followed by
watching one of my best and oldest friends fall

apart over memories of his dad, and now
I'm sitting in a chapel, looking at a black-and-white photograph of Bill

in his high school football jersey, fading into flowers. And here I am,
between my wife and another best and oldest friend, and I'm staring

at Bill, lying in his casket, eyes closed to this world and all its problems,
and I think maybe that's not a bad idea, and I close my eyes,

squeeze my wife's hand, and open them again, looking
for what comes next

Glorietta in Hashbury

"Glorietta, come on over here. We got joints here, baby." Chaka offered Glorietta a mangled cigarette paper wrapped badly around a lumpy mass. She sat down on the floor next to Chaka, with the joint in her left hand, and watched to see what would happen next. Clemmie, two tall, thin men she hadn't met, and a young girl who looked to be about 12-13 leaned here and there against the walls, waiting quietly with their own joints. Djuna lit six tall candles stuck into the tops of empty wine bottles in the middle of the floor, and Chaka reached out his hand. She gave him one, and he put his joint in his mouth and drew in air through it while he held the candle flame to the other end.

"Ever smoked before?" Chaka asked her suddenly, smoke spilling out of both sides of his mouth and curling around his face.

"Once or twice," she said. She and Josie had experimented in Josie's family garage back in Fresno before she ran away to San Francisco.

"Joints or cigs?"

"Cigs. No joints before." Maybe she shouldn't have admitted that, she thought, but it popped out. How many times had that happened in her life and made her sorry? Too many to count. But Chaka didn't seem to mind.

"Just lay back baby and smoke it slow and easy. You be fine." Djuna sat down on the other side of Chaka and leaned against his leg. She placed a sketchpad and a piece of charcoal next to her right hand on the floor.

Glorietta's tailbone hurt where she had broken it as a child, and she wished there were pillows on the floor. She backed up to the wall and rested her back against it. When the candle arrived, she got the joint lit. The first lungful of smoke didn't have much effect on her. It was very much like a cigarette, except harder to keep the weed inside the wrapper, she thought. This sharing of drugs was what she had heard about, this and the demonstrations. And love or sex, but she saw nothing leading that way yet. That's why she had decided Haight-Ashbury was her destination when she ran away. It was the place everyone wanted to be now, in 1968, if they could.

"Binnie, got some chords for us?" Chaka asked, blowing a smoke ring.

The darker of the two thin men got up from his cross-legged position, put his lit joint behind his ear, and walked through a door Glorietta hadn't noticed before. He came back carrying a speaker and then went back for another one, each one three feet tall. They were attached to long cords that ran back through the door. He followed the cords back and after a minute, the sounds of the Jefferson Airplane *Surrealistic Pillow* album came from the speakers, softer than Glorietta had expected but with a wonderful clarity. Grace Slick sang "White Rabbit," and as Glorietta smoked, she began to feel like she was sliding up and down the cadence, riding on the notes. Almost like cross-country skiing, but with no effort at all. When there was a pause between verses, Grace held the note and Glorietta saw a rainbow of flavors fanning out from the note she sat on.

The young girl sat on Glorietta's right and Chaka on her left. "I'm Mia," the girl said, then yawned and lay down with her head in Glorietta's lap. Chaka reached over and massaged the back of Mia's neck for a minute, then patted Glorietta on the head and returned to making rhythmic gestures with his right hand in time with the off beats of the music. "You feelin' it, baby?" he asked.

"Yes," Glorietta said. She didn't want to talk or even move. No one did. Except for Djuna, who sketched a line on her drawing every so often, they all sat motionless, listening and smoking, eventually using up the last of their joints and putting the small butts in a copper bowl next to the candles. No one had roach clips, a device Glorietta had read about but never seen. She wondered if someone would get the shreds of weed out of the remains and repackage it for the next round.

When the music stopped, Binnie got up and went out, and after a short time, Sergeant Pepper came through the speakers. Glorietta's music-ride feelings seemed to be specific to the Airplane sound, but she heard every drum beat from Ringo Starr feeling twitches in her arms with each drumstick strike she heard him make. The melody seemed negligible, only the drumbeats had meaning. It was a code, but instead of active mental work to unravel it, she must relax and let it float to the surface of her brain.

Glorietta fell asleep there. The next thing she knew it was morning, quiet, and a stream of sunlight shone on her face. And something wet and a little rough touched her cheek. She opened her eyes, and saw a black cat, face to face with her, licking her cheek with a pomegranate pink tongue. Djuna came into the room and looked down at her. "Want to wake up now? It's pretty early," she said. She wore a midnight blue long dress, tie died in ever-darkening blues from top to hem, with white flecks that looked like stars here and there.

"I guess so. What should I do?" Glorietta said, sitting up and stretching her stiff muscles. The cat made surprisingly loud noises stalking and jumping around the room. Probably it was noticeable because there was no background noise, Glorietta thought.

"How should I know? Will you stay here?" Djuna asked.

"I'd like to. Do you think it's okay?"

"Chaka said you could," Djuna said. "He's, well sort of the boss, I guess."

"I don't have money for rent," Glorietta said.

"Oh, no big deal. We don't pay rent."

"Why?"

"Something about Binnie's uncle, but don't ask. Anyway, it's okay just to stay. And we co-op food. Whoever has bread, it's shared."

"Oh. Maybe I can find some way to make some."

"Well, don't worry. That's the important thing. If we need to demonstrate, we don't want to be tied down to a job."

Chaka came in, stretching and scratching his head. "Hey Glorietta, you plan to stay on?"

"I guess. Don't have anywhere else to go. And I'd like to help with demonstrations."

"Got a beef with the war? Or what?" Chaka asked.

"Yeah. Why do we have to go over there and get killed?" Glorietta wasn't sure if he was looking for her to say something Marxist, but she couldn't recall any quotes from Marx, Davis, or Marcuse, so she hoped not.

"Right. Welcome, then. We'll get you to help out with the veggie garden, is that okay? Ever grow anything?"

"Yes, not much edible though. Mostly flowers."

"Djuna will show you. And maybe sometimes you can panhandle with Clemmie at the opera. Do you sing or play an instrument?"

"Not really. They'd probably pay for me to be quiet."

"Well, hmm. Maybe dance? Clemmie plays violin—she'd say it's a fiddle."

"Yes, a bit. I can clog."

"Well, we'll see. Anyway, we have some food today, so eat. May or may not have some tomorrow."

Glorietta thought that sounded rather ominous. She'd been without food for two days hitchhiking to San Francisco from Fresno after her stepdad Ron had beat her up again, sleeping in bushes along the road between rides. She was used to the bruises, but not hunger. She followed Djuna into the kitchen. There was a loaf of bread and a bottle of plum jam. Djuna neatly severed slices from the bread. Each of them took one and spread it with jam. It tasted like a June wind loaded with fruit aromas. Glorietta normally didn't like jam, or any sweets in the morning, but this was sublime. And she expected coffee, but there didn't seem to be any.

"Coffee, maybe?" she asked.

"Not today. Maybe tomorrow." Djuna laughed. "Just relax and enjoy what we have. It's always different, but we get along. You'll be fine."

"Okay," Glorietta said, following Djuna outside to the garden.

JUDY KOHNEN

Life Chasing Desire

I have been sitting on a log,
basking in the sun for a long time
waves carry my coastal Island,
balancing earthly burdens. During stormy
floodwaters, a Cowichen tribe
once sheltered inside my caves
when they emerged, worshipful,
they named this emergent land
Shkewetsn, basking in the sun, after me.
They hid my frog image in purses
for fortune, to prevent losses. When
they desired peace, warrior chiefs
whittled my face into guardian totem poles.
Of course, it is not always me
sitting on the log, basking in the sun.
I pass the tradition to the next generation
but all frogs look the same to humans.
I sunbathe, watch logs and plastic and birds
in the surf and ferries carrying people,
creatures who do not embrace the world.
Basking in the sun, I listen to rocks eroding
I never see the moment a rock turns to sand
but when it does, the sea surges and sings.
My tongue reaches for a dragonfly, choosing,
and the insect captures my wisdom.

Contemplations with an Egg

This is the thinking of
my little egg; it has noticed my
morning windows open to
Santa Ana winds swirling,
sensing winter's ambient
desert temperature.
Egg sits like a pearl in salt water
measuring low pressure systems
pushing smoke from the
San Gabriel hills over to the ocean,
toweling-clean the air.
It can hear the radio news
scandal and reports of
fires and mud and guns
ravaging households
delivering grief and
seasons of survivors.
My little egg understands pressure,
an intensity of unrecoverable,
the launching of ballistic
missiles from North Korea.
It wonders about timing,
transformations and living,
how the sky can hold steel,
and where in California
nuclear weapons explode,
near, inside, or far away?
There is a rattling, sensations,
vapor squeezing through tight places,
heat beading on fragility,
boiling, and the final let go. To where?
Somewhere inconsolable.

A Day at the DMV

I woke up in a good mood. I had studied the rules booklet from cover to cover, taken the practice quizzes, and had made an appointment. Confidence oozed out of every pore; nothing could stop me. Because of my age I had to take the written test to renew my driver's license. I hadn't been to a DMV office for years. My husband had. As I ritualistically consumed my oatmeal and fruit, he looked over at me and said, "I'll go with you for moral support." The last time he had said that to me was years ago when I was diagnosed with breast cancer. How bad could this be?

He insisted on leaving early, so we arrived at the DMV half an hour before my appointment. We found a parking spot right away. "Piece of cake," I said.

My husband replied, "We'd better go in as I don't know my way around this new office."

When we entered, about fifty people were sitting in a waiting area. *Do they all have appointments?* Another group of about twenty-five were standing in line behind a large sign, NO APPOINT-MENTS. "Where do I go?" I asked my husband. He wandered off in one direction, and I in another. When I looked around, people were walking in a confused stupor like question marks waiting for answers.

Ending up back at the NO APPOINTMENT line, I looked to the right, and there, in much smaller lettering, I read Appointments and the Disabled. *Interesting combination.* Nobody was in line.

I approached the clerk, "I have an appointment," dutifully producing my confirmation number, which she ignored.

"Did you complete an application?" the dour lady asked.

"No," I replied.

She handed me a half sheet of paper, directing me by pointing to the vicinity of the far corner of the building.

My husband had rejoined me and accompanied me to the designated area.

We both said in unison, "That says testing area."

"Yes," I said, "I can't go in there."

As retired teachers, we are both highly conscious of the need for test security. I asked somebody wearing an official name tag, "Where do I go to fill out an application for a driver's license renewal?"

Her response, "Oh, go to that line in the testing area."

Raising his eyebrows in disbelief, my husband said, "I'll wait for you out there."

Within the so-called secure testing area were a group of people filling out applications on computers, a handful of others taking the test, and a line to which I was headed with relatives of the test takers milling about. The clerk kept shouting at an Asian lady to put away her cell phone. Even though a large sign bragged about being able to take the test in ten different languages, the sign banning cell phones was in English.

I completed my application and returned to the same line. A mother with three children all under the age of six was trying to fill out her application on a computer while two of her children were running in and out of the queue. I learned that the eldest, Edmundo, was supposed to be looking after his younger brother Rodrigo. Every two minutes she would ask, "Where's your brother?" Those of us in line would answer, "He's over here." This continued until I reached the desk. My babysitting duties completed, I handed over my paper. My thumbprint taken, I was then told to go to the waiting area until my assigned number was called.

I joined my husband.

"Now what?" he said, smiling.

"Why didn't you tell me it would be like this?"

"I didn't want to discourage you."

"I've been trying to figure out the system," chuckled my husband. "There's no sequence or pattern because there are letters and numbers, so you can't figure out how close you are to being called. L 42 follows G 86, for example."

"So much for a restroom break," I said.

After listening to the calling of random numbers for a while, I began to laugh.

"What's so funny?" asked my husband.

"It's like playing bingo."

"N 55, snakes alive."

"G 22, two little ducks."

"B 66, clickety click."

"Bingo! My number was called."

After another thumbprint, an eye test, and payment, I was directed to the camera section. Step 5. A young photographer, with a pained expression on her face, took my picture then sent me back to the testing section to finally take my test. By this time, I felt I had forgotten everything I ever knew about the rules of the road.

Using my thumbprint, I logged into the computer. Nothing happened. I tried again. MISMATCH. SEE TECHNICIAN flashed across the screen. I changed computers and logged in once more. Nothing. My confidence shattered and my blood pressure off the charts, I attempted to get the attention of the same "cheerful" photographer who had now changed roles and was answering questions from people in the infamous line. After several "excuse me's" and wild gestures, I succeeded. I explained the problem.

She reassuringly replied, "I'll have to bring another technician."

Ten minutes later she returned with notes scribbled on a yellow post it. Now I was logged in, I began to take the test, conscious of my neighbor who kept muttering to himself, "But I studied. I don't understand," interspersed with long sighs. I missed one question about pulling a trailer on the freeway. When am I going to be doing that? Mission accomplished, seven steps and two hours later, I returned to the clerk.

When I rejoined my husband, he asked, "Did you pass?"

"I missed one."

"Congratulations."

Grabbing his arm, I said, "Let's just get out of here."

"Do you want to go for a coffee?" he asked.

"No. What I really need is a gin and tonic."

CORONA PUBLIC LIBRARY

Led by Andrea Fingerson

Horse Number Four

Mae never understood how It got into the house; yet, *It* always did. An unwashed dish, a forgotten chore, a look that wasn't perfect, and It would slither along the floor and slide up his Wrangler jeans. When It did, everyone did what they were told. She had seen what happened when they tried to ignore it. It would grow big in him. She had seen It pick up guns; she had seen It put barrels in ma's mouth. She had seen It make ma climb in Mae's bed at night and apologize.

"He wasn't like this before the war, Mae. He was a sweet man but It got him." Mae preferred to be outside amongst the horses.

Things got better when her cousin Skye came to stay. Ma muttered something about Skye's parents being her dad going to someplace called the VA. Mae didn't mind; Skye was ten just like Mae and liked horses, too. Together they would ride out there on the plains near Grants, New Mexico with the mesas off in the distance, their baby-blonde turning-brown manes waving in that New Mexican wind. Out there, It couldn't get in.

"Mae? Skye? Get in here now!"

The girls would look at each other. Skye would roll her eyes. Mae would never dare; instead she would dismount and deflate as they steered the horses back to the barn in the back of the double wide where they lived.

With Skye, being inside was better too. Skye brought horses. Dozens of plastic horses in dozens of Ziploc bags. Mae had a few plastic horses she kept in a cigar box above her bed.

"Take them out!" Skye would demand of Mae.

Mae followed orders.

"I'll give you two stallions for that brown mare," Skye bargained.

Mae figured two was better than one. The deal was sealed. Mae took the stallions and slid them across the bed while Skye unloaded her brown mare along with several other plastic horses on the bed. That's when Mae saw a plastic painted pony with four painted spots. Mae pointed her finger,

"What do you want for that?"

"You mean, Horse Number Four?"

"Yeah, I'll give you my black stallion for her."

"Nope," Skye shook her head, "My dad gave me that one."

This made Mae want it more. She reached back to the shelf above her bed and took down another cigar box that kept her savings.

"I think I have ten bucks here," Mae said, "Ten bucks for Horse Number Four?"

Skye shook her head again; Mae wanted to poke her in the eye.

That night when everyone was asleep, Mae did what she never had done. She stole. She stole Horse Number Four. She put him in the bottom of her horse box. With the crime complete, she whispered, "Horse Number Four."

Skye discovered Horse Number Four's disappearance the next afternoon. She dumped out her Ziploc bags and screamed,

"Mae, did you take Horse Number Four! Where is Horse Number Four?"

Mae told the first lie in her life.

"No."

Skye wasn't dumb; she screamed.

Mae begged her to stop.

"Stop it! I didn't take Horse Number Four. Stop it before someone comes in."

Skye didn't stop. She screamed louder. Mae grew panicked, and put her hand over Skye's mouth.

Too late. The faint sound of Hank Williams muffled by Ford 150 tires became louder and louder. Mae released Skye mouth and begged Skye to stop screaming, but the heavy boots walked up the doublewide stairs, and the aluminum door almost broke from the shove he gave while Skye screamed even louder. Mae closed her eyes tight, put her hands over her ears. He took one look at the scene and It slid up his pant leg and crawled inside.

"What the hell is going on here?"

Mikal howled, "Mae took Horse Number Four!"

"Horseshit!" he stormed, "Mae, where's Horse Number Four?"

Mae said nothing.

Its voice hissed, "Mae, I said where is Horse Number Four?"

Mae's mouth wouldn't move. It grew furious, stomped into Mae's room, found the box and returned to the living room.

"Mae, I am going to ask you one more goddamn time, where's Horse Number Four?"

Mae's mouth disappeared.

That's when It took the box and threw it at the wall. Shatters of wood and plastic horses like a fireworks display. Everyone stopped. Skye walked across the room to the shrapnel, picked up a little plastic horse and announced,

"Horse Number Four."

Mae's eyes closed. She felt It grab her jacket; It dragged her outside.

"No child of mine is going to be a thief. You got that, Mae?"

Mae's eyes still closed.

It said louder with a slap across the face.

"I said, 'you got that?'"

Mae managed a nod.

"Now get out there and cut yourself a switch." It grabbed her shoulder, gave her a shove towards the creosote bushes by the doublewide's side.

Mae followed directions.

"Pull down your pants, Mae Sue. Get what's coming to you."

Mae did what she was told.

It took the switch and hit her behind. It became hungry. It whipped her back, her shoulders, the backs of her legs. Tears and blood fell upon the earth. It grabbed her jacket and shoved her back in the house. She found the sofa where Skye sat watching a Cyndi Lauper video. It hurt to sit down.

It kept muttering caught up in its fury,

"No good goddamn kids! Thieving little shits!"

It stomped towards Skye, grabbed Horse Number Four, opened up the wood-burning stove and threw Horse Number Four into the flames. Skye screamed. Mae stayed silent.

It slapped Skye across the face.

"Stop your sniveling, you hear? Or you're the next one to get a switch!"

Skye stifled her cries; Mae went to lie down on her bed, too sore to sit.

Later, when he had drunk enough beer and passed out, Syke opened on Mae's door and whispered,

"Can I come in?"

"Yeah."

"Are you hurting?"

"Yeah."

"Sorry."

"Sorry too."

"Pa gets mad sometimes."

"Mine too."

"Yours too?"

"Yeah, that's why I'm here. Ma says I can't come home until pa gets the war that he brought with him out of the house."

"Ma says things like that."

"Can I sleep with you?"

"Yeah," Mae made room on her bed. Skye got in and spooned Mae.

"That's the end of Horse Number Four," Skye joked, sort of.

Mae had no words. Mae's eyes closed. She tried to dream.

Months went by. Skye went back to Albuquerque. Ma muttered something about divorce.

Years went by. Horses turned into boys. Mae turned into a woman that looked like a boy, all straight up and down. Boys didn't notice her, but Mae noticed Kurt Clark. She knew she never got what she wanted, so she drew what she wanted instead. Sketchbooks full of Kurt Clark.

"Why do you always draw Kurt?" her friends would ask.

She shrugged like she didn't know. Truth was she was trying to capture something in these sketches besides his trademark pinched blue eyes and sideways smirk. He reminded her of New Mexican wind; both could kick anybody's ass. She tried to capture that. She never could.

Shortly after Mae barely graduated from high school, Kurt took a liking to Mae when he saw one of her sketches of him while she was on break at the local Dairy Queen.

"I like how you draw me," he threw her his smirk, "You want to be my girl?"

Mae was over the moon at Kurt's question until a baby grew.

Mae closed her eyes tight.

"I don't think I should have kids," she whispered.

Kurt told her they'd figure it out.

They did for a while. The baby turned into two, twins. Mae found out when Kurt was in jail.

"I had some warrants, Mae. It's time to come clean, do my time and then get on with things."

Mae was not built to have kids with her straight up and down ways and certainly not built for twins. They fell upon the earth premature. She waited for Kurt while the twins incubated from aliens to babies.

"You can take them home now," they told her. She had no choice;

she took them home. Kurt was released, got a job at the Dairy Queen too and said to Mae,

"Let's get on with our dreams."

She was unable to dream, scared if she could, It would return. It did.

"Mae, what the fuck is this?" it slithered up the card table that served as the dinner table and crawled up Kurt's Wrangler leg.

"Food?" she replied.

"It's shit!" it shoved the plate away. The twins began crying.

"Make it yourself!"

It didn't like that. It grabbed her by the shirt and pulled her outside, punched her face, kicked her side.

"What did you say to me?"

It snarled.

"I said, 'do you want me to make you something else?'" Mae asked while blood from her mouth onto the earth.

"Exactly! Now, get in that house, woman, and cook me some real food."

She followed directions. She followed

Its directions until one night Kurt brought home a gun. The flashes of what Mae seen drove her to do something she never thought she would do, leave. Walking nearly two miles in the New Mexican wind to her Pa's trailer. Ma had left long ago for some country rock singer. This had destroyed Pa who was taken to that place they called the VA for several weeks; when he came back, he never drank again and somehow this changed him; Mae now knew what her ma had meant when she said her pa had been a decent guy before the war. He was when It was not around. Mae knocked on the door.

Even though It hadn't lived in the trailer for a few years, she still worried It would open the door. It didn't. Instead her pa who seemed smaller now opened the door.

"Pa?"

"Mae?"

"Can we stay here for the night?"

Pa held the door open for her and her boys.

Kurt pulled up in somebody's Camaro the next morning.

"Mae, what the fuck?"

Mae's eyes shut.

"I can't do this."

"Yes, you can and yes, you will."

Pa came outside. Kurt looked at him. Pa looked at him.

It hissed in Pa's eyes. Kurt got back in the Camaro. Kurt left. Mae's eyes stayed shut.

"Mae, why don't you go up to Albuquerque and stay with Skye?"

Skye had made a life for herself in Albuquerque after messing up twice as a teen by having two boys before she was 18 with two different men. Skye had finally 'gotten her act together' as Pa said and gone to cosmetology school and was now a hairdresser making 'big money.'

Mae followed his suggestion.

Pa brought her and the twins, who were replicas of Kurt, pinched blue eyes, sideways smirks and his wind bus tickets to Albuquerque to be with Skye. Skye was glad to have Mae and the babies. She let them stay and Skye showed Mae how to get by. Mae got a job a Piggly Wiggly and saved enough money to rent a doublewide with a barn in the back. Her twins screamed, fought, ran all over the place. It found her again, that thing. She was the only thing it had left.

It entered her and screamed,

"Shut the fuck up! Just shut the fuck up!"

The twins didn't listen.

It made her throw things. It made her say,

"Get the fuck off the couch or I am going to kick your ass."

It hit her children in the ways she promised she never would. This was how it was.

One day Skye pulled up with a horse trailer attached to her Ford 150. Mae went to

outside to greet her.

"Mae, you know my new boyfriend, Bob?" Skye asked.

"Well, I got a horse that Bob doesn't know what to do with. He found a foal that he can't say no to. This one here, she's old and Bob doesn't have room, so he is wondering if you want a horse?"

Did Mae want a horse?

"Of course!"

Skye opened the trailer. Mae's heart stopped. A horse, a brown mare. They led it into the barn. Their brown manes blowing in the wind.

"One thing," Skye stopped for a moment, "she's pregnant. Do you know how to deliver a horse?"

"Yes!" Mae lied for the second time in her life.

When she wasn't working or yelling at her boys, she would read about animal husbandry. She got all the books she could at the local library. For the first time in her life, she learned. Mae explained to the boys the mare would have a baby soon. They enjoyed watching the mare get fuller.

It rarely came into the house although it sometimes did.

Mae woke them one night.

"Boys," she whispered, "let's get out to the barn. It's time."

They followed directions. She gave orders.

"Now, when I ask you for something, you've got to do it, okay?"

They did what they were told. They handed ma whatever she asked for: water, scissors, gauze. They watched ma struggle, pull and yank. A new being fell upon the earth.

Mae was excited, "Boys, boys, get the sponges, let's wash this pony off."

The twins took turns wiping the birth off the newborn's coat.

"No way!" Mae said. It appeared to be a painted pony with brown spots.

The boys looked up at her. Mae's eyes closed.

"Boys, can you count the spots?" she asked.

"One, two, three, four."

Mae's eyes stayed closed.

"Boys, are there any more spots?"

"Nope."

Mae's eyes and mouth opened.

"Horse Number Four!"

They never understood why she cried and laughed at the same time covered with blood and birth screaming,

"Horse Number Four! I'll be a goddamned."

She never understood how it happened either; yet, for one suspended moment, It ceased to be.

HEATHER RIOS

Home Sweet Home

Horrendous hurricane hails havoc on hen house
Officials Overlook obvious offenses against
Men with more melanin
Endless evictions and economic friction
Sanctioned sermons in certain sanctuaries
Weather warnings whether wayward western waves or world-
    wide warming
Equality for everyone—embryos the exception
Evacuations and emigration
Trafficked teens tailor to tasteless temptations
Hasty halt to humanize the hungry homeless
Ongoing obliteration of occupation opportunities
MAYDAY! MAYDAY! Malignant militant missile mayhem!
Exalted Emmanuel! Express Your empathy!

Silence

Women in black at the Golden Globe Awards on Sunday sat in silence as Oprah Winfrey gave an impassioned speech about women having the courage to speak out against sexual harassment and sexual assault. She indicated the silence was over.

Reflecting on Oprah's speech I did a stroll down memory lane regarding sexual assault and sexual harassment in my years in college and later in the workplace. My first recollection regarding this issue was being date raped at age eighteen as a freshman in college. Listening to the women speaking out in the #metoo movement, I realized that I wasn't asking for it. That my "no" meant "no." Looking back, I was just thankful that the statistic of the one in four women being raped that it was me and not my daughters.

After my divorce I went to work at the County Department of Public Social Services. I was warned by coworkers to watch out for Bob. Our desks faced each other without a partition. Bob was known for telling dirty jokes which were followed by, "Does that offend you?"

"Yes, Bob, it does. Please don't do that again." And he wouldn't ... for a while and then after the next dirty joke we would repeat the same conversation, like a broken record. That was Bob being Bob. That's how it was.

My next recollection about a significant episode of inappropriate behavior came when I was in my early forties. The women reading this will understand that I did not relish having my annual exam, especially with a new doctor. It's always awkward to sit naked covered by a hospital gown and be examined by a stranger even if there was a nurse in the room. I was ushered into an exam room and asked to put on a gown. "The doctor will be right in." The doctor, accompanied by his nurse, came in without a word and walked over and started touching me.

"Excuse me!" He didn't stop. "Excuse me," still not stopping. "What is your name?" I raised my voice.

"Oh!" He seemed startled, "Dr. Gomez." After telling me his name he had me lie down.

The doctor ran both hands from my ankles up the front of my legs to the top of my thighs. I was forty-two, and had never been touched that way during my annual exam. When he began the exam and he hurt me I said, "Ouch," he pushed harder. At the end of the exam the nurse returned with some paperwork and said, "I am so sorry."

"Does Dr. Gomez have complaints?" Silence...

I filed a complaint with the insurance company. I never received anything in writing or an apology for the mistreatment. I should be thankful they allowed me to move out of that Health Maintenance Organization to a Preferred Physical Organization where I could choose my own care provider. That's how it was back then. Silence...

At Risk Management in a large University and Medical Center where I worked, a male coworker "went off on me" one morning before my supervisor was in the office. I was so upset I left work and made it downstairs before I started crying. Sobbing, I drove home. I called the supervisor and through my sobs, left a message on her voice mail that I would not be back in the office that day. I spent several hours on the phone with the Employee Assistance Program (EAP) looking for guidance on how to work with this coworker. When I returned to work my female supervisor did not ask about my tearful message nor my absence. Silence.

Several weeks later when the same coworker went off on me again, I left for lunch with my friend who managed another department. She recommended I report the episode. When I returned to my office to speak to the vice-president above my female supervisor, he reported that my coworker had already briefed him about the episode. After reporting to the Vice President (VP) the incident was followed by silence. After weeks and weeks of silence, at my insistence, I asked for a meeting to review the problems with my supervisor, the VP and the coworker. The coworker and I were asked to meet separately with the Employee Assistance Program counselor, have a joint session and then return for another individual meeting with the EAP counselor.

"I never went back to the EAP. Did you?"

"Yes, I did," I said which was followed by silence.

My insistence at discussing the working relationship resulted in a letter in MY personnel file. When the next incident happened with another employee occurred, my coworker no longer worked at the University and Medical Center thanks to my courage to put his behavior on record.

As Disability Management Coordinator, Human Resources Department in a large university, I placed qualified individuals with disabilities in non-competitive placements following federal and state laws. The Director of Physical Plant, a "big cheese," objected and so I was called into a meeting with the "big cheese" and the Assistant Vice Chancellor, a "bigger cheese."

I explained the law and the options and left the decision to the cheeses. The "bigger cheese" followed the law, much to the "big cheese's" disappointment. Several months later the "big cheese" walked up to the HR Booth at the Benefits Fair and picked up the stress balls that we were giving away, throwing them at me "Please stop!" I protested. After repeated protests, I put down my hands. The Director continued throwing the stress balls until one of the balls bounced off my boob and hit the woman next to me in the eye. I reported the incident to female Director of HR to file a complaint.

She came into my office, shut the door, and explained how this same director had harassed her.

My complaint was ignored. Silence.

The changes in our world with regard to women's rights regarding sexual assault and sexual harassment are significant and encouraging. In my thirty-year recollection it appears that I spoke up. I am hopeful that my daughters and granddaughters will not have these types of experiences and when they speak up, will not be followed by silence.

Anna and Oscar

It was the Fourth of July when Oscar first noticed Anna Walgren. The Swedish Church celebrated the holiday with a picnic at Gage Park and he spotted her across the park. An angel dressed in white with her black hair blowing in the breeze, she laughed as the group of children she was playing with tried to catch her but she was too fast for them.

Oscar had been patient with Anna. They had grown up together in the Swedish community in Topeka, Kansas. Older by six years, Oscar had had his eye on Anna since that first fourth of July at the Swedish Covenant Church picnic. His father had been the pastor at the church since his father immigrated from Sweden to settle in Topeka. Oscar and his other siblings were all born in Kansas. Anna must have been about 13 when he first noticed her. She was a raven-haired beauty and drew lots of attention from the boys. He knew immediately that she was the one he wanted to marry even if it did take another 12 years before she said, "yes."

It felt like a lifetime since the small wedding with family at Oscar's parent's home on Clay Street in Topeka. Anna would have been content to stay single but as the years went by her mother made it clear that would not happen. Anna had plenty of suitors vying for her attention and she enjoyed the chase. The thought of being someone's wife never crossed her mind. When Oscar asked her mother for Anna's hand in marriage, Inga Walgren was thrilled. Anna's protests fell on deaf ears so the wedding was arranged. Oscar was older and had already purchased a home at 110 Elmwood Avenue, in Topeka. Inga was delighted to accept Oscar's invitation to live with the newlyweds in the small white house on Elmwood Avenue. That sealed the deal even though Anna might have to be dragged down the aisle, kicking and screaming. In the end, Inga knew her daughter would do what she was told.

The wedding day had been beautiful. Anna awoke early and sat, brushing her long black hair.

Her hair shone like obsidian as the light from outside streamed into the room where she sat on the window seat. Her thoughts had been as dark as her raven hair, thoughts of one of her former beaus. He had gone to Harvard to become a lawyer and she was sure she would never see him again. Besides, she was a poor girl from a broken family. At least that was how Anna felt. Who would want a bride from the wrong side of the tracks, raised by a single mother?

Anna thought of Oscar who wanted her to have the best of everything. She smiled as she thought of all the clothes he bought her. Purchased at JC Penney's, downtown, her favorite was the pale blue long dress with the wide brimmed hat. There were the boxes of dresses, lingerie, shoes and accessories. Since the wedding was only family she chose a simple ecru sheath with a high lace collar, very stylish for the day. She was, after all, almost considered an old maid at twenty-five.

"Anna, hurry up! You don't want to be late for your own wedding." Inga shattered the daydreaming.

"Yes, Mother. I'll be right down." Anna piled her black hair up but as always, there were wisps that escaped and framed her porcelain face. Hurriedly she slipped into her dress and shoes. She glanced in the mirror before she headed down the stairs for the last time as Anna Walgren.

Inga had arranged a carriage to take them to the Parsonage next to the Swedish Church. Erik had picked up the carriage and waited patiently in front of the small house. Anna smiled at her brother and climbed in the carriage. Although her father-in-law to be was the pastor, Anna insisted that they be married in the living room of the parsonage. The couple and guests had enjoyed a light lunch before the newlyweds boarded the train to the World's Fair in St. Louis, Missouri.

It felt like a lifetime since the carriage ride to the Pierson's house, the wedding, lunch and the ride to the train station. Boarding the

Atchison, Topeka and the Santa Fe Railroad for the trip to St. Louis, Oscar and Anna headed to their new life together. Oscar was a good man. Anna was sure she would love him in time. He certainly had spared no expense where she was concerned.

It was 1904. Anna and Oscar walked hand-in-hand as the couple entered the St. Louis World's fair. Oscar had planned everything and it wasn't until the last minute that he told Anna of their honeymoon plans. She hadn't left Topeka since she and her mother settled there from Sweden.

"You are the 10,000th visitor! Congratulations, you have won that playhouse with shipping anywhere in the United States!" the salesman gestured excitedly to a large wooden playhouse near a display. Anna was not used to being the center of attention and blushed crimson.

She turned toward Oscar and asked, "What would we do with a playhouse?"

"Get it ready for our family." Oscar, smiled at his new wife.

"Oh, Oscar," Anna blushed again.

"You made me wait long enough to marry you! I hope you won't make me wait for our family too."

Anna turned to the man who had congratulated her. "Thank you. What do we need to do?" The man ushered Anna and Oscar over to the playhouse where the photographer was waiting. His tripod with the large box camera was ready to take their picture in front of the playhouse. After the picture they were guided to a table to complete their name and address for shipping. Anna had never thought of herself as lucky but maybe things were changing.

So many firsts: the first train ride, the wedding night and now the World's Fair. Oscar's voice pulled her back to the present, "Look. That's the famous Ferris wheel from Chicago!" Off in the distance was the enormous structure. The crowds were as big as the Ferris wheel. The World's Exposition at Forest Park spanned 1,272 acres and welcomed 22 countries including exotic places like Japan, China, Ceylon and the Philippines. The newlyweds had never seen anything like it.

"It's the biggest attraction called the Pike. I read it has been in storage since the 1893 exposition held in Chicago. Let's go ride it." Oscar grabbed her hand and they were off through the crowds. Anna thought about the courage her mother had bringing Anna and her younger brother, Eric to America. "I can do this." Anna said it more to herself than her new husband. After all it was only a ride on a Ferris wheel, not like starting a new life in a new country with two toddlers. The couple headed toward the Ferris wheel, taking in the exhibits along the way. A Swiss chalet, a Buddhist Temple, and the Palace of fine arts, were just some of the sights. Oscar bought tickets and the couple joined the long line of people waiting for an experience of a lifetime. Anna said a silent prayer as they were ushered into their seat and strapped in. In a moment they moved away from the ground, swinging back and forth as the operator loaded the people below them. They inched higher and higher until they reached the top of the world. Anna was nervous so high up. She heard Oscar chuckle. "What's so funny?"

"I was just thinking about how long we've known each other. You were worth waiting for."

"You know Mother. She wanted me to finish school so I could take care of my children like she had to." Anna thought of their unusual family of three. Most families had a father and mother but her mother raised her and Eric alone, earning a living birthing other's women's babies. Oscar sensed her nervousness sitting on top of the world. "Don't you worry. I'll take care of you Anna."

The Schwinn Bicycle

I didn't have a Schwinn bicycle. Mine was an orange Monarch. It had wide beachcomber handlebars with tassels hanging from each grip. There was a thick-wire seat on the back for passengers. Each of the wires ended in a small round reflector encircled by a white cover. Another thick-wire contraption was on the front of the bicycle. It had a spring-loaded clasp for book bags or small grocery bags. An adventurous friend of mine, Tom, decided one day to ride on the front, facing me on the bike. It turned out he was heavy enough to flatten the front tire to the point that the wheel frame hit the pavement, making the wheel less than round. I rode it that way the rest of the time I had the Monarch.

Santa brought me the bike one year. It was a 24". I longed for the 26" Schwinn I saw in the bike shop downtown. Every time we went to town, I would make an excuse to go to the bike shop. The 26" black Schwinn represented the big kid I wanted to be. With this bike I could ride with the big kids. I would have what all the other big boys in the neighborhood had: a 26" black Schwinn bicycle.

It was obvious to my parents that I had been bitten by the Schwinn bug. At every meal I would bring up the idea that I really wanted that bike. I devised plots where I would finally find a way to convince Dad that I really needed a bigger bike. I had Dad adjust the seat up daily so that it would not stay in the flange it built to fit into. I would explicitly point out that my knees were not able to extent to their full length while riding the bicycle.

Finally, Dad had enough. One night when I was pleading my case for a larger bike, he brought out the red power mower. Dad spent time making sure the motor was tuned and oiled. On every Tuesday evening, he would come home and mow the grass. This day was a Tuesday. Dad asked me to get off the bike and come over to the mower. In the garage was a small one-gallon box red can of gas. Dad grabbed the gas tank cap and pulled out the spout. With the spout turned over, he screwed the cap back on the rectangular red can. Bending the spout over the gas tank, Dad unscrewed the cap. On the opposite side of the gas can there was a little yellow cap. Dad showed me that you how to release the small cap to allow the gas to flow out of the can. Otherwise, the gas wouldn't flow. With one hand he held the handle at the top of the can. With a nod he gestured for me to lift the bottom of the can to pour the gas into the tank on the mower. Soon the gas was overflowing the tank. The smell of gas pouring out is distinct in my experience. That evening, I got full nose of the smell that never left me.

"Full," he pronounced. "We don't want to pour gas all over the driveway. It's a waste." I got to put the cap back on the tank on the mower and the spout back into the can and replace the cap.

Dad got to the point. His bent index finger was wagging in the air right in front of my face. His face was stern. I knew these were my orders. "Every Tuesday when I come home from work, you can mow the yard. If it rains that day, we'll do it the next day. Every time you mow the grass, you will get $1.00. If you use the clippers around the trees and next to the bushes, you will get another $0.50. I will pay you after I inspect to see if you got everything mowed and trimmed. When you get the $65.00 you need to get your new Schwinn, we'll go down to the bike shop and get it."

I was ecstatic. I could use a power mower, the hand clippers, and collect $1.50 per week. I started running around the driveway, jumping up and down. I didn't bother to think about the math problem Dad had just presented to me. At $1.50 per week, it would take me sixty-five weeks to get the money together to buy the 26" Schwinn I coveted. I pleaded, "Dad, I'll be in high school before I save the money at that rate."

Suddenly Dad became a little stern. He yelled pointing at the mower, "You have to do the work first!"

Pointing out the lever I had to push with my index finger to get the mower started, he showed me how to pull the rope that got the engine to turn. The three-foot rope had a wooden handle on one end and a knot on the other. On the top of the mower was metal circle with a notch, just the size of the knot at the end of the rope. Dad pointed out that the procedure was to put the knot in the notch and wind the rest the rope around the metal circle. Since I was left handed, Dad showed me how to put my foot on the mower so it wouldn't move when I pulled the rope.

I pulled the rope. The mower made a mechanical sound, a farting sound out of the muffler, but it didn't start. Dad looked at me with that amused prideful look. "It never starts the first time. Try again." I looked over at the open garage door. My mother was standing there. She was holding my sister, Susie, back. At three years old, she was anxious to show me how to start the mower. Mother had one arm around Susie and the other over her mouth, blocking whatever it was she wanted to say.

I put the knot at the end of the rope in the slot and wound the rope around the metal circle very carefully. Dad gave me the nod to try again. I put my foot on the mower again, grabbed the wooden handle. Face squinted, eyes closed, lips together, I pulled the rope with both hands as hard as I could. I heard the sound of the engine starting. I wrapped the rope around the mower handle triumphantly. Mother had both arms in the air cheering. Susie came right up between me and the mower handle, reaching up to push the mower. Mother had to come over quickly to keep her from running off with the mower while it was running.

With the mower running loudly, we depended on sign language. Dad pointed to the grass in the front yard. I pushed the mower toward the front yard. He walked backwards in front of me and the mover, pointing for me to move the mower closer to the edge of the concrete driveway.

"If you don't overlap you will leave too much, you will be busy using the hand clippers on your hands and knees trimming it up. You'll be out here until sundown." He was yelling in my ear over the sound of the mower. The neighbors heard him, `I am sure. Soon I was moving along just like I knew what I was doing. The fresh-cut grass streamed out of the side of the mower. The fragrance that followed filled my nose, refreshing me with every turn of the mower. Dad stayed in front of me walking backward through the first three turns around the front yard. Every now and then he would point in one direction or the other. When I had made all the rounds to complete my first cutting of the front yard, we walked the green grass to admire our work together. I had a feeling of accomplishment. I was doing the work my dad did. Dad pointed out to me the places where I didn't overlap enough. There would be rows of long grass between the cut rows. In some places, he would say, "Good you got that corner. I never get that corner. I always have to come back to it."

Dad asked me, "Would you like to get the mower over here to take care of the misses or do you want to use the hand clippers?" I opted for the mower. I ran over to get it. Dad joined me, watching to see if I followed directions. He let me do what he had instructed me to do. The first pull it started. He smiled that prideful smile and said, "It's easier to start after it's been running a while."

This time Dad went in front of me and pointed out the spots we had missed. About that time, the sun was setting. Dad looked around the corner of the house at the back yard. "We'll get the backyard tomorrow afternoon. Let's put the mower away for now. The next day, I kept asking my gramma, "When does Dad get home?"

She told me, "Watch the clock! When the big hand gets to the six and the little hand is between the five and the six, then it will be time."

"How long is that, Gramma?" I asked over and over again.

Patiently, she kept answering my questions. Soon I saw the Jeep panel truck pull up out in front. Dad got out and locked it up. He walked up the driveway. I met him at the front of the garage. "Let's do the back, Dad!" He smiled that prideful smile. Soon we were getting the back yard mowed. Mother came home from work. Mother, Gramma, and Susie all watched from the back porch. We mowed back and forth, up and down. Finally, it was done. We took our walk around to see what we missed. This time it was less than last time. It took only a couple of passes to get the misses done. I got the hand clippers out. I carefully opened them. I enthusiastically cut the grass next to the I trees I couldn't reach with the mower.

When everything was put away, Dad gave me that prideful look and handed me my first $1.50 to save up for my new black 26" Schwinn bicycle. I ran in my room and found a white bank bag I had been saving just for this purpose. I put three shiny 50-cent pieces in the bottom of the bag. I tried to imagine what $65.00 of 50-cent pieces would feel like in this bag. I flipped the bag around my head, yelling "Yippee!"

Soon I became confident enough to get the mower out myself and mow the grass and trim it after school, before Dad got home from work. When Dad got home, he would walk the yard with me and check my work. He would always say, "Bring your clippers!" He would always find a blade or two I missed. After a while, I realized that this was his way of making me accountable and teaching me there was a way of doing things that didn't require a "do-over."

One day, we were walking around the yard, looking things over. Dad pulled his hat off his head and wiped his brow. He looked at me with that prideful smile, "I've been waiting for this day!" he announced. "I don't think you need those clippers today!"

I jumped around the yard with my hands in the air. Dad handed me the silver half-dollars, four of them. "I've been saving these for you! You are doing a great job!" I thought my head would pop off. I took the four half-dollars and put them in the bag. I flung it around my head again. Dad came into my room. "How many have you saved in that bag?"

I poured them out on my bed and counted them out. I had eighty-four half dollars. Dad asked me, "How much is that?" I counted them out by two's and found that I had $42.00. I didn't bother to do the math to realize that the half dollars I had earned mowing the grass could not have equaled $42.00. I completely missed the obvious. Someone was adding half dollars to my bag without my knowledge. Dad was walking out the door of my room, "Bring your bag! Let's go." I couldn't imagine where we were going. Dad answered my questions emphatically when we got in the car. "We are going to the bank!"

Soon we drove up to the parking lot in the back of the bank. On the car seat, I spotted a little book. It looked very official. I picked it up and opened it. I saw my name and Dad's at the top of the first page. There was a number at the top. There was also an amount listed on the line on the first yellow page of the book. The entry was dated the Saturday before. In the column farthest to the right was an entry: $20.00. When Dad parked, he said, "This is your bank account. I hope you will make many deposits." We walked into the bank through the back door. Dad shook hands with a couple of the men seated at the desks inside the bank. They all spoke to me by name and smiled.

When we got to the place where there was an opening in the marble counter to do business, Dad told me that I should take my half dollars and put them in the bank to make them safe. "What about my black 26" Schwinn?"

Dad replied patiently, "It will be here when you need it. Put your bag and your book on the counter. The teller will count out the coins and deposit them into your account." I stood by patiently. The teller put my eighty-four half dollars in a drawer behind the counter where I couldn't see them, then stamped the date in my bank book and entered the amount of the deposit and the balance: $62.00. I beamed. I almost had enough money to buy my new Schwinn. Dad reached for my bank book, put it in his shirt pocket and said, "Now let's go see if they still have that 26" black Schwinn" My heart was about to jump out of my shirt. Dad reached for my hand. We walked hand-in-hand out the bank front door. We walked around the sidewalk to the parking lot in the back where we parked. Soon we were driving to the bike shop. I didn't dare say a word.

Soon we were parallel parking in front of the bike shop. The owner was a neighbor.

His boys walked to school with me. I greeted him, "Hi, Mr. Chilton!" He knew me and my dad. I ran past the other customers in the sports store. We passed by the small bikes and quickly moved on to the taller models at the end of the row of Schwinns. There it was: a black 26" Schwinn bicycle. Dad looked at me with a smile, "Is this the one?" I yelled at the top of my lungs, "YES!" Soon Dad was writing a check for the amount of the price of the bicycle. I was confused, "Wait I just put my money in the bank." Dad had a serious look on his face, "You keep your money. Save it for college!"

Dad finished writing the check and handed it to Mr. Chilton. Next, he came out from behind the counter and moved the bike away from the display. "Let's have you sit on the seat, Alan. We may have to adjust the seat." If my heart hadn't jumped out of my shirt yet, it was about to do just that. I stood next to the bike, swung my right leg over the seat. Dad held the bike up with me perched on the seat. "Let's see if you can reach the pedals when you're seated," Mr. Chilton offered. I sat there with my hands on the grips, holding on for life. The air was full of what I came to know as "new bike smell." It was the smell of the new rubber tires, hand grips and new paint. It was exhilarating. I couldn't wait to get it home and ride it up and down our street. Mr. Chilton checked the air pressure in the tires, made adjustments with his air compressor in the back of the store and checked each tire again.

The rubber tires made a low-pitched squeaky sound as I guided it carefully across the shiny store hard wood floor. I was careful not to bump into the glass cases as I moved toward the front door. Dad held the door open, then out to the car in front of the store. I waited for Dad to get the gate open at the back of his 1956 two-door mint green Ford station wagon. We both lifted my new black 26" Schwinn in the back. Dad closed the gate.

Soon we were in the front seat. Dad started the V8 engine and put it in gear. After a couple of turns to get out of the parking place, we were off to home to deliver the bike. Dad did his usual approach in the sloped-toward-the-house driveway. He would turn quickly into the driveway, put the transmission in neutral, take his foot off the break and let the car run into the back of the garage. Without the back wall of the garage, we would have ended up in the white plank fence on the back of our lot. The back of the garage had a definite bow toward the bottom of the siding. The wall was clearly off its foundation.

When the car came to rest with a metal hitting wood sound, Dad put it in park and turned the motor off. Next, he would take that bent index finger and make a low whistling sound. This was my cue to get out. Otherwise, I would be subject to several minutes of tickling. I didn't have time for that today. I jumped out of the car while Dad headed into the house. I was left to get the bike out myself. I opened the top of the gate and he the bottom portion. My bike was still there safe.

I heard Dad yell, "Grace and Suzie, I'm home!" On entering the back door of the house, there was what we called a landing with steps into the basement straight ahead and two steps up into the kitchen on the left. To the right was some hooks for all of us to hang our jackets. Dad always sat on the step going into the kitchen to unlace his work boots, replacing them with light brown soft house slippers. In the midst of him taking off his boots, Suzie would come up behind him, put her arms around his neck and hug him, splattering the back of his head with kisses, saying loudly, "Daddy, Daddy, Daddy!".

While all this was going on, I was lugging my bike out of the back of the station wagon. Soon I had it on the concrete driveway. That new bike smell was intoxicating. I pulled up the kick stand with my right foot, raised my foot over the seat. Soon I was astride the bar between the seat and the handlebars, my feet on the ground. I walked the bike to a spot where I felt secure, the metal bar pushing my jeans up into my crotch. I took a deep breath. I turned the right pedal around so that it was at about 10 o'clock. I put my right foot firmly on the pedal. I stood up, putting all of my weight on that pedal. In seconds I was sitting on the seat securely while the bike carried me up the driveway toward the street. I looked both ways. The coast was clear. Now I had both feet on the pedals moving forward faster with each turn, I turned the bike to the right and headed up the hill. My feet were moving the pedals in a rhythmic motion, my feet pushing forward and then downward to propel the bicycle up the hill. Soon I was standing up straight on the pedals. The breeze hit my face, my hair standing straight up.

My heart was jumping out of my chest. Soon I had worked hard enough to get to the top of the one-half-mile-long twenty-degree incline hill. I triumphantly made a circle around the intersection, the plateau. I put the brakes on and stood for a moment with my feet on the ground. I peered down the hill toward my house. I couldn't see Dad standing with Mom and Suzie at the end of the driveway, looking up and down the hill. There were enough trees between us to hide me at the top of the hill. I decided to test the limits of me and my new bike. I put the right pedal in a ten o'clock position, putting all my weight on it.

I was off at a speed I had never, ever achieved. I headed down hill and kept pedaling to go faster. Soon I had reached the point of discomfort where I had to stop pedaling. I was thoroughly enjoying the wind blowing my hair around my ears. One by one I could see the neighbors watching me hurl down the hill. Kids who saw me cheered me on. Others jeered. I clearly had the attention of all who had ventured out to their front yard that evening. Among the observers were Mom, Dad, and Suzie. Mom was holding Suzie, her arms around Mom's neck. Dad had removed his work sunglasses, so I could see his eyes getting bigger as I zoomed by our driveway. My mother had one hand over her mouth again. Her eyebrows were high on her forehead.

I reached the end of the street without incident. I turned the bike around again and headed home. Dad, Mom and Suzie were standing at the end of the driveway, waiting for me to return. "That was quite a show, young man!" Dad said sarcastically. You're lucky I wasn't backing out of our driveway. Is that how you're going to ride that bike all the time?" I turned my head away from Dad and smiled ear to ear.

Mom just looked at me plaintively, "Time for dinner!" I put the new bicycle in the garage, closed the garage door and joined my family at the table for dinner.

A person in my life....

When I was a youngster of about 4, my grandmother was my caregiver during the day. I mostly had her to myself. My mother worked for an attorney in town. His name was Mr. Foot. I guess that was a good name for an attorney. He could really put his foot down in negotiations. My Dad worked as a surveyor. We lived in a small university town that was growing quickly. This town was founded on the barbed wire industry. There were monuments in special places to that industry. The mascot for the high school teams was a bird called a "barb." Our team was always the Barbs.

My grandmother raised six children with her husband on the farm that belonged to the man who invented barbed wire with his partner. Her husband, my grandfather, was a ranch hand. He died at the age of forty of tuberculosis. My mother was the youngest of the six. She was two when her father died. My grandmother made a living for her and her six children working in the big house on the farm where my grandfather worked. Her job was to iron in the basement. She ironed everything: sheets doilies, shirts, underwear. Anything that was cloth was ironed.

My grandmother continued that particular skill to the day when she was my caregiver. She would spend her mornings ironing everything in the house made of cloth, including sheets and pillowcases. I used to watch her iron from the other room. She thought I wasn't watching, but I remember her pushing and folding the sheets and pillowcases around the ironing board. The thing I remember most was that she would whistle hymns while she ironed. Very young I knew many of the hymns from the hymnal at church. My grandmother didn't attend church, but she knew the melodies by heart. One of her favorites was "In the Garden." This hymn was one we asked our friend, Gene, to sing at her funeral service. It has become a standard at all the family funerals since hers. She used to say that she didn't think she should attend church since she didn't have the money to contribute. I think of her whistling the tunes every time I sing one of her hymns in church. Frequently a hymn from her hymn book will pop in my head. I just hum along as if I was listening to her whistle the tune in the kitchen by the ironing board.

Gramma walked with a significant limp. I am sure she would have had a new hip today, but then those who suffer this malady just put up with the pain. She never complained and never used a cane. She would not take help getting up and down steps. If one of us would try to help her she would wave us away as if we were in the way. She was the helper in our lives. On days when the weather would allow, I would go out and play in the yard. I was a very curious little guy, so I would tend to wander off. I would go off to other homes in the neighborhood and knock on the door to find out if there were any kids who wanted to play. I would find kids in many homes and we would swing or play tag in their yard. Sometimes they would come to get me as well. When it was time to come in, my grandmother would step out onto the front stoop and whistle loudly. If I didn't hear it right away, the other kids would let me know that "gramma" was calling. Gramma would keep whistling until I appeared in front of her. If I took too long by her estimation, she would scold me for not coming right away. She would say,

"I don't have time for your nonsense."

One of my early memories was the annual spring trip to the cemeteries where we would wash the stones and plant what I knew to be "cemetery flowers" on the graves. In the oldest of the cemeteries there was a hand pump on the well we used to get water for the flowers. On my grandfather's grave, gramma's husband, we would plant one for the head, two for the shoulders, and two for the feet. Frequently we would stop there on our way to and from places, get the bucket out of the trunk, and water the flowers. At each stop we would fill the bucket at the well, throw water on the stone and wash it clean. The red marble would shine in the sun. We could clearly read "William Columbus Metcalfe 1880-1920." Gramma was a widow for forty-six years.

Years later, I brought my boys to the cemeteries before Memorial Day to wash the stones and plant cemetery flowers.

One of the things about a boy that my gramma could not tolerate was dirty ears. If she saw a speck of dirt on my ear she would grab me and take me to the sink to clean my ears.

Although she was a very caring person, she was not gentle when cleaning my ears. It taught me a lesson that my ears should always be clean. Some days we would visit my aunt's house who had five boys, all older than me. Her husband "worked at home." At the sight of gramma and me walking up the walk they would all run. Gramma would stand on the front stoop of their house and whistle. Pretty soon we were all lined up by age waiting to get their ears cleaned. Of course, I was first, since I was the youngest. This memory was one we all shared. Years later we would all share this memory of our gramma cleaning our ears and her standing on the front stoop whistling for us to come, get in line and take our ear cleaning like a man.

On special days I would go on a cab ride with my gramma to my mother's office in town. We would sit together in the back seat, watching the cab driver make the turns and stop at the stop lights. I would, of course, chat up the driver. My gramma was sometimes mortified at my questions. "How many kids do you have?" "Where do you live?" "Where do you go to church?" Gramma would hand the driver a silver dollar and he would flip it in the air as he held the door for us to get out. I watched to make sure he caught it. I was sure I would have a chance to pick it up from the pavement. I had no such luck. His eyes were fixed on the shiny silver dollar spinning in the air, all the way up and right back into his hand. He would hold it up and admire it, then put it safely in his pocket. I learned many lessons in life from my gramma. One was the work ethic. Every day was a productive day for her. She would never complain about her work and she would always have a pleasant smile and a positive greeting even though she was in pain 24/7. In my later years, I have tried to emulate her positive attitude even though I experience some of that pain she had in her life. Recently I heard from one of my colleagues that it was nice to see me smile when I came to work in the morning. The person talking said it brightens their day to see me cheerful even though they knew my life has had challenges. I know that it's the memory of my gramma that keeps me cheerful even when I have pain and don't feel that cheerful all the time.

In those days the doctor would come to the house. When she was sick, Dr. Telford would pull up in the middle of our driveway in his shiny black two-door Cadillac, get out with his big black leather doctor bag and come to the door. He would never knock. He would just come bustling in the house. He knew where her room was so he would hustle through the house to her room, saying good evening or morning.

A major malady of my gramma's was her gallbladder. Dr. Telford advised her many times that she had to get it removed. Then the surgery that would solve this problem would be majorly invasive. Gramma was dead set against this surgery. She would not succumb to the Dr.'s repeated entreaties to get it done as soon as possible. When the problems that come with this malady became unbearable, she finally went to the hospital for treatment. Dr. Telford had to give her the news that she had developed cancer in her gallbladder. They did the surgery the doctor had prescribed years earlier, but it was too late. The cancer had spread all over her body. When she was discharged from the hospital, Dr. Telford advised that Gramma should go in a nursing facility. Of course, she wanted to go home. My mother honored her request. The care she needed was too much for my mother to provide on her own. Mom ended up hiring assistance to come in a relieve her for a few hours of the day. When Gramma was so sick and in pain, they all decided that she should go into a nursing home. The facility was a new one in our city. It was very pleasant and clean. It was called Green Acres. A couple of months and a couple of weeks in the nursing home passed, then she died with all of her children gathered around her.

I was sixteen when Gramma passed at the age of 78. The funeral was well attended by all her children, grandchildren and great grandchildren. Old friends came to the visitation and told stories about years passed by. I couldn't help but wonder where all these folks had been when she was living. Our friend, Gene Duncan, who sang hymns on the local radio station, sang "In the Garden" and "The Lord's Prayer" at her service. She was buried in the old cemetery next to the big house where she worked next to her husband. The high school where I attended that year was in full view of the cemetery. Gramma, my mother and I all graduated from the same high school. I remember standing there hearing the passing bells ring while we went through the burial service. I looked at my watch to see that I had just missed English class and then soon I would miss French. When it was over, the adults gathered around the stones and talked, reminiscing, discussing Gramma's life and committing to keep the family ties strong even though we all knew that family matriarch was gone. Life would never be the same.

ALAN VANTASSEL

Morning Eye Wax

When I wake up in the morning, I sometimes have to re-orientate myself. I have to think "Where do I live?" "What year is it?" Sometimes I have to remind myself that I don't have to wonder how my son, Keith, is doing this morning. I don't have to listen to see if I can hear him breathing in the next room. I don't have to get out his blood sugar meter to have him prick his finger one more time to check his sugar level. I don't have to plan my day based on the reading that appears on the meter. I don't have to ask him how he feels and make sure he gets his breakfast. I also don't get to hear him say, "Good morning!" and get his morning hug. I don't get to hear him say, "Love you, Dad." I don't get to ask him about his plans for the day, where he is going and who is he is seeing. I don't get to take him to the doctor and hear once again that he really isn't taking care of himself very well. I don't get to hear the Ozzie disc once again that magically appears in the CD player in my car. One of his favorites was "I'm coming home, Mamma." He could sing along and have a great time all on his own just enjoying the music.

When I hear someone talking about the loss of a child, I have been struck dumb. I have not been able to enter into a conversation about their loss or to share my own. I just listen intently and can't articulate a response. I know that a conversation about a loss could be therapeutic for me as well as the other person, but the words just don't come. Recently I have been doing my best to bridge the gap and express my feelings to the person I hear expressing theirs.

Yesterday, I had the opportunity to sit in a dentist chair getting ready for an extraction.

This situation is not something I looked forward to. The woman, Linda, who was helping me get ready was a woman about my age. I attempted to make small talk with her. Eventually we got around to talking about our kids. Usually when this topic comes up, I just listen. The person doing the talking usually has been a more successful parent than I was, so I just listen. I noticed that she was a little reluctant to discuss, so I threw out another probing question, "How many children did you have?" She responded "three boys." I also said. "I had three boys also." I probed some more. She still seemed reluctant. I said, "What are they doing now?" I expected to hear that one was a doctor, another a state senator. Linda started with "My oldest is up north. He has a job, doing well." I probed again, "What about the others?" Linda still seemed reluctant.

"My second boy is in the wind. We don't hear from him." I said, "I have one of those too." I looked at her with anticipation. Linda finally said, "We lost the third boy recently." I didn't expect to hear this response. She said, "He just passed in April, three months ago." I was a little tongue-tied. I managed to spurt out, "I lost a son also." She said, "I'm not over it yet." I responded, "Mourning is a process. It takes time." She got busy with the task at hand. I could see that she wasn't ready to talk much about her loss. I empathized with her reluctance completely, I ventured, "I lost my son nine years ago. He died from the effects of long-term Type-one diabetes." I continued, "It doesn't get easier." I wanted to say, "It just becomes a part of you. It has become a part of me." Just then the dentist walked in and the moment passed. I will try to talk to her again. I didn't mention the exclusive club we both belong to. It's not the kind of club you try to get into, but it is a club where we have something profound in common.

There is a couple in my church who lost their son one year ago. I have been sitting back silently listening to them go through their mourning very publicly. I have admired their ability to discuss their feelings, to talk about their loss. I have heard the father talk about how he has guilt feelings. He thinks he should have been a better father. In his mind had he been a better father, he would still have his son. Last Sunday they brought flowers to commemorate the one-year anniversary of his passing. They told a story about his preference for that particular flower. I admired their ability to express their feelings.

I was recently talking to a lady who was my bridge partner for the day at the senior center. I asked her about her family. She told me she had a family of four children, all boys. I probed a little more. I asked her what they are doing today. She hesitated a little and said, "They have all passed." I was a little taken back. I stammered that I lost one also. She looked at me in a way that I thought she was making contact with me in some way. I had observed Anna to be a woman who enjoyed life. She always had a smile. She was always on time for bridge. She knew her bridge up and down. I found I couldn't slip a trick by her. I asked if she had any grandchildren. She replied that she had two from one of her sons. I asked if they lived close by.

She said "Yes." I said you get to see them often then. She replied that it wasn't often, but she had seen them recently. Anna went on to say that it was very nice to see them. She smiled again, a warm smile. Anna went on to sort her cards and get on with the game. I admire Anna for her ability to get up and face life every day, finding entertainment and laughter in the joys she has in her life. I am learning from these life examples slowly. It has taken time for me to learn to communicate about my personal loss. My goal is to get better at it. I feel that people who have had losses are put in my life as examples of how I should live, happy to be alive and happy to have had a great life filled with people with whom I have loved.

Author Biographies

Margit Andersson was born in Sweden and has lived in Hemet for the last 14 years. She was always interested in literature and in writing. Since she retired she attended UC Riverside and obtained a degree in Anthropology. She now volunteers at the Western Center of Natural History in Hemet. Margit enjoys reading, traveling and learning new things.

Ernie Benzor grew up in the community of Casa Blanca. His mother was secretary and his father was head custodian where he went to school. Everyone knew him. Ernie loved to make things and music—especially rock n roll. In his first trip to Disneyland he was very interested in how the rides worked. At age 32, he started working for Disney as a mechanical designer. With interests in design and music, Ernie enjoyed jobs with theme park companies, and trips to recording studios. He recorded many songs. Today Ernie is retired, 71, and feels he's had a good life.

Patty Brown has lived in San Bernardino, Riverside, and Orange counties her entire life. She started attending the Redlands Joslyn Joy Writers with Mae Wagner Marinello when she retired. Her husband (Steve Brown) had been in the class since his retirement. He would come home and talk about the prompts, the people, and how much fun the workshop was. When she attended for the first time she only intended to sit and watch and listen. Mae said "no way", tossed her a notebook and said, "Write!" The workshop has become like family and is a regular part of the week.

Steve Brown was born in the East Texas Piney woods in 1938. He finished school in southern New Mexico and from there went into the Navy. Always an unstoppable reader, he started to write to pass time on shipboard. Story after story flowed each more pornographic than the last. His shipmates loved it but the Navy didn't, so his budding career as an author came to a sudden halt. Years passed and with them came the more regular elements of life. Finally in retirement, he saw a flyer for Mae Wagner Marinello's workshop and the old urge to smear ink on paper flared up again. Here we are! Wow! What fun!

CelenaDiana Bumpus, BA, is the author of the poetry collection, *Confessions* (1998, The Inevitable Press). Her personal essay was published in *Street Lit: Representing the Urban Landscape* (2014, Scarecrow Press). Her poetry has appeared in past issues of *Writing from Inlandia, Verse/Chorus: A Call and Response Anthology* (2013, Scarecrow Press), *Invisible Memoirs* (2014, Memoir Journal), *Orangelandia: The Literature of Inland Citrus* (2014, Inlandia Institute), *Pen 2 Paper Online Journal* (2014), and *On The Rusk* magazine (2015). As the owner of Islands for Writers, she is the host of the popular 'Tuesday Literary Series.' Her website is www.islandsforwriters.blogspot.com.

José Chavez has retired as a bilingual teacher and dedicates his life to writing. He's had poetry published in the *Multilingual Educator Journal, Acentos Review,* and *2017 Inlandia Anthology*. His award-winning bilingual children's poetry book: *Estrellitas y Nopales-Little Stars and Cactus*, was published in 2017. Authors like Gary Soto, Francisco X. Alarcon, and Juan Felipe Herrera have been inspirational. He is currently finishing a second bilingual poetry book for children, lives in Moreno Valley, CA, is married, has three grown children.

Wil Clarke spent 9 weeks in hospital and rehab with WNV, several months combating herpes, and has just finished doing 5 months of chemo for the cancer. He wishes to thank Jessica Carrillo, his Inlandia Workshop leader, and Celena Bumpus, his fiction/non-fiction writing teacher, for their continuous, strong encouragement to actually enter a few words into the computer when he had no desire to do so. Long may they live!

Retired from part-time work as an editor/proof reader, **Sylvia Clarke** is enjoying a slower life, catching up a bit on reading and doing a bit more writing. She and her husband Wil spend most of their time together at home, going to appointments, or out walking Katie, their dog, in the fields near their home.

Deenaz P. Coachbuilder, Ph. D., is a writer, educator, artist, and environmental advocate, wife, mother and grandmother. Her poetry, commentaries and essays have been published internationally. Deenaz' book of poems, *Imperfect Fragments*, has been received with critical acclaim in the U.S. and abroad. Her most recent volume of poems is *Metal Horse and Shadows: a soul's journey*. Her paintings in oil and mixed media have been displayed in a variety of venues. Deenaz is the recipient of several awards, including President Obama's "Volunteer Service Award." She is actively involved in literary, community, and social justice organizations, in the U.S. and India.

Carlos Cortés is the Edward A. Dickson Emeritus Professor of History at the University of California, Riverside. His books include his memoir, *Rose Hill: An Intermarriage before Its Time* (Heyday) and a book of poetry, *Fourth Quarter: Reflections of a Cranky Old Man* (Bad Knee Press), which received honorable mention in the 2017 International Latino Book Awards. Cortés served as the Creative/Cultural Advisor for Nickelodeon's *Dora the Explorer* and *Go, Diego, Go!*, for which he received the 2009 NAACP Image Award. He also performs his one-person autobiographical play, *A Conversation with Alana: One Boy's Multicultural Rite of Passage*.

Laurel Vermilyea Cortés studied Spanish and Comparative Literature at San Diego State. She is retired from the University of California, Riverside, where she served as Management Services Officer in the Department of Literatures and Languages. Laurel always considered herself lucky to be working in the exact environment of her choice.

Deborah Dybowski lives in Riverside County, California.

Jerry Ellingson lives in Redlands, California. As someone new to the community, she has had the excitement of discovering many new wonders in the Inland Empire. A recent discovery is the family of Joslyn Joy Writers in Redlands. Here, Jerry's goal is to record family stories so her genealogy work will not only have photos and statistics, but stories that should be told. She is a retired teacher with a Bachelor's degree in Dance and English. Her Master's degree is in education. The greatest joys in her life have been teaching graphic design and computer to adults and her role as a mother and grandmother.

Ellen Estilai, formerly executive director of the Riverside Arts Council and the Arts Council for San Bernardino County, has taught in universities in Iran and California. Her essay "Front Yard Fruit," originally published in *Alimentum*, is included in *New California Writing 2011* and was selected as a notable essay in *The Best American Essays 2011*. A Pushcart and Orison prize nominee, she has published in *Phantom Seed; Broad!; Snapdragon; Ink & Letters; Heron Tree; (In)Visible Memoirs 2; HOME: Tall Grass Writers Guild Anthology*; and *Shark Reef*, among others. Ellen is a founding board member and past-president of the Inlandia Institute.

Nan Friedley is a retired special education teacherand graduate of Ball State University. Her writings have been published in *Indiana Voice Journal*, a poetry chapbook, *Short Bus Ride*, the *Writing from Inlandia* anthologies, and *Three*, a nonfiction anthology collection. Nan lives in Riverside and participates in the local writing workshop.

Hazel Fuller is a native Californian. During her junior and senior years in high school she worked in the school library. That experience prepared her for a job at the San Bernardino County Library where she worked several years. After moving to Ventura, she worked in the Ventura County Library while attending night classes at Ventura City College. She continued working in libraries, first for the Dept. of Defense, then for the Dept. of Interior, until her retirement. Hazel lives in Redlands in a Victorian house she is restoring. She joined the Joslyn Joy Writers in January 2018. Besides writing, she enjoys reading and traveling.

Richard Gonzalez was born and raised in San Bernardino where he learned simple tasks in the grocery business from his parents. He joined the Navy and achieved the rank of Sonarman First Class. He attended San Bernardino Valley College and majored in engineering and physics, then graduated from Fresno State with a degree in economics. He worked with the fledging War On Poverty, directed the Equal Opportunity Program at UCR, and served as Executive Director of the Chicano Federation of San Diego County. He became Building Official for the City of Colton, and retired as Building Plans Examiner for the City of Redlands. Mr. Gonzalez has served on various public agency commissions and civic organizations in the San Bernardino area.

Renee Gurley, MA MFA, attends the Corona Critique Group with Andrea Fingerson. She has been published in *Coping Magazine*, *Lehigh Valley Woman's Journal*, and *The Hungry Eye*.

Doralba Harmon nacio en Colombia y es la mayor de ocho hermanos. Algo que define su personalidad es su positivismo y la fe que tiene en el poder de su mente, su inagotable fortaleza interior, lo cual descubrio a la temprana edad de 13 años, a travez de un libro que no sabe como llego a sus manos. Ella siempre ha creido que cuando el alumno esta listo, el profesor aparece. Esta filosofía de vida ha hecho que su existencia sea plena, armoniosa, feliz, sin ningún problema de salud, estrés o amarguras a sus 79 años de edad.

Tim Hatch writes poetry that explores themes of abuse, fragility, and our human obligation to one another. He earned his MFA at Cal State San Bernardino, and his poetry has appeared in *East Jasmine Review*, *The Vehicle*, *Touch: The Journal of Healing*, *Apeiron Review*, and *Cholla Needles*. He teaches composition at Riverside City College, and Cal State San Bernardino. His collection of poetry, which has gone through several titles, will be forthcoming whenever he gets his act together.

Laura L. Mays Hoopes is Halstead-Bent Professor Emerita of Biology at Pomona College. She's married with two grown children. She completed a creative writing certificate at UCLA in 2009 and an MFA at San Diego State University in 2013. Her memoir on becoming a woman scientist, *Breaking through the Spiral Ceiling*, was published in 2011. A dual biography called *Opening Doors:*

Joan Steitz and Jennifer Doudna of the RNA World was published in 2019. She has over 20 published stories and articles in magazines and newspapers. Hoopes won the California Writers' Club Jack London Award in 2013.

Maria Jaquez has spent much of her life helping others to realize their potential. She has taught mental health empowerment classes as well as politics at various colleges. She loves animals, especially cats because "cats know what they want and won't settle for less." Curious like her beloved cats, Maria has a wide range of interests such as knitting and crocheting with the *Happy Hookers* (a knitting group). She practices yoga, Tai Chi, and meditation, and enjoys learning foreign languages such as French and Italian as well as drawing and painting.

Joan Jones was born in Barbados, then immigrated to Trinidad at age ten, and the U.S. at seventeen. Joan is a Vietnam era United States Air Force veteran. Joan graduated from the University of Nebraska at Omaha in 1986 with a Bachelor of Science (BS) degree in Biology, and in May 1987 she graduated from The University of Nebraska Medical Center, College of Pharmacy with a Doctor of Pharmacy degree. Joan managed a hospital pharmacy from 1992-2000, after which she became a Pharmaceutical Consultant for the Department of Public Health. She retired in August 2014 to pursue her passion of writing poetry, and stories.

Robin Longfield was born in Chamblee, Georgia, but grew up in Midway City, CA, a very small unincorporated area between Huntington Beach, and Westminster. She is a graduate of Fountain Valley High School, and received a B.A. in English/Creative Writing from U.C. Irvine. In September, 2018, Robin retired after 30+ years in the real estate financing field. She is grateful for her long-suffering husband, John, her 2 amazing, beautiful daughters, and all of her family and friends. She believes in adventures, magic, laughter, and the power of words to change, inspire, and enlighten.

Merrill Lyew is a retired geographer. His job functions demanded frequent business travel to the metropolitan areas of Latin America, with sporadic visits to the provinces. These trips were always engaging, exciting, eventful, and packed with multitudes of story-lines, most of which went unnoticed, but enough remained unforgettable and might become the subject of some his storytelling.

Phyllis Maynard has been retired for several years, having spent most of her employment as a confidential secretary in the Corporate Finance Department of Alfred M. Lewis, Inc. (grocery wholesaler to divisions in Riverside, San Diego and Northridge, California, in addition to divisions in Arizona, Nevada and Texas). When the A.M. Lewis company closed (after 80 years), Phyllis went on to work in the Creative Writing Dept. at the University of California, Riverside continuing her secretarial duties for (and becoming friends with) many of the esteemed department faculty. She is currently working on an illustrated children's book about four Dalmatians.

Morris Frank Mendoza was born at Riverside Community Hospital in 1948. He grew up in the Casa Blanca neighborhood and attended Riverside schools. He has lived there his entire life. He served two years in the Army and four years in California National Guard. He's been married to Rosie for 38 years and they have three children. He retired as a clerk after 40 years in the U.S. Postal Service. He's been actively involved in his community since 1970. Currently, He's the Secretary of the VFW as an Adjutant. He volunteers at Catholic Charities in the community garden and food distribution programs.

Marvin Meyer was born on a farm in Western Oklahoma in 1936. He spent most of his early years farming there; he also became a bricklayer, a surveyor and an engineer of many types, including civil, hydraulic, flight and safety. Marvin worked as a California Registered Safety Engineer through most of his civilian work life. He also spent 34 years as an Air Force Reserve aircraft mechanic and flight engineer with over 6,000 hours in the air.

Marvin currently resides in the Inland Empire with his wife, Barbara. They have been married for over 60 years and raised three children.

Rose Y. Monge was born in Agua Prieta, Sonora, Mexico. She is one of ten children—five of whom are educators. Facilitating memoir classes at the Goeske Center and the Tesoros de Cuentos have been a joy and an un-expected learning experience after retiring as an educator in 2008. She values the opportunities to learn and to teach others. Her parents' sacrifice in bringing the family to the United States doesn't go unnoticed. Writing their legacy in memoir is an honor due to their unwavering faith and love. She hopes to inspire others to write their life stories.

Krystal B. Moon is a twice published author with an affinity for writing short stories. From romance to tragedies and everything inbetween, she writes it all—when she has the time between juggling her own business and family life. Krystal writes for the joy of the craft and hopes each reader falls in love with her characters like she has.

Chuck Morris lives in Riverside County, California.

Kimmery Moss was born and raised in Southern California. She was educated at the University of Southern California, graduating with a degree in Creative Writing and a minor in Political Science. She now enjoys living in the Inland Empire with her husband, two dogs, and four chickens.

Roberto Murillo is also known as "Tex" in Casa Blanca.

Patti Naqvi is a retired English teacher who lives in Upland, California and is an active participant in the Inlandia Ontario Workshop. She enjoys writing historical fiction often set in her native England. Based on her experiences living in Pakistan, she has self-published a memoir called *Hands Across Two Cultures* and has written an account of her childhood in Edinburgh, Scotland, a city immersed in history.

Cindi Neisinger believes curiosity will lead you to your passion. Her interest in the National Historic Landmark, The Mission Inn

Hotel and Spa in Riverside, California, inspired her Children's Book, *Mouse Wedding at the Inn*. She did not start off with the intention of writing. However, after taking many online writing classes, participating in a writers' critique group and attending writing workshops throughout the Inland Empire and the Inlandia Institute, she was hooked. Currently, she is writing a Kindle Series of short stories. She enjoys serving on the Inlandia Institute Advisory Council.

Gary Neuharth lives in Redlands, California where he is a member of the Joslyn Writers Group. He has studied art, sculpture, and writing at San Bernardino College, La Sierra College, and Loma Linda University. Gary was in the Air Force during the late 1950s. While in the Air Force he worked as a technical illustrator in Loan, France. He also taught art in service clubs and exhibited his paintings in Paris and Venice Beach, California. The Bohemian life and the Beat Generation have inspired Gary's art and writing. Gary has published more than a hundred poems, many of which have been included in his art exhibits.

Jane O'Shields-Hayner is a writer and visual artist, living in the foothills of the Santa Ana Mountains in Southern California. Her stories travel cultural, political and spiritual terrain and explore how they bump, meld and bleed into one another. Jane writes creative non-fiction, fiction and poetry. Her recent work has been published in *Tiferet Journal, Friends Journal, Lady Liberty Lit., The Manifest Station* and *Western Friend*. Jane is currently completing a trilogy of short stories written in homage to Kurt Vonnegut, Jr. and she is writing the memoir of her pilgrimages through California inspired by Woody Guthrie's song "Deportees," also known as "Plane Wreck at Los Gatos Canyon."

S. J. Perry grew up in a small town on the Kansas prairie, went to college, became an English teacher, got married, moved to the Inland Empire, and helped raise two great kids. Now retired, he spends his days walking, puttering around the house, and volunteering. He's still learning.

Cindi Pringle's first-grade teacher wisely predicted she would grow up to be a writer. Following a communications career that included print and broadcast journalism in Wisconsin, and public affairs and marketing at California State University, San Bernardino, Cindi is focused now on a renewed excursion into creative writing. She also is devoted to animal welfare as a local shelter volunteer who assists with pet therapy visits at an acute-care facility.

Phyllis Reis was born in Gadsden, Alabama. Her family relocated to Riverside, California in 1957. For forty years Phyllis worked in law-enforcement in Riverside County as a Riverside Deputy Sheriff and Marshal retiring, from service in 2018. Phyllis resides in Riverside County, California.

At birth my mother gave me the name of **Maria Rodriguez**. Ever since entering school at five years old in Stockton, California, I have officially been called **Mary**. I was born in Merced, on May 22, 1939, and raised in the East Los Angeles. I have lived in Riverside for almost 30 years. I am a new writer; although in my late 30s, when my husband was away on business trips and I felt alone and lonely, I would sit up in bed and write poetry. I thank the Inlandia Institute and CelenaDiana Bumpus for giving me this opportunity submit my voice in writing.

Rowena Silver, a native of Winnipeg, Canada, now living in Riverside, is a founding editor of *Epicenter Magazine*. Her work has been widely published in such journals as: *Ariga, Bridges: A Feminist Journal, European Judaism, Writer's Digest, Standards: University of Colorado, Pudding House Publications, Guardian Unlimited, Heyday Books, The San Fernando Journal,* and *Dissident Editions.* Rowena has also written several plays which have been performed in Los Angeles and San Francisco, including "The Disputation," a sonnet series, with Mark Steven Scheffer and "The King of Montpelier," an operetta. A video of "The Disputation" is available on YouTube, featuring the late Michael J. Cluff.

Kristine Shell lives in Redlands, California, where she participates in the Joslyn Writers Group. Kristine is a retired school administrator and teacher. She holds a Bachelor's degree in English and Secondary Education. She also holds Master degrees in Elementary Reading and School Administration. Kristine has been a member of the Inlandia Institute since October, 2016.

Donna Slezak resides in Riverside County, California.

Lillian Rodriguez Solorio was born at Riverside Community Hospital and attended schools in Riverside. She has worked in many jobs. At 20 years old, she was certified as a preschool teacher and worked as a bilingual teacher at Highgrove Elementary School. At the same time, she multitasked as a mother of two daughters, a wife, community and church activist, and attended night classes at local colleges. The family moved to Northern California but later returned to Riverside where she worked as a Substance Abuse Counselor for 20 years. She writes to leave a legacy for her daughters and family members.

Craig Stone lives in Riverside County, California.

Shirley Petro-Timura is a freelance writer. She is a Riverside County Public Schools teacher, having taught for over 30 years. Presently, she is seeking an agent for her completely finished and edited (finally!) first novel.

Gudelia Vaden (Delia) is a retired preschool teacher with a BA degree in Liberal Studies with Bilingual-Bicultural Emphasis from Cal State University in San Bernardino. Delia grew up in the San Joaquin Valley, near Merced. She is married to Thomas Vaden and they have a son, Patrick, and a daughter, Natalie. She cherishes her granddaughter, Natasha, as well as 3 bonus grandchildren: Julius, Kara, and Violet. Delia has learned much from her fellow Inlandia students and workshop leaders. She can be frequently seen walking her small black and white Chihuahua in the Hillcrest community of Riverside.

Thomas Vaden is a retired statistician with a MS degree in Mathematics from the University of Missouri at Columbia. Originally from St. Louis, Tom enlisted in the Air Force during the Vietnam

War, spent time in Colorado where he learned how to figure skate, then transferred to Castle AFB in the San Joaquin Valley where he met his future wife, Delia. Tom resides in Riverside with his wife Delia and a very spoiled black and white Chihuahua named Pepper. His son Patrick lives in Riverside, his daughter Natalie lives in San Francisco, and his granddaughter, Natasha, a recent graduate of the University of Oregon, lives in San Marcos.

Scharlett Stowers Vai's heart belongs to Casa Blanca, a barrio in Riverside where she was born on May 1, 1952. She was raised as both Black and Chicana by an entire community. She attended Casa Blanca Elementary School and in her 20s was hired there as a preschool teacher. She considers herself a social activist and always speaks her mind. She's a vital presence in her community as she belongs to the Community Action Group, the Brown Berets and the Baby Boomers. She has lived in Casa Blanca for 66 years and says that she will live there for the rest of my life.

Alan VanTassell grew up in a small university town on Northern Illinois in the 1950s. He graduated from DeKalb Senior High School in 1968 and from Northern Illinois University in 1972. In 1973, Alan enlisted in the U.S. Navy and spent his four-year enlistment at Naval Air Station, Point Mugu. On separation from the military Alan returned to Illinois and began teaching in a town called Harvard. After a career teaching high school, he retired in 2017. Alan lives with his wife, Sarah, in Redlands. They have three Labradors. Alan has long yearned to see Homer's red, red sea since he read Homer's work as a young man.

Sarah VanTassell lives in Redlands with husband Alan.

Frances J. Vásquez is a native of the Inland region and was raised in Highgrove. She pursued higher education at Riverside City College and the University of California, Riverside where she earned BS and MBA Degrees. She wrote her Master's Thesis on the status of Chicano leadership. She has a diverse background in public service and served as International Director/CEO of Other Cultures, Inc.—a student exchange program focused on México,

Central America, Canada, and the U.S. An aficionada of arts and culture, she loves attending and organizing cultural events. She serves as past president of the Inlandia Institute.

Jose Luis Vizcarra was born in the city of Chihuahua, Mexico to a single mother. His mother relocated him to the United States when he was fourteen years old. During the Vietnam War, Jose served in the United States Army. After returning home from the Army, he applied for and received his United States citizenship. After using his GI Bill to pay his thirteen years of college education, he taught elementary school teacher and adult ESL for 33 years. He is now very passionate about educating people about to better apply their finances. He is currently writing two books on financial education.

Romaine Washington is the author of *Sirens in Her Belly*, Jamii Publishing 2015. The collection of poems was placed on BET's must-read list in 2016. She is a fellow of The Watering Hole, South Carolina and the Inland Area Writing Project, University of California Riverside.

Duncan Webb resides in Riverside County, California.

www.ingramcontent.com/pod-product-compliance
Lightning Source LLC
Chambersburg PA
CBHW020505020726
47493CB00001B/188